Interpersonal Encounters in Contemporary Travel Writing

Anthem Studies in Travel

Anthem Studies in Travel publishes new and pioneering work in the burgeoning field of travel studies. Titles in this series engage with questions of travel, travel writing, literature and history, and encompass some of the most exciting current scholarship in a variety of disciplines, with research representing a broad range of geographical zones and historical contexts. A key feature of books published in the series is their potential interest to a wide readership, as well as their originality and potential to break new ground in research.

Series Editor

Charles Forsdick – University of Liverpool, UK

Editorial Board

Mary B. Campbell – Brandeis University, USA
Steve Clark – University of Tokyo, Japan
Claire Lindsay – University College London, UK
Loredana Polezzi – University of Warwick, UK
Paul Smethurst – University of Hong Kong, China

Interpersonal Encounters in Contemporary Travel Writing

French and Italian Perspectives

Catharine Mee

ANTHEM PRESS
LONDON · NEW YORK · DELHI

Anthem Press
An imprint of Wimbledon Publishing Company
www.anthempress.com

This edition first published in UK and USA 2015
by ANTHEM PRESS
75–76 Blackfriars Road, London SE1 8HA, UK
or PO Box 9779, London SW19 7ZG, UK
and
244 Madison Ave #116, New York, NY 10016, USA

First published in hardback by Anthem Press in 2014

Copyright © Catharine Mee 2015

The author asserts the moral right to be identified as the author of this work.

All rights reserved. Without limiting the rights under copyright reserved above,
no part of this publication may be reproduced, stored or introduced into
a retrieval system, or transmitted, in any form or by any means
(electronic, mechanical, photocopying, recording or otherwise),
without the prior written permission of both the copyright
owner and the above publisher of this book.

British Library Cataloguing-in-Publication Data
A catalogue record for this book is available from the British Library.

Library of Congress Cataloging-in-Publication Data
The Library of Congress has cataloged the hardcover edition as follows:
 Mee, Catharine, 1978– author.
 Interpersonal Encounters in Contemporary Travel Writing : French and
  Italian Perspectives / Catharine Mee.
   pages cm. – (Anthem Studies in Travel)
 Includes bibliographical references and index.
 ISBN 978-1-78308-037-3 (hardcover : alk. paper)
 1. Travel writing–France–History. 2. Travel
writing–Italy–History. 3. Interpersonal relations in literature.
 I. Title.
 PQ307.T73M44 2–14
 840.9'32–dc23
                2013048650

ISBN-13: 978 1 78308 420 3 (Pbk)
ISBN-10: 1 78308 420 0 (Pbk)

Cover image: Ella Maillart montrant le livre d'Owen Lattimore *The Desert Road to Turkestan*, Province de Ts'ing-Hai, Chine, 1935 © Musée de l'Elysée, Fonds Ella Maillart

This title is also available as an ebook.

CONTENTS

Acknowledgements   vii
List of Abbreviations   ix

1. Encountering, Travelling, Writing   1
   Encounter   1
   Travel Writing and Tourism   6
   Voyage/Viaggio   10
   Chapters   12

2. Strategy, Authenticity, Ethics   17
   Strategy   18
   Authenticity   21
   Ethics   26

3. Guiding   33
   Authenticity and Mediation   34
      Guides and guidebooks   34
      The gatekeeper   38
      An authentic encounter   43
   Translation and Voice   47
      The invisible translator   47
      Representation strategies   50
      Authorship and readership   53

4. Hosting   59
   Hospitality and Authenticity   60
      Invitation versus reservation   60
      Back to the bubble   62
   Freedom   65
      Hospitality as control   65
      The world is my playground   68

The Nature of Encounters	73
Reciprocity	73
Time and friendships	77

5. Staring   83

The Stare of the Travellee	84
The gaze, the stare and the travel encounter	84
The travellee as starer	86
The traveller as staree	91
Photography and Encounter	94
Tourists and cameras	94
Photography as intrusion	96
Photography as interaction	99

6. Challenging   107

Economic Power	109
Justification: Rickshaw Riders	112
Distancing: Prostitutes	115
Dilemma: Beggars	119

7. Accompanying   127

Absent Friends	129
'That most ambiguous of personal pronouns'	129
A question of genre	133
Alter Ego or Mirror?	136
Chance Companions	141

8. Concluding   147

Notes	151
Bibliography	173
Index	185

ACKNOWLEDGEMENTS

The research for this study has been generously funded by the Arts and Humanities Research Council and The Queen's College, Oxford. Lincoln College, Oxford has also provided several travel bursaries and book grants.

I am particularly indebted to Professor Charles Forsdick, whose advice and support have been instrumental in the development and publication of this study. I am also especially grateful to my two PhD supervisors, Dr Toby Garfitt and Professor Martin McLaughlin, who oversaw the initial stages of this research project as my PhD thesis and provided invaluable feedback and encouragement. I would like to thank the five anonymous reviewers, whose comments and suggestions have been extremely helpful in revising the manuscript. I would also like to thank Professor Guido Bonsaver, Professor Michael Sheringham, Dr Giuseppe Stellardi and Dr Wes Williams for their comments on earlier versions of parts of the study. I am very grateful to Dr Loredana Polezzi for her advice and I would also like to mention Dr Ed Welch, Dr Clare Harris and Professor Lino Pertile for help on specific points.

Earlier versions of some sections have been presented at a number of conferences: 'Literature Travels' at the University of Wolverhampton in September 2005, the Society for French Studies conferences at the Universities of Leeds and Liverpool in 2005 and 2008, and the 'Borders and Crossings VI' conference at the University of Palermo in September 2006. I am grateful to the organizers of those conferences for the opportunity to present my work and to the audiences for their feedback. I have carried out research in a number of libraries in Oxford, principally the Bodleian and the Taylor Institution, as well as the Bibliothèque Nationale de France, the Biblioteca Nazionale Centrale di Firenze and the Widener Library in Harvard, and I am grateful to the staff of those institutions for their assistance.

Finally I owe a huge debt of gratitude to family and friends for supporting me throughout, and especially to my parents, to whom I dedicate this book, and my husband for their love, advice and patience.

LIST OF ABBREVIATIONS

The following abbreviations are applied to primary texts when more than one text by the same author is used. All other primary texts are identified by the author's name only.

Afrozapping	Ramazzotti, Sergio, *Afrozapping: Breve guida all'Africa per uomini bianchi* (Milan: Feltrinelli, 2006).
Asie	Guillebaud, Jean-Claude, *Un voyage vers l'Asie* (Paris: Seuil, 1979), reprinted in *La traversée du monde*, presented by Jean Lacouture (Paris: Arléa, 1998), 95–208.
Birra	Ramazzotti, Sergio, *La birra di Shaoshan: Viaggio nel paese natale di Mao* (Milan: Feltrinelli, 2002).
Buonanotte	Terzani, Tiziano, *Buonanotte, Signor Lenin* (Milan: Longanesi, 1992; repr. Milan: TEA, 2004).
Carnets	Ollivier, Bernard, *Carnets d'une longue marche: Nouveau voyage d'Istanbul à Xi'an* (Paris: Phébus, 2005).
Chambres	Bernheim, Nicole-Lise, *Chambres d'ailleurs* (Paris: Arléa, 1986; repr. Payot et Rivages, 1999).
Chronique	Bouvier, Nicolas, *Chronique japonaise* (Paris: Payot, 1989) reprinted in *Œuvres* (Paris: Gallimard, 2004), 495–669.
Colline	Guillebaud, Jean-Claude, *La colline des anges: Retour au Vietnam* (Paris: Seuil, 1993), reprinted in *La traversée du monde*, presented by Jean Lacouture (Paris: Arléa, 1998), 419–516.
Couleur	Bernheim, Nicole-Lise, *Couleur cannelle* (Paris: Arléa, 2002).
Croisades	Guillebaud, Jean-Claude, *Sur la route des croisades* (Paris: Arléa, 1993), reprinted in *La traversée du monde*, presented by Jean Lacouture (Paris: Arléa, 1998), 517–652.
Festin	Weber, Olivier, *Le grand festin de l'Orient* (Paris: Robert Laffont, 2004).
Indovino	Terzani, Tiziano, *Un indovino mi disse* (Milan: Longanesi, 1995; repr. Milan: TEA, 2004).

Journal	Bouvier, Nicolas, *Journal d'Aran et d'autres lieux* (Paris: Payot, 1990), reprinted in *Œuvres* (Paris: Gallimard, 2004), 945–1037.
Marche I	Ollivier, Bernard, *Longue marche: À pied de la Méditerranée jusqu'en Chine par la Route de la Soie: I. Traverser l'Anatolie* (Paris: Phébus, 2000).
Marche II	Ollivier, Bernard, *Longue marche: À pied de la Méditerranée jusqu'en Chine par la Route de la Soie: II. Vers Samarcande* (Paris: Phébus, 2001).
Marche III	Ollivier, Bernard, *Longue marche: À pied de la Méditerranée jusqu'en Chine par la Route de la Soie: III. Le vent des steppes* (Paris: Phébus, 2003).
Oriente	Rumiz, Paolo, *È Oriente* (Milan: Feltrinelli, 2003; repr. 2005).
Poisson	Bouvier, Nicolas, *Le poisson-scorpion* (Vevey: Bertil Galland, 1981), reprinted in *Œuvres* (Paris: Gallimard, 2004), 721–811.
Porte	Guillebaud, Jean-Claude, *La porte des larmes: Retour vers l'Abyssinie* (Paris: Seuil, 1996), reprinted in *La traversée du monde*, presented by Jean Lacouture (Paris: Arléa, 1998), 653–763.
Radici	Aime, Marco, *Le radici nella sabbia: Viaggio in Mali e Burkina Faso* (Turin: EDT, 1999).
Routes	Bouvier, Nicolas, *Routes et déroutes: Entretiens avec Irène Lichtenstein-Fall* (Geneva: Éditions Métropolis, 1992), reprinted in *Œuvres* (Paris: Gallimard, 2004), 1249–1388.
Russies	Weber, Olivier, *Voyage au pays de toutes les Russies* (Paris: Quai Voltaire, 1992; repr. Payot et Rivages, 2003).
Saisons	Bernheim, Nicole-Lise, *Saisons japonaises* (Paris: Payot et Rivages, 1999; repr. 2002).
Uomini	Rumiz, Paolo, and Francesco Altan, *Tre uomini in bicicletta* (Milan: Feltrinelli, 2002; repr. 2004).
Usage	Bouvier, Nicolas, *L'usage du monde* (Geneva: Droz, 1963), reprinted in *Œuvres* (Paris: Gallimard, 2004), 59–388.
Vado	Ramazzotti, Sergio, *Vado verso il capo: 13.000 km attraverso l'Africa* (Milan: Feltrinelli, 1996; repr. 2002).

Chapter 1

ENCOUNTERING, TRAVELLING, WRITING

Encounter

Sergio Ramazzotti collects beer bottle labels as travel souvenirs, as he tells his Chinese interpreter Celia, in *La birra di Shaoshan*: '"Le incollo in un libro, come in un album di fotografie. Ogni etichetta è un incontro"' ('I stick them in a book, like a photo album. Each label is an encounter').[1] He prefers beer labels to photographs because they oblige him to reconstruct the person's face and voice from memory (*Birra*, 60). The label represents an encounter, and the collection of labels or encounters is both the sum of the journey and the part that Ramazzotti chooses to keep as a souvenir. Throughout his journey in China Ramazzotti strives to understand the country, always searching for something, without knowing exactly what he is seeking. His frustrated encounter with China becomes an encounter with Celia instead, whom he attempts to relate back to China: 'Celia […] era la piccola Celia ed era tutti i cinesi e forse la Cina stessa' (79; Celia […] was little Celia and she was all the Chinese and perhaps China itself). The tension between traveller and interpreter is constant: he is alternately impressed and disappointed by her; he lectures her, she protests. He attempts to circumvent the formality of their acquaintance, but she insists on the economic basis of their relationship. He is undecided whether or not he desires her physically, while she attempts to navigate his vague quest and vocal preconceptions, all the time worrying that his questioning and criticizing of her country pose a threat to herself and her family. The beer labels of Shaoshan prove elusive, adhering stubbornly to their bottles, and besides, Celia doesn't even drink beer. Eventually Ramazzotti renounces his attempts to comprehend China and thinks he has won Celia over because she toasts his decision. He contemplates burning his whole collection of beer labels: a symbolic gesture to cease representing and symbolizing and leave past encounters to memory. Then they are both arrested; China finally confirms his expectations and Celia leaves him with a defiant beer label for his album, an instruction to represent her, perhaps. Ramazzotti set out to visit

China, but the principal subject he chooses for his account of that journey is his awkward, unresolved, troubled encounter with this individual Chinese woman, Celia.

Ramazzotti's choice to prioritize the encounter is shared by other travel writers, who populate their narratives with characters met during their journeys. Some highlight encounters from the outset: Gianni Celati dedicates *Avventure in Africa* 'a quelli che abbiamo incontrato' (to those whom we met), Olivier Weber declares in the opening sentence of *Voyage au pays de toutes les Russies* that 'Ce ne sont pas des chapitres, mais des hommes rencontrés' (These are not chapters, but men encountered).[2] Others reflect back at the end of their journeys: Bernard Ollivier thinks of the many characters who have kept him company on his 'longue marche' (long walk) across Asia as he completes the final kilometres: 'On s'émerveille que j'aie pu faire ce chemin en solitaire, mais j'ai rarement été seul' (People are amazed that I could do this journey on my own, but I have rarely been alone).[3] Encounters form the backbone of many travel narratives, which become collections of portraits and interactions.[4] Nicolas Bouvier's *L'usage du monde* is, in his own words, a 'gigantesque ménagerie' (vast menagerie) of characters.[5] In François Maspero's *Les passagers du Roissy-Express* encounters are collected as so many photographs, reproduced alongside the text, while Tiziano Terzani's *Un indovino mi disse* catalogues a long series of meetings with fortune-tellers.[6] Not all encounters are brief; some travellers establish lasting relationships, for example with their guides, as in Corrado Ruggeri's *Farfalle sul Mekong*, or their hosts, as in Nicole-Lise Bernheim's *Saisons japonaises*, or their travelling companions, as in Jean-Claude Guillebaud's *La colline des anges*.[7] Such examples demonstrate the importance of interpersonal encounter in contemporary travel, a fact already noted by Franco Trequadrini in 1980, writing about twentieth-century Italian travel literature: 'Nel nostro secolo il viaggio serve un'esigenza di riscontro, di dialogo, di testimonianza' (In this century travel meets a need for comparison, for dialogue, for personal stories).[8] The statement is echoed twenty-five years later by Olivier Hamburzin, in his study of French travel literature of the same period: 'L'Autre est un personnage-clé de la littérature voyageuse du XXe siècle' (The Other is a key character in twentieth-century travel literature).[9] Despite the significance of interpersonal encounter in travel and its narratives there is a lack of critical attention to the subject, a failing that this study aims to address by analysing encounter in a range of contemporary travel writing. The meaning of the term encounter is not as straightforward as it might appear, and the first task is to clarify its uses in the context of travel.

In her study of Italian travel literature, Gaia De Pascale suggests that the principal motivation of voluntary travel today is contact with 'l'altro da sé' (the self's other), but she recognizes that 'altro' is not necessarily a person; it can refer to landscape or place.[10] When encounter is evoked, in both travel writing and studies of travel, it often denotes a general experience involving a vague confluence of place, culture and people as a collective. This is encounter between the traveller and the other as a concept, often idealistically elusive or mystical, rather than an individual person. The exotic appeal of unknown people(s), as much as unknown places, is a long-established motivational trope. Encounter in this evocative sense seems attractively easy; gathering a collection of strange and colourful others could be as simple as peeling off beer labels and sticking them into an album. Experience often belies ideals, and Ramazzotti, like every traveller, is confronted with the reality of the person facing him, in his case Celia. Italian anthropologist Marco Aime observes that tourist advertising emphasizes encounter with nature, history or tradition, but he draws attention to the fact that 'a gestire quella natura, quella storia o tradizione sono individui, persone' (managing this nature, this history or tradition are individuals, people).[11] Even when travellers purposely seek encounter with places and concepts, they must constantly deal with actual people; Ramazzotti travels to encounter China, but his narrative is dominated by his encounter with Celia. Travellers spend a considerable amount of time meeting and contending with people as concrete individuals and it is interpersonal encounter in this sense that is the theme of this book.

A travel encounter occurs every time a traveller comes into contact with another person. It involves two particular individuals, at a particular location in space and time. Verbal interaction is not always necessary; the exchange of a glance or a gesture, the faintest mutual acknowledgement can constitute an encounter. Sometimes the most remarkable encounters last a few moments and are prolonged no further, while others develop into relationships. An encounter is significant; it constitutes an event, as indicated by the writer's choice to include the encounter in the travel narrative. Any encounter that is selected for representation, regardless of whether it is fact or fiction, is consequently endowed with significance. Encounters are as essential to travel as place; they shape and define journeys in ways that we will explore throughout this study. Exotic fantasies dissolve when faced with the practicalities of interacting and negotiating with individuals. Travel writing might evoke the appeal of the utopian other, but it constantly narrates specific encounters, between individuals, in particular contexts. Before elaborating on the particularities of these contexts, I will tackle the thorny question of vocabulary and address the 'other' problem.

Travellers encounter such an array of individuals in such varied circumstances that no single term embraces them all adequately. While the traveller is the self at the centre of the text, whose perspective provides the filter through which the reader glimpses the other, 'O/other' is a rather inhuman term, implying distance and difference that are rarely reflected in narratives of interaction. Other also carries the exotic and mystical connotations that I wish to avoid. 'Local' is an improvement on 'native', but implies assumptions about identity and immobility that are often belied; those encountered by travellers may not be any more local than the travellers themselves. 'Interlocutor' appeals for the emphasis on interaction and communication, but is rather technical and, besides, conversation does not always take place. I therefore use these terms sparingly, and opt by preference for a fourth: 'travellee'. Travellee was coined by Mary Louise Pratt to make a pairing for traveller to correspond to colonizer and colonized. As she explains: 'This clumsy term is coined on analogy with the term "addressee." As the latter means the person addressed by a speaker, "travelee" means persons traveled to (or on) by a traveler, receptors of travel.'[12] Travellee is clumsy but useful because it circumvents assumptions about identity in terms of cultural, national or racial affiliations. Instead of merely designating the inhabitants of a place, it encompasses everyone who comes into contact with the traveller, regardless of their identity. Applying a term that defines the travellee solely in terms of his/her relation to the traveller runs the risk of neglecting individual identities, but since the traveller remains the focal point of the text, to whom all incidents happen and other characters relate, the travellee's presence in the text is always conditional on his/her encounter with the traveller.

Travellee does have its disadvantages. It implies an active traveller, perpetually acting upon a passive travellee: observing them, photographing them, conversing with them, translating them and finally writing about them. Yet encounters are reciprocal and the traveller is also acted upon by the travellee, who, despite the grammatical implications of the term, is far from being a passive, 'travelled all over' character.[13] Bouvier's much quoted reflection on travel applies here: 'On croit qu'on va faire un voyage, mais bientôt c'est le voyage qui vous fait, ou vous défait' (*Usage*, 82; You think you're going to make a journey, but soon it's the journey that makes you, or unmakes you). The English translation of *faire* encompasses both 'to make' and 'to do'. Travel certainly makes the traveller – it is an eminently self-forming activity – but it also does something to the traveller, or rather things are done to the traveller, not only by the journey, but also by the people the traveller encounters along the way. The traveller is driven, fed, guided, misled, interpreted for, hosted, stared at, accosted, arrested, befriended, insulted, accompanied, seduced, suspected, welcomed and so much more. The agent of all these helping and hindering actions, which make a journey and make a traveller, is the travellee. In order to reflect this and with the aim of countering the grammatical passivity of travellee, the chapters that follow are entitled with active verbs, taking the travellee as subject and describe the actions s/he performs to or for the traveller.

When two individuals encounter each other, they meet at a particular place and time, in a particular context, brought together by particular circumstances, concerned with particular hopes and desires, inscribed with particular personal histories and identities, distracted by irritations and preoccupations particular to the occasion. Nationality, race and gender are three fundamental attributes of identity, which naturally receive considerable attention, but there are many other aspects of identity and context that come into play when individuals encounter each other.[14] Others include, but are not limited to: age, social status, education, class, linguistic abilities, the dynamic of the relationship (employer–employee, chance acquaintance), the reason or cause for the encounter, the influence of other people (employer, mutual acquaintance), state of health (fatigue, pain, illness), comfort (extreme temperatures, (in)adequate clothing, (un)comfortable mode of transport), expectations (preconceptions, prejudices, stereotypes), motivations and desires, mood and disposition, personality (sociability), cultural habits (manners, social norms), wealth, religion, mobility (dwelling or travelling, right to free movement), personal history and life experience, the state of the weather, and other contemporary concerns (anxieties, preoccupations). All of these factors combine to create a unique situation. Some of them will be conscious, others unconscious, some shared, others private, some forgotten. Some are known to both parties, some to only one, some to neither, and each has varying relevance depending on the situation. When the encounter is rendered into a written narrative some aspects will be emphasized, others exaggerated, some will be forgotten, others edited out, many will be fictionalized, so the reader will also have an incomplete picture of the encounter. The relevance of some of the factors listed may seem obscure, such as the weather or a person's state of health, yet travellers suffer when they are ill-adapted to unfamiliar climates and are vulnerable to illness or accident, circumstances that affect their emotional state, their mental availability, and therefore their interactions with others. The emphasis on such key aspects as nationality, race and gender is understandable, but they should not obscure all others completely. Clearly I do not propose to take account of every factor in every encounter, but I do examine issues such as relative wealth, the dynamics of interaction, linguistic abilities, freedom of movement, expectations and circumstances, in order to clarify some of these more neglected features of travel encounter.

The combination of all these different factors and contexts creates tensions between the encountering traveller and travellee. Aime recognizes that one of the reasons why types of tourism that prioritize encounters are not mass phenomena is this complexity and difficulty of meeting people, compared to gazing at monuments or scenery.[15] People are harder to visit and represent than stones and landscapes. They rarely stay put for a start, making them more difficult to locate; scheduled encounters do not happen, others stumble into a journey by chance. People have minds of their own, they do not always conform to expectations, they can be awkward and intimidating, they can answer back. Encounter is hard work: 'An encounter with Others is not a simple, automatic thing, but involves will and an effort that not everyone is always ready to undertake.'[16] The tensions between Ramazzotti and Celia result from their different preconceptions, expectations and desires, from the dynamics created by the monetary exchange that is the basis of their relationship and the disparate linguistic skills that render the traveller dependent on his interpreter. Their different ages and sexes also contribute to the tension, as well as the discomfort of staying in a hotel without hot water (e.g., *Birra*, 12–13, 16, 50).

The following chapters examine many of these tensions and contradictions, as well as moments of agreement and harmony. Each chapter takes as principal context a common practical activity that brings travellers into contact with travellees: guiding and interpreting, hosting, staring and photographing, challenging and finally accompanying. Within these contexts tensions emerge between, for example, the practical or functional reason for the encounter and the desire for more meaningful contact, the need for time to create lasting connections and the pressures of constant movement, interacting with a travellee during a journey and representing that interaction in a text addressed to a distant reader. Travellers and travellees constantly encroach on each other's personal spaces, limit each other's freedom, contravene each other's conventions. Encounters disrupt journeys in unexpected ways, they shape journeys, are integral to them, generate the narratives that retell them, and are therefore a rich subject for the study of those narratives. The remaining sections of this chapter outline the corpus of this study, by clarifying my definition of travel writing, its relation to travel practices and its contemporary manifestations in French and Italian.

Travel Writing and Tourism

It can seem meaningless to define a narrative as a travel narrative, since the word travel encompasses such a wide range of practices, from beach tourism, to political exile, to commuter journeys, to religious pilgrimages, to business trips, to military manoeuvres to name but a few.[17] Travel writing also overlaps with other genres, especially ethnography, journalism, autobiography and the novel.[18] While the breadth of the field is its richness, classificatory boundaries are necessary to a critical study and although I do not intend to launch into a detailed definition of the genre here – not least since this has been done thoroughly by others – I will set out the key features of the texts that will be examined in this study.[19]

Jan Borm provides a helpful distinction in his essay 'Defining Travel' between 'travel writing' (or travel literature or *littérature de voyage*), which describes a wide range of texts dealing with the theme of travel, and the 'travel book' (or travelogue or *récit de voyage*), which is more specifically the mostly nonfiction genre.[20] The former, broader category would incorporate fictional works, such as Homer's *The Odyssey*, Swift's *Gulliver's Travels*, Italo Calvino's *Le città invisibili* or Michel Houellebecq's *Plateforme*. The texts examined in this study fit into the latter category, labelled by Borm as the travel book and described as 'any narrative characterized by a non-fiction dominant that relates (almost always) in the first person a journey or journeys that the reader supposes to have taken place in reality while assuming or presupposing that author, narrator and principal character are but one or identical'.[21] Although Borm applies travel writing and travel literature interchangeably, I prefer to use travel writing (or travel text, book or narrative for lexical variety) to describe the mostly nonfiction genre and travel literature as the broader term for literature that takes travel as its theme.[22] The intention is not to imply that travel writing is never literary, but rather to separate narratives that are ostensibly nonfiction from fiction, and those where travel is the principal subject from those where travel is one theme or trope among others.

Borm writes that the reader of the travel book supposes the journey to have taken place in reality and I would add that travel texts deliberately cultivate the impression that they are strongly rooted in real experiences. Odile Gannier evokes the autobiographical pact between reader and writer to suggest that such a contract of mutual expectations and obligations also exists in travel writing.[23] I do not intend to either confirm or refute any correspondence between text and reality, but rather to draw attention to the representation of events as real. Although travel writers use many of the devices of narrative fiction, they also create a reality effect by other means, such as the coincidence of author, narrator and protagonist, or the presentation of the author as a character.[24] The places visited are real places and are described in a believable manner, while paratexts also contribute, such as photographs, subtitles giving details of the journey, or information printed on the book jacket. Style can be another factor, since simpler styles are associated, not necessarily justifiably, with more truthful accounts.[25] The use of these and other devices creates authorial authority and gives readers the impression that what they are reading is factual.[26]

Even when writers set out to tell the truth, creating a representation of reality is no simple task, but it also raises ethical questions about the importance of veracity and the implications of mistaken or intentional inaccuracy. From an ethical or even legal perspective the correspondence between representation and reality can be crucial, especially if a book is accused of misrepresenting people or events.[27] From a purely literary, aesthetic or critical perspective, it is important for a book to create the impression, even if it is an illusion, that it represents real events, allowing for a degree of suspended disbelief.[28] Failing to do so may contravene the implicit rules of the genre and break the contract of expectations with the reader, since a writer can make anything up, but not everything can be lived in the world.[29] Otherwise the text may wander successfully or not into the territory of another genre, such as the novel.[30] The reality effect in travel writing also matters because the genre has long served an informative purpose, providing information about real places in an accessible, entertaining format, originally for readers who were unlikely ever to see the places described, now for readers who are often travellers and tourists themselves. The chapters that follow examine the ethical implications of the relation between reality and text for encounter and its representation and demonstrate how this issue helps to delineate the boundaries of the travel genre.

I focus on a core group of travel texts, which vary in style, but are united by an interest in interpersonal encounter. They might be described as rather conventional travel books, narrating tales of voluntary, temporary travel with principally cultural or experiential motivations. The selected texts belong in the category of predominantly nonfictional travel writing, rather than travel literature, since the reality effect has important implications for the representation of encounter and fictional narratives create a different contract of expectation with the reader. They have been chosen on the basis of thematic, rather than aesthetic or literary criteria; most are more innovative or original in terms of what they say about travel, rather than how they say it. Given this thematic focus I use a broad range of texts to discuss different aspects of the travel encounter, rather than concentrating on particular authors or focusing on particular texts. Theme therefore takes priority over the oeuvre or biography of individual authors, befitting the nature of this study, but references to author-based studies, where these exist, are included in the bibliography.[31] Since it does not make sense to use a completely new corpus for each chapter, the same authors and texts recur in several chapters. While it is difficult to make generalizations about a wider genre based on any selection, it is hoped that the common patterns identified in this particular body of texts are relevant to others.

Recent travel writing exists within the context of tourism as a major economic force, motivating the cross-border mobility of people and money on a massive scale.[32] Like tourism, travel writing is a manifestation of the culture of leisured travel that has become so highly valued among those who can afford to participate. It has long been noted that pioneering travellers open up new routes for mass tourists, albeit often unintentionally, and travel writing publicizes destinations to an audience who are increasingly able to follow in the traveller's footsteps.[33] The genre plays a role in defining travel practices, helping to shape and perpetuate the culture of travel.[34] Despite the connections between travel writing and tourism, travel writers are keen to distinguish their traveller-protagonists from their fellow tourists: the central character of most travel books is a self-defined traveller and specifically not a tourist. Denigration of tourism is as old as the practice itself and antitourism has been a feature of travel writing since there were tourists for writers to scorn.[35] In fact, antitourism has become such a convention of travel writing that originality might best be sought by assuming a tourist identity.[36] Travel writers construct the identities of their traveller characters in opposition to the stereotypical tourist, denigrating the negative qualities of the tourist, to emphasize better the positive qualities of the traveller.[37] Problematically, this often means scapegoating tourists to exonerate travellers of responsibility for some of the more negative aspects of tourism.[38] The activities, practices and beliefs of tourists and travellers overlap more than the latter may admit, blurring the division and raising questions about its descriptive value. However erroneous or distracting it may be, travel writers perpetuate the distinction, maintaining it rhetorically if not practically. I therefore use the word traveller to designate the protagonists of travel texts, but I do so only in order to maintain a distinction between the author as travel writer and the character as traveller, not because I believe that the division between travellers and tourists is either accurate or constructive. Chapter 2 examines how the representation of encounter plays a role in antitourist discourse.

Clearly, it is crucial to consider travel writing in the context of contemporary tourism and therefore logical to turn to studies of tourism to illuminate certain aspects of the genre. Travel as a subject invites research from a wide range of disciplines and has become a focal point for interdisciplinary approaches.[39] Travel writing itself shares historical roots and ongoing links with anthropology and ethnography. Studies of tourism are particularly useful in countering some of the stereotypes and undermining the tourist–traveller dichotomy by moving beyond such distinctions to examine the motivations behind them.[40] Research into the interactions between tourists and their hosts also helps to shed light on interpersonal encounters in travel writing.[41] In the following chapters such studies provide background and insight into such issues as the search for authenticity, the dynamic between traveller as employer and guide or host as employee, the use of tourist services, and the dynamics of tourist photography.

Voyage/Viaggio

In the first section I introduced some of the many contexts that shape the travel encounter. National identity is one context that receives considerable attention and would seem pertinent to a study examining authors from France, Italy and Switzerland.[42] This is not, however, a classically comparative study, in the sense that it focuses on the theme of encounter above and beyond the national contexts specific to the primary sources addressed. I do not aim to provide a survey of travel writing in either French or Italian, but rather to use these literatures as material for a thematic study, thus complementing studies that do address specific national contexts, by presenting identity and encounter in a different way.[43] I aim to analyse the interactions of multiple identity and circumstantial contexts, precisely by shifting the emphasis away from nationality; I do this by considering material in two European languages. Including both French and Italian has the advantage of highlighting similar trends across national boundaries, while limiting the scope to a realistic field of study. While these two languages are natural choices given my own area of expertise, it is hoped that the issues raised and conclusions drawn will be relevant to those working in other language areas and fields. Considering texts in their original language enables a closer focus and makes a wider range of texts available than would be in translation, while English translations are provided for all examples and quotations to ensure accessibility. I therefore limit my exploration of the genre and its treatment in both languages in this section to some brief observations, which provide background for the chapters to come.

Travel writing has enjoyed a renaissance in both France and Italy from the late twentieth century and continuing into the present. Michel Le Bris suggests that 1975–78 signalled the beginning of a new movement in not only French but also wider European travel literature, although in Italy this shift is more marked in the 1990s, a decade that also saw a peak in French travel literature.[44] In France one of the most obvious manifestations of this interest has been the *Pour une littérature voyageuse* movement and its accompanying annual Étonnants voyageurs festival, initiated in 1990 in Saint-Malo. The movement's manifesto, written in reaction against the perceived stagnation of French literature, contains essays by 11 authors, including Le Bris and Bouvier, proposing diverse and sometimes contrasting views on travel and literature.[45] Although the festival and movement embrace a broad range of cultural expression, the manifesto itself proposes travel as a catalyst for literature in particular and as a way of relating to the world and discovering oneself. There is no equivalent in Italy on the scale of either *Pour une littérature voyageuse* or Étonnants voyageurs, although some recent cultural initiatives suggest a move to recognize travel literature, including L'albatros premio e festival per la letteratura di viaggio, running since 1998, and the annual Festival della letteratura di viaggio, inaugurated in 2008.[46]

The increasing popularity of travel writing has been accompanied in both France and Italy by a growth in studies of the genre. Both countries have long histories as major destinations for tourists from all over the world: France is currently the number one international tourist destination, while Italy is number five.[47] In terms of their self-identity, the French seem to consider themselves more readily as travellers than the Italians, whose research tends to focus on Italy as a destination for travellers, rather than a provenance of travellers.[48] This is reflected in the two main research centres on travel literature in each respective country: the Centre de recherche sur la littérature des voyages (CRLV), founded in 1984 and based at the Sorbonne in Paris, and the Centro interuniversitario di ricerche sul 'Viaggio in Italia' (CIRVI), founded in 1978 and based in Turin.[49] Significantly, as its title suggests, the CIRVI almost exclusively addresses travel literature about Italy, namely the Italian travels of usually non-Italian travellers, while the CRLV gathers researchers working on travel literature in its broadest understanding, though French travellers and their journeys abroad unsurprisingly occupy the central focus. Altogether, travel writing written in the late twentieth and turn of the twenty-first centuries has received little attention, though this is largely due to the lack of critical distance. The importance of encounter in this period has been acknowledged, but encounter in the sense in which I describe it above has not been tackled, though some studies have approached broader issues of self and other. The 'editorial effervescence' in travel writing in the last few decades makes this period particularly fascinating for study, and the lack of critical attention to date makes that study all the more urgent.[50]

Although French and Italian tourists do not leave their respective countries with the same frequency as the British or Germans, they do holiday abroad in significant numbers: in 2011 Italians made about 15 million and the French about 23 million journeys abroad for holidays or personal reasons.[51] Tourism in France developed along patterns common to much of Western Europe, influenced by innovations in transport technologies and the democratization of travel, as well as the advent of the paid holiday.[52] For much of the twentieth century, the most significant movement of Italians was the economically motivated displacement of emigration, rather than leisured tourism. However, the postwar economic boom and changes in lifestyle and affluence have transformed the Italians into travellers and tourists themselves, alongside other Europeans.[53] It is interesting to note that studies of tourism in both languages often insist on its common European roots, beginning with Thomas Cook's tours and Baedeker's guides, neither of which originated in either country.

Even the Italian studies include the Grand Tour, despite the fact that for a long time Italians were the hosts, not the tourists.[54] This suggests that tourism is perceived as a practice shared across Western Europe, despite national differences in rates of development and particular trends.

Travel is an eminently border-crossing activity, calling for a comparative and interdisciplinary approach to the study of both the practice itself and the texts that take it as a theme.[55] Travel writing is a transnational genre and although particular forms may be more salient in particular national literatures, the principal features are translated into different languages. Hagen Schulz-Forberg points to the many translations of travel writing, which create a citation network across Europe.[56] Translation is particularly important for travel literature, especially in France and Italy, where a large number of the texts published, both new and reissued, are translations, so that studying travel texts strictly within national canons does not necessarily reflect the way in which they are read.

National differences are not a central concern in the chapters that follow, largely because the encounters I consider seldom bring to the fore issues specific to particular nationalities and rarely call national identity into question. The travellers often share more in common as white, European or Western tourists than they differ because of being French or Italian. They refer to themselves by their racial, religious, regional or continental identity, as well as by their national identity.[57] It is important not to be too reductive, and to avoid suggesting that all European, or Western, travellers can be treated together and reduced to the same characteristics, but the same is true of nationality: no individual should be reduced to his/her nation. National differences might be more salient in a study that examines the reception of travel texts, publishing strategies, or specific geographical or historical contexts. Deliberately grouping writers of different nationalities together better enables focus on some of the many other contextual factors that influence encounters. Michael Cronin's *Across the Lines* provides a precedent to my approach.[58] Cronin uses a mixture of sources, written in English, French, Gaelic and Italian, in order to highlight aspects of language and translation in travel writing that are not necessarily unique to particular nations. The texts chosen here also cover a range of travel destinations across the world, once more shifting the focus away from the specifically national or geographical, to other determining aspects of the travel encounter.

Chapters

Travellers and travellees encounter each other in different circumstances and for different reasons, but I focus on several of the most common contexts that bring them together, all of which centre on actions performed by travellees to or for travellers. With the aim of avoiding defining travellees in terms of presumed or fixed social or cultural identity, the chapters are entitled with verbs describing these actions: guiding, hosting, staring, challenging and accompanying. This selection does not claim to cover all encounters between travellers and travellees, but it does represent some of the most significant forms of interaction.

The pursuit of encounters is a deliberate approach, or strategy, that coincides with others evident in travel writing and the culture of travel in recent decades. Before embarking on an analysis of specific encounters, Chapter 2 examines several of these strategies and their common points with encounter. I begin by briefly highlighting the connections between encounter and three common themes: antitourism, fears of and responses to the end of travel, and deceleration. I then examine the role of encounter in the traveller's search for authenticity, a much-discussed concept in tourism and travel writing. Encounter has the potential to both enable the traveller's access to authenticity, in terms of information and 'back regions', as well as providing authenticity through the interaction between travellers and travellees. Discourses of travel frequently express value judgements designating 'better' and 'worse' ways of travelling, and this ethical dimension of travel writing is the final subject of discussion in Chapter 2. Issues relating to authenticity and ethics influence many of the encounters in subsequent chapters.

Guiding is arguably the most fundamental action that travellees perform for travellers, making this subject a natural choice for Chapter 3, the first of the chapters focused on specific types of encounter. My analysis of guiding develops directly from the strategies addressed in Chapter 2, particularly authenticity and ethics. Guides enable access to place, culture, information and people, and are especially well placed to assist travellers in their search for authenticity. The traveller–guide relationship is hindered, however, by the complex circumstances and multiple factors outlined above. Tensions emerge because of conflicting expectations and loyalties, while the authenticity of the relationship itself is undermined by the employer–employee dynamic. The potential importance of the guide to the success of a journey is undeniable, but travellees are not always credited for their role. This chapter examines how travel writers attempt to acknowledge travellees, but also how they frequently fail to do so, reflecting some of the limitations of the travel genre and setting out key points about agency that underlie the representations of travellees addressed in later chapters.

Providing hospitality, whether food or shelter, whether as employees of the tourist industry or as hosts welcoming guests into their private home, is another major travellee activity and is therefore addressed in Chapter 4.

Hospitality sets encounters within specific contexts, which call into question several common discourses of travel. Continuing on the theme of authenticity from Chapters 2 and 3, the private home of the travellee is a potentially authentic environment, but the experience of being hosted tests the limits of the desire for authenticity when competing with other needs such as privacy and comfort. Within the travellee's home the traveller is a guest and subject to the host's control, creating further tensions and undermining another ideal: freedom. This also exposes the boundaries of leisured travel, as revealing comparisons are made between the experiences of tourists and those of immigrants. Hospitality brings to the fore two more general aspects of the travel encounter: reciprocity and duration, both of which are threatened by the very mobility of the traveller, whose proposed solutions are examined in the final section, laying the ground for the encounters examined in subsequent chapters.

Encounters do not always involve sustained verbal interaction, but can occur with the briefest of visual exchanges. Chapter 5 therefore moves beyond the more sustained interactions of guiding and hosting to examine brief encounters rooted in the visual. The traveller is usually the one who observes all others, but here I turn the tables and focus instead on the traveller as object of the travellee's stare. Pursuing the issue of limiting freedom from Chapter 4, this chapter examines one specific way in which travellees control travellers. Travellers are forced to negotiate identities imposed on them by travellees, but they also resist and return the stare. The gap between journey and narrative is particularly evident when travellers use their texts to recover their authority. The second part of the chapter explores the role of the camera in the traveller–travellee encounter, continuing the theme of reciprocity from the previous chapter. Photography is both a disrupting and a creative force, depending on the traveller's approach and the travellee's response.

Chapter 6 focuses on another form of brief but significant encounter: challenging encounters, which are unplanned moments that interrupt the flow of a journey, arresting travellers, perturbing them and raising ethical dilemmas. These encounters often occur against a background of inequality, highlighting the disparate level of wealth between traveller and travellee, which contributes to their ethical implications. The economics of travel, which has already cropped up in previous chapters, is addressed in more detail here. The chapter focuses on meetings with travellees playing three specific roles: rickshaw riders, prostitutes and beggars, each with their particular moral connotations. The specific circumstances of these encounters shape the travellers' deliberations and responses, but the fact of addressing the travel text to a home readership also influences the presentation of autobiographical traveller-protagonists.

Travellers are usually solitary characters, remaining alone between encounters, but they sometimes join forces with others. The final chapter addresses these travelling travellees, who accompany travellers for all or part of their journeys, whether brought along from home or met on the road. The different treatment of companions, depending on when and where they are first encountered, reflects on the boundaries of the journey and its narrative, helping to mark the separation between home and away. This final chapter rounds off the study by returning to questions of genre and how encounter contributes towards setting generic boundaries for travel writing. Companions are often remarkable for their absence, but their presence, though infrequent, is strategic. Like tourists, examined in Chapter 2, companions serve to define the identity of the protagonist as traveller, once more shaping the understanding of travel promoted and perpetuated by travel writing.

Chapter 2

STRATEGY, AUTHENTICITY, ETHICS

Il viaggiare in treno o in nave, su grandi distanze, m'ha ridato il senso della vastità del mondo e soprattutto m'ha fatto riscoprire un'umanità, quella dei più, quella di cui uno, a forza di volare, dimentica quasi l'esistenza […].

Gli aeroporti, falsi come i messaggi pubblicitari, isole di relativa perfezione anche nello sfacelo dei paesi in cui si trovano, si assomigliano ormai tutti; tutti parlano nello stesso linguaggio internazionale che dà a ciascuno l'impressione di essere arrivato a casa. […]

Le stazioni invece no, sono vere, sono specchi delle città nel cui cuore sono piantate. Le stazioni stanno vicino alle cattedrali, alle moschee, alle pagode o ai mausolei. Una volta arrivati lì, si è arrivati davvero. (Terzani, *Indovino*, 12–14)

(Travelling by train or ship, over long distances, has restored my sense of the world's sheer size and above all has led me to rediscover a section of humanity, the majority, whose existence one almost forgets, because of always flying […].

Airports, false as advertising messages, islands of relative perfection, despite the collapse of the countries in which they are located, all resemble each other now; they all speak the same international language that gives each person the impression they are arriving home. […]

Train stations don't, however, they are real, they are mirrors of the cities in whose heart they are planted. Stations are close to the cathedrals, the mosques, the pagodas and the mausoleums. Once you arrive there, you have really arrived.)

These few extracts from Tiziano Terzani encapsulate the themes of this chapter: encounter as a strategy, authenticity and ethics.[1] I open with a discussion of three modes of travel or attitudes to travel, which I call strategies, that all relate directly to encounter. While Terzani does not mention tourism by name in these passages, his criticism of swift anonymous air travel brings to mind tourism and its stereotypical faults. Terzani clearly identifies himself as a traveller, who has 'really arrived', as opposed to the tourist, who hops from airport to airport – introducing the first theme: antitourism. He laments the homogeneity of airports and their monolingualism, recalling fears that globalization is wiping out the diversity that motivates travellers, thus threatening to end travel itself – the second subject for consideration here. His comparison between the merits of the slower train or ship and the shortcomings of the hasty plane relate to another discourse, common in contemporary travel writing: deceleration or slow travel, the third strategy in the opening section. Antitourism, the end of travel and deceleration are themes that have been examined closely by others studying travel writing, but they provide background to many of the encounters discussed in the following chapters and I will focus on this connection here. Terzani specifies that travelling by train or ship enables encounters, putting him back in touch with a humanity forgotten in the air.

Terzani associates airports with 'false messages' and stations with the 'real', where one 'really' arrives, which brings us to the theme of authenticity. For Terzani the airport is a fake environment, artificially created to reassure through homogeneity, while the station is an authentic place, located at the heart of the city, reflecting its genuine character in all its diversity. The search for authenticity, though frequently discussed and maligned, underlies much travel and tourism, particularly in travel writing. While authenticity is often a quality of places, as suggested by Terzani, it can also be a quality of relationships and encounters. Chapters 3 and 4 focus specifically on authenticity, since the guides and hosts whom travellers encounter alternately enable and prevent their access to authentic information, experiences and relations.

The final section of this chapter examines a theme latent throughout the passages from Terzani. He clearly expresses value judgments about different ways of travelling: the superiority of the ship or train over the plane. For Terzani choices between modes of travel are not merely a question of convenience or lifestyle but also have ethical implications, and it is this ethics of travel that concerns us here. Relations between the self and others are central to ethics, while travel also raises its own ethical questions, making this theme particularly relevant to the travel encounter. Ethics underlies all the encounters addressed in this book, but especially those in Chapter 6, where travellers face ethically challenging encounters with rickshaw riders, prostitutes and beggars. The more ethical, more authentic, slower, antitouristic, unusual way of travelling that Terzani advocates brings him into contact with a humanity that he had almost lost, with the individual travellees whom he encounters on his journey.

Strategy

Antitourism is a common trope in travel writing, as we have seen in Chapter 1, and the traveller's identity is largely shaped in opposition to the tourist. Among the various character flaws that the stereotypical tourist exhibits is a lack of interest in encounters. As Tzvetan Todorov puts it: 'Le touriste est un visiteur pressé qui préfère les monuments aux êtres humains' (The tourist is a hurried visitor, who prefers monuments to human beings).[2] Todorov suggests that the tourist's aversion to encounters is partly due to a lack of time, but he also adds, 'L'absence de rencontres avec des sujets différents est beaucoup plus reposante, puisqu'elle ne remet jamais en question notre identité; il est moins dangereux de voir des chameaux que des hommes' (The absence of encounters with diverse individuals is far more relaxing, since it never puts our identity into question; it is less dangerous to view camels than people).[3] The tourist industry often contributes to this impression by minimizing, managing and even preventing encounters between tourists and travellees, as we shall see in Chapter 4. Whether or not tourists live up to their asocial stereotype, antitourist assumptions follow the portrait Todorov outlines, whereby the tourist positively shuns contact with unfamiliar others. The deliberate pursuit of encounters is therefore a useful strategy of self-distinction for antitourist travellers: 'Insistence on the primacy of human intercultural contact in travel is of course consistent with binary constructions of travel as antithetical/superior to tourism, where tourism is overwhelmingly conceived as a practice biased against the interpersonal encounter.'[4] This is not to suggest that encounters only appeal as an antitourist tactic, it is merely one of many motivations. Nonetheless, an encounter with an individual can develop into a significant event in travel: famous monuments are immobile and well signposted, while weeding out or stumbling across a particular person and enjoying a meaningful moment of connection may be more unique and memorable, not to mention story worthy.

Mass tourism is one of the factors that have contributed to the perception that travel itself may be coming to an end. This does not mean a literal end to displacement, which is thriving, but the end of a certain culture or kind of travel, the end of certain possibilities for encounter with difference. The lament usually follows a pattern: the democratization of travel that has produced mass tourism has resulted in a qualitative degradation in the practice of travel. Travel has become banal and commonplace, it is no longer a risk or a challenge through which to prove oneself, while cultural differences have been levelled by global homogenization and the blank spaces on the maps have all been filled.[5]

Charles Forsdick identifies discourses of the decline of diversity throughout the twentieth century and even earlier, suggesting that decline is always in process and never reaches its conclusion.[6] Gérard Cogez and Olivier Hambursin both note that despite travel being in constant crisis throughout the twentieth century, French writers continue to produce travel books.[7] Others writing on French travel also contradict the purported demise of both travel and travel writing, while Forsdick and Feroza Basu examine some of the ways in which French writers innovate and reinvent travel.[8] Gaia De Pascale notes briefly that fear of the end of travel characterizes Italian travel writing of the eighties and nineties.[9] Both French and Italian writers mourn changes in travel, but both continue to find solutions, as demonstrated by the trend for deceleration, examined below.

Encounter with radical difference may no longer be possible, but the conditions for encounter have never been better. An increasing population and increasing opportunities for movement can only lead to greater opportunities for people to meet each other. Whether or not one believes that a global monoculture is inevitable, a crowded planet does increase the potential for encounters. New human beings are created at a far swifter pace than new tourist attractions or natural wonders. Michael Cronin explores Benoît Mandelbrot's concept of fractal geometry: 'The shapes or fractals in this new geometry allowed infinite length to be contained in finite space.'[10] Cronin suggests that it has applications for travel, particularly in countering the 'discourse of exhaustion', or the end of travel.[11] This fractal approach is applicable to encounter: if tourists focus on individuals, rather than wider cultures or places, there is an infinite possibility for encounter and also for travel.[12] The decline in linguistic diversity, though a tragic loss in itself, further facilitates encounter: if more people speak fewer languages, then communication becomes easier. Furthermore, changing attitudes to race, gender and class broaden the opportunities for encounter between people who would have avoided contact in the past. The difficulties of encounter mean that it remains one of the great challenges of travel, one of the few that has hardly been altered by any of the developments that revolutionized travel and tourism in the twentieth century.

The 'slow food' movement originated in Italy, so it is no surprise that 'slow travel' has followed. This trend responds to both the end of travel and antitourism, while favouring encounter. De Pascale's book *Slow travel* advocates decelerated journeys, providing practical information and a bibliography of travel writing that exemplifies the practice.[13] Terzani's *Un indovino mi disse*, which supplied the quotation opening this chapter, is one of Pascale's choices. Terzani recounts the challenge he set himself in 1993 to avoid planes for a year and travel only by land, while continuing his work as a journalist. The change reinvigorates travel for him, altering his perception of distance and space, giving him a new attention to detail and a sense of discovery and adventure (*Indovino*, 12). Paolo Rumiz is another proponent of slow travel, choosing the bicycle and the slow train as his preferred means of transport and disparaging the car and the plane.[14] He insists that Italians need to travel slowly to perceive places and distances differently: 'L'Italia ha un grande bisogno di un viaggio lento. Da noi si è smesso di viaggiare: ci si sposta' (*Oriente*, 26; Italy really needs slow travel. We have stopped travelling: we move instead). Another Italian example is Sergio Ramazzotti's journey in *Vado verso il Capo*, in which he undertakes to cover the length of Africa from Algiers to Cape Town, using only public transport, as an alternative to the Paris–Le Cap rally.[15]

Forsdick and Basu both identify and analyse a trend for decelerated travel, particularly walking journeys, in French travel writing in the late twentieth century.[16] Walking becomes a protest against the speed of mechanized transport, but is also a way of experiencing the world and one's own body differently. Bernard Ollivier's 'long walk' from Istanbul to Xi'an, recounted in the three volumes of *Longue marche*, is one example of this trend. Other decelerated journeys in French include Nicolas Bouvier's tale of driving from Geneva to the Khyber Pass in *L'usage du monde* and François Maspero's month-long exploration of the RER B line in Paris, narrated in *Les passagers du Roissy Express*.[17]

Duccio Canestrini, who also advocates taking one's time, argues that the main purpose is to 'moltiplicare le occasioni di contatto con le persone' (increase the opportunities for contact with people).[18] While some decelerated travellers may have other priorities, slow travel certainly facilitates encounter, making encounter both a motivation for and a consequence of deceleration. Feroza Basu identifies this as a particular feature of French walking journeys, and links it back to antitourism: 'By positing pedestrianism as the only true means of equitable interpersonal encounters […] travel writers reinscribe into their practices of travel that which has been theorized as the most reprehensible omission of touristic travel: human intercultural contact.'[19] Ollivier often asserts that walking helps him to meet people (e.g., *Marche I*, 94–5), but other types of decelerated movement also favour encounter; Jean Chesneaux argues that long-distance train journeys provide opportunities for contact.[20] Ollivier and Chesneaux make an interesting comparison, since the latter cites his encounters with Chinese passengers on trains, while the former has great difficulties encountering anyone in China, no matter how slowly he moves, because of his lack of language skills; clearly a slow pace is not enough to guarantee meaningful encounters.

Authenticity

Authenticity is another connecting thread linking travel writing to tourism and another weapon in the antitourist's arsenal. Superficiality is a common stereotype of tourism: tourists are accused of failing to comprehend or access the destination culture, while the tourist industry cossets them in bubbles of comfort and familiarity, screening them from the places they are supposed to be visiting. This approach is thought to exclude the possibility of authentic travel experiences, a situation further compounded by the commercialization of tourism and the commoditization of culture: principal sources of inauthenticity.[21] Prioritizing authenticity is therefore another way for travellers to distinguish themselves from tourists. This is not a recent development; James Buzard describes authenticity as a mark of antitourism in nineteenth-century travel literature.[22] As well as being an antitourist strategy, authenticity has wider significance for travel writing, since the pursuit of authentic experiences is a natural course for travel writers who wish to present accurate, or at least convincingly realistic, representations of their travel destinations.

Authenticity has been the subject of much debate in the study of tourism, since Daniel Boorstin's attack on the inauthenticity of tourism and Dean MacCannell's response that tourism is a quest for authenticity in reaction to the alienation of modern society.[23] MacCannell argues that tourists seek out the authenticity they are denied by modern society in the lives of other peoples, yet they are often foiled in their quest by the staging of tourist sites, which prevents them from accessing the authentic 'back regions'. The studies that have followed have taken less homogenizing approaches to tourists, suggesting that authenticity is only a priority for some, while others place greater value on pursuits such as recreation, quality family time or the acquisition of status amongst peers.[24] Maxine Feifer identifies the 'post-tourist', who is not duped by the staged authenticity of tourist attractions, but approaches them playfully, accepting their inauthenticity and even revelling in it.[25]

The traveller-protagonists of travel writing usually share much in common with tourists who do prioritize authenticity. Recreational tourism, which provides relaxation as an antidote to work life, might make a good setting for a novel, but travel writing requires a greater engagement with place or culture.[26] The flippancy of the post-tourist is rarely reflected in travel writing in French and Italian; antitourism and authenticity remain serious values.[27] Travellers tend to resemble those tourists for whom travel is an educational or cultural experience, who seek knowledge and engage with people and their culture. Such tourists and travellers look for the hidden realities they presume to be masked behind external appearances, and in so doing they repeat what Marie-Paule Ha describes as: 'the Western ways of interpretation, whose ultimate goal lies in penetrating as deeply as possible beneath the surface in order to retrieve the Truth or decipher an enigma'.[28] Corrado Ruggeri, for example, visits the Thai village of Ko Pannyi, which has been transformed into a tourist attraction: 'Tutto finto, a uso e consumo del turista che si accontenta della recita' (115; Everything is fake, for the use and consumption of the tourist who is satisfied with the performance).[29] The traveller is not duped by this false spectacle and his guide invites him backstage to see the real village, saying '"Vieni, andiamo a vedere qualche briciola di autenticità"' (116; Come on, let's go and see a few scraps of authenticity). Ruggeri makes a direct link between tourism and inauthenticity, while distinguishing himself and his experience of the village from the tourists. The word 'authenticity' is not necessarily used, but the sentiment is expressed through the assertion of particular values. Nostalgia for past societies and a corresponding interest in those that are non-Western and perceived to be nonmodern is typical of the concept of authenticity described by MacCannell.[30] This is also characteristic of writers such as Terzani, who laments the building of a new highway into Laos, which will bring hordes of destructive tourists, or the development of Singapore, which has become 'la Betlemme della nuova grande religione: la religione dei consumi, del benessere materiale, del turismo di massa' (*Indovino*, 31 and 193; the Bethlehem of the great new religion: the religion of consumerism, of material wealth, of mass tourism). Once more, tourism and inauthenticity go hand in hand. The means of travelling, such as using slower forms of transport, may also suggest a desire for authenticity; Ollivier explicitly distinguishes himself, the 'voyageur authentique' (authentic traveller), from tourists in jeeps who cross the country to see and photograph it but 'n'en franchissent pas la porte' (*Marche I*, 305; don't cross the threshold).[31]

Although researchers of tourism have expressed some impatience with the debate about authenticity,[32] it continues to be used in studies of tourism and remains useful to travel writing.[33] Authenticity is a complex term with a wide variety of meanings and applications, and is open to varied interpretation.[34] It is as elusive a concept as truth, but it also has connotations of tradition, continuity, sincerity. Authenticity can be a quality of objects, of cultural practices, of facts and information, of relationships, of feelings, of oneself. These notions are interrelated but are often vague and necessitate different schemes of corroboration. In some cases we look to others more knowledgeable than ourselves to confirm the authenticity of something: we might turn to an art historian for the authentication of a painting as an original, or to an Italian for an authentic recipe for *melanzane alla parmigiana*. While these examples are open to debate even among the experts, other instances of authenticity, especially in terms of relationships or feelings, are a matter of personal opinion. Tourists and travellers come across or seek out all of these different types of authenticity at different times during their journeys and they often turn to others to verify the authenticity of their experiences. For the purposes of this study I use authenticity in its broadest understanding in relation to travel experiences and encounters. Since it is a highly subjective category, I do not aim to find objective defining criteria, but focus instead on analysing travel writers' own subjective notions and especially their navigation of the different paths to authenticity. I limit myself to three of the areas where authenticity is relevant to travel writing: information, 'back regions' and encounters.

The authenticity of information or knowledge may be important to travel writers for whom accuracy is a major concern, but there is nothing straightforward about verifying the authenticity of a piece of information. Ning Wang clarifies the distinction between objectivist and constructivist approaches: the former defines authenticity as an objective, innate quality of an object or cultural practice, while the latter describes it as a constructed, attributed value.[35] The constructivist approach is useful because it emphasizes both the indeterminacy of authenticity and the fact that it is up for negotiation.[36] The second area where authenticity is useful to travel writing is the concept of back regions, which MacCannell has adapted from Erving Goffman for specific application to tourism. In MacCannell's words, Goffman's original division proposes that in social establishments 'the front is the meeting place of hosts and guests or customers and service persons, and the back is the place where members of the home team retire between performances to relax and to prepare'.[37] MacCannell connects this division with concerns in modern society about authenticity: 'This division into front and back supports the popular beliefs regarding the relationship of truth to intimacy. In our society, intimacy and closeness are accorded much importance: they are seen as the core of social solidarity and they are also thought by some to be morally superior to rationality and distance in social relationships, and more "real". Being "one of them", or at one with "them", means, in part, being permitted to share back regions with "them".'[38] Following on from this, MacCannell concludes that many, though not all, tourists are in search of authentic back regions, but he suggests that tourists are foiled because false back regions are deliberately staged to imitate the authenticity they seek, while the real back regions are kept out of their reach. The commercialization of tourist sites is a major factor determining their inauthenticity and the pursuit of the authentic back regions is also an escape from the commercial.[39] In terms of encounters, the most interesting aspect of authentic information and back regions is that each usually requires the intervention of a mediator. Just as Ruggeri is dependent on his guide to lead him to the authentic back region of Ko Pannyi, travellers require the help of others to put them on the right path to authenticity, and in this they are no different to tourists. Such assistance comes from a range of sources, both human and written, both local and conational to the traveller. Guides, interpreters and hosts play particularly significant roles as mediators, as we shall see in the following two chapters.

The constructivist approach is useful in drawing attention to questions of how authenticity is constructed, but also who is doing the constructing, the authenticating. The mediator's principal qualification for presenting authenticity to the traveller is some form of knowledge, but this raises questions such as whether the 'local' knowledge of experience is more valid than the 'expert' knowledge of reading and research, sanctioned perhaps by Western institutions.[40] Travel writers choose to whom they attribute the power to authenticate: although mediators are in a position to authenticate for travellers, writers, through their own representations, exercise the power to authenticate the authenticator.[41] Ollivier, for example, often distrusts the knowledge of local people about the old caravanserais he visits along the Silk Route. He places more confidence in the information he has learned from books, mostly written by Westerners, including Jean-Baptiste Tavernier's seventeenth-century *Six voyages en Turquie et en Perse*, although he also conducts a long interview with local historians at the University in Erzurum (*Marche I*, 33 and 237–8). Since authenticity is so subjective, the debate between tourists and antitourists about the authenticity of their personal travel experiences is often rather unfruitful, while examining the negotiations over the power to authenticate, as I do in the following chapters, can provide a useful antidote to such wrangling.

Authenticity is not limited to objects, experiences or information but, as suggested by MacCannell in the quotation above, it is also associated with closer and more intimate relationships between people, making it particularly relevant to the theme of encounters. This aspect of authenticity has been addressed in various ways in studies of tourism, with considerable reference to philosophical interpretations of the concept.[42] In an early approach to the authenticity of encounters in tourism, Philip Pearce and Gianna Moscardo suggest extending MacCannell's regions to include the people whom tourists encounter as potential sources of authenticity themselves.[43] More recently, Wang proposes applying 'existential authenticity' to tourism, following Heidegger, encompassing both 'intrapersonal' authenticity, achieved through bodily feelings and self-making, and 'interpersonal' authenticity, involving the tourist's relations with others.[44] Travel is widely considered to be an excellent path to self-development and self-discovery, making intrapersonal authenticity particularly relevant to travel writing. Travel texts, especially those of a more autobiographical nature, often represent the traveller's inner journey as much as the journey in the world.[45] Since this study focuses on travellers' relations with others, Wang's interpersonal authenticity is more directly relevant here.[46] Wang concentrates on family ties and touristic 'communitas', a notion he borrows from Victor Turner, where the usual social structures and hierarchies disappear in the liminality of tourism, allowing for more spontaneous and genuine relations between tourists.[47] Interpersonal authenticity need not be limited to the tourist group, but can apply to relations between tourists and the people they meet, whether employed in the tourist industry or encountered beyond its bounds.[48] The traveller characters in travel writing do differ from tourists in the sense that they often travel alone, positively avoiding other tourists and prioritizing instead encounters with locals, which means that they are more likely to experience interpersonal authenticity in these kinds of relationships.

Authenticity in the encounter between two people implies that the relation is based on genuine, spontaneous sentiments, requiring that each be true or genuine to him/herself and to the other. Therefore the traveller's perception that his/her interlocutor is being genuine is of importance in creating the impression of an authentic encounter. Trust is a key element, since one of the major factors interfering with the authenticity of travel encounters is the suspicion of ulterior motives. Many of the encounters between tourists and travellees are bound by financial relationships determined by the tourist industry, where tourists pay for services carried out by travellees. This contributes significantly to the perceived inauthenticity of such relationships, especially when tourists know that part of the service is a semblance of friendship. An authentic relationship is therefore one that either does not have a financial basis or where this is transcended through the authentic expression of honesty and friendship.[49] In the context of global tourism, travellers have many relationships that are primarily economic and are therefore motivated to transcend the monetary basis of these relationships whenever possible. This aspect of authenticity is particularly relevant to the encounters I study, since many of these involve travellees who are employed by the traveller, such as guides and interpreters, as we shall see in the following two chapters.

Ethics

The recent 'ethical turn' in literary studies has revived interest in an area that has always been central to both literature and the criticism of literature, but has become neglected, or disguised under the banner of causes such as feminist criticism, Marxist criticism, or postcolonial studies.[50] Although ethical criticism carries unsavoury implications of moralizing, censoring or the didactic, it can be envisaged more positively as a debate or dialogue, rather than judgement, about the issues that are central to our lives and to the literature that represents them. Ethics is an important but also rather neglected aspect of travel literature.[51] In some ways this lack of attention is surprising given the weight of ethical debates surrounding travel and tourism, particularly in terms of their impact on environment, culture and society. Perhaps it should not be so surprising, given the persistent distancing of travel writing from tourism, a separation that is refuted by two recent studies that do take an ethical approach to the genre: Patrick Holland and Graham Huggan's *Tourists with Typewriters* and Debbie Lisle's *The Global Politics of Contemporary Travel Writing*.[52] Relationships with others are at the heart of ethics, making it especially relevant to the theme of the interpersonal encounter, while representation, the very essence of travel writing and its study, also raises ethical questions.[53]

Martha Nussbaum, who approaches the connections between ethics and literature from the perspective of moral philosophy, identifies the central question of ethics as that formulated by the ancient Greek philosophers: 'How should one live?'[54] Nussbaum proceeds to argue that literature, especially novels, examines and answers this central question, and that literary theory should also concern itself with such enquiry.[55] According to Nussbaum, literature contributes because 'Literary works […] are not neutral instruments for the investigation of all conceptions. Built into the very structure of a novel is a certain conception of what matters.'[56] Although Nussbaum focuses on novels, her proposals for an ethical approach to literature apply to other genres: Richard Freadman argues that autobiography inevitably addresses the central ethical question, since how people live is the genre's very subject, while John Wiltshire applies Nussbaum's arguments to pathography (narrative accounts of the experience of illness by patients or carers), asserting their importance for bioethics.[57] Travel literature is another genre with ethical relevance. If novels answer 'How should one live?', then travel books address 'How should one travel?'

One might argue that travel writing answers the question 'How does one travel?', but not 'How should one travel?', disputing the suggestion that it expresses value judgements about different ways of travelling. Addressing the ethical in literature is not a matter of imposing something from outside, but rather focusing on an issue that much literature consciously deals with already.[58] Ethical issues are already present in travel writing; the common recurrence of antitourism clearly demonstrates beliefs that there are better and worse ways of travelling. If travel writers criticize the ways certain tourists behave it is because they believe that those behaviours are incorrect, inappropriate or immoral, revealing their own ethical values. Travel and tourism are not merely recreational, they raise ethical issues, though these differ in the course of different journeys: a beach holiday on the Côte d'Azur implies different, and probably lesser, ethical questions than a trip to North Korea. Travel is also ethically important as a valued means of self-development. One of the reasons why travel is valued so highly is its role in shaping people, by confronting them with experiences and challenges. People expect travel to change them and they expect it to change them for the better. Although it is difficult to identify direct connections between travel writing and the actions of its readers, since values and choices are gradually constructed through interactions and conversations with multiple sources, travel writing is nonetheless a significant forum for discussing the ethics of travel and helping to shape each traveller's own ethics.[59] The question of how one *should* travel is therefore absolutely relevant to a discussion of the genre. The intention here is not to set out a code of ethical conduct for travel writers and readers, but rather to examine the ethical issues that travel writing addresses, directly or indirectly, as they arise in relation to interpersonal encounter. The values asserted and perpetuated by travel writing convey the ethics of travel, often according to authors' assumptions about their readers. While travel writing is ethically important for a range of reasons, I will focus here on several related specifically to interpersonal encounter: intercultural relations, representation and relative wealth.

As the blank spaces disappear, as the human population increases, as transport and communications technologies bind us closer together, it is increasingly difficult for any social group, and perhaps any individual, to live in isolation from those whose lifestyle, culture, language, religion, and/or race differ from their own. As we live in increasing proximity, even without travelling, constructing positive relationships across such identity boundaries becomes essential. This connectedness and its challenges are addressed by Kwame Anthony Appiah in his book *Cosmopolitanism*, subtitled *Ethics in a World of Strangers*.[60] Travellers are, and always have been, at the forefront of intercultural contact, whether they are the explorers and navigators of past centuries, tourists on a package holiday, or immigrants arriving in a new country. Interpersonal encounter between two individuals is the most basic form of human interaction and when the two individuals concerned, like most travellers and travellees, are from different cultural backgrounds, then it is the most basic form of multicultural relation. Interpersonal encounter across such divides can deteriorate because of clashing values, misunderstandings, disagreements and even violence, as we shall see in the course of the following chapters. At the very least, travellers and travellees often find themselves stepping on each other's toes, encroaching into each other's space: physical, psychological, metaphorical. As Appiah constantly asserts, what we need is dialogue and conversation, both literally between individuals and metaphorically through literature and art.[61] Travel writing is already taking part in that conversation in both senses.

As well as dealing with how one should travel, travel writing also addresses the question 'How should one write about travel?' The text is a dialogue between writer and reader, or implied author and implied reader, and travel writers usually – if often incorrectly – assume that their readers share their own culture; travel writing brings home stories about elsewhere.[62] It is also the representation of another dialogue, with that supposedly passive figure, the one who is always discussed behind his/her back – the travellee. Many of the ethical problems of travel writing as a genre arise from the fact that it is always a conversation about someone else, going on in their absence. Despite the ethical complexity of representing other cultures and peoples, travel texts remain important channels for cross-cultural exchange. By paying close attention to the character of the travellee, I will show how their active role emerges even in a text written by another, but also how it is suppressed.

Tourism raises ethical issues concerning, for example, environmental sustainability, cultural impact and social interactions. Sustainability, responsibility and ecotourism are all labels describing attempts at constructing more ethical approaches to tourism, while codes of conduct abound.[63] The environment and sustainability have attracted particular attention in recent years, but since I focus on the interpersonal encounter at the individual scale, I concentrate on another ethical issue related to tourism: inequality. Tourism is a multibillion-dollar industry and a luxury product in a world where wealth is increasingly unevenly distributed. This imbalance is to the great benefit of tourists, as Canestrini bluntly comments: 'È chiaro che lo sviluppo del turismo di massa nei Paesi economicamente sottosviluppati è legato alla disparità economica: se il Guatemala fosse caro come la Svezia, gli scandinavi non ci andrebbero più' (It's clear that the development of mass tourism in economically underdeveloped countries is linked to economic disparity: if Guatemala was as expensive as Sweden, the Scandinavians would no longer go there).[64] Zygmunt Bauman argues that increased mobility widens the gap: 'Rather than homogenizing the human condition, the technological annulment of temporal/spatial distances tends to polarize it.'[65] Economic forces influence encounter in different ways. First of all, the traveller often encounters the travellee as a service provider, so the encounter is defined as an economic transaction from the start. Secondly, broader global inequalities directly affect the encounter between two individuals in terms of the disparity in their own personal wealth, which can create situations with ethical implications. What, for example, can the tourist or traveller buy? What should be for sale? Tourism itself is the purchase of services and experiences, but does this include the personal histories of guides, a question addressed in Chapter 3, or an individual's photograph, examined in Chapter 4? Chapter 6 delves further into such questions, analysing travellers' responses to the ethical dilemmas faced when encountering travellees whose standard of living trails far behind their own.

Travel texts connect their readers to people and places that they may never encounter themselves and, like Nussbaum's novels, broaden our own limited experiences.[66] Literature, including travel literature, has the capacity to create empathy, enabling and encouraging readers to identify with characters and situations that are often totally alien, totally outside of their personal experience. Travel writing appeals because it is entertaining and, as Nussbaum also points out, its power, like that of novels, derives from this ability to entertain.[67] Nussbaum lists several features of novels that are also features of an Aristotelian ethical position. Although she focuses on particular novels, which address philosophical and ethical questions directly, several of the features she identifies can also be found, to a greater or lesser extent, in travel writing and contribute likewise to its ethics. Nussbaum associates the priority of perceptions and the priority of the particular: 'The subtleties of a complex ethical situation must be seized in a confrontation with the situation itself, by a faculty that is suited to address it as a complex whole. Prior general formulations lack both the concreteness and the flexibility that is required. They do not contain the particularizing details of the matter at hand, with which decision must grapple; and they are not responsive to what is there, as good decision must be.'[68] Ethics is not based on general rules alone, but on responses to concrete, contextualized situations, taking into account the many factors in play. This allows for the flexibility to respond to new and unanticipated aspects of a situation, as well as contextually relevant features, and the uniqueness and relevance of particular people and relationships.[69] Nussbaum praises the novel's ability to find the balance between appealing to common human nature and emphasizing the particular instance.[70] Travel writing might not always provide the same thick descriptions that Nussbaum finds in Henry James's novels, but it does attend to the concrete and the particular in ways that provide enlightened representations of ethically complex encounters, as we shall see in Chapter 6. Nussbaum also defends the ethical value of the emotions, countering Plato and Kant's emphasis on the rational by arguing that the emotions are also necessary to decision-making.[71] Travel writing, like novels, represents the emotional responses of characters to events and portrays ethical decisions in all their immediate richness and complexity. Finally, Nussbaum points to the importance of contingency, of 'uncontrolled happenings', in ethical understanding.[72] Every traveller knows, and perhaps even hopes, that their journey will entail unpredictable events and the ability to respond to the unexpected is a quality of the stereotypically ideal traveller.

Some travellers wring their hands over actions and decisions, while others plough on obliviously. Certain travel writers take a direct interest in the ethics of travel and travel encounters, such as Francesco Piccolo and Jean-Claude Guillebaud, among the authors whose texts I examine. Even those who do not set out with ethical questions in mind find themselves confronted with dilemmas and their responses contribute to discussions about how one should travel and how one should write about it, albeit often reluctantly, unconsciously, incompletely or counterproductively. Holland and Huggan suggest that, in a positive sense, travel writing can encourage its readers to reflect on their own travel practices, but that it also 'frequently provides an effective alibi for the perpetuation or reinstallment of ethnocentrically superior attitudes to "other" cultures, peoples, and places'.[73] Travel writing often asserts and perpetuates existing norms and values, but at other times it questions or challenges ideas and assumptions. I echo Holland and Huggan, who state that *Tourists with Typewriters* 'makes a pitch for the ethical value of travel writing, even as it demonstrates that travel narratives are unreliable in the extreme'.[74] Travel writing expresses an ethics of travel, and encounter is valued as a strategy, particularly because of its potential to counter some of the most commonly perceived threats to travel, such as mass tourism, commercialization, speed and homogenization. It remains to be seen whether encounter is a successful strategy and what obstacles, tensions and limitations interfere with its success. By examining encounters within some of the complex contexts introduced in the previous chapter, the following chapters seek answers to these questions.

Chapter 3

GUIDING

Il est aisé – et d'ailleurs de bon ton – de se moquer des voyages de groupe mais, pour qui ne parle ni ne lit le chinois, c'est encore la seule manière d'être assuré d'avoir vu quelque chose. Se lancer seul, aveugle, sourd-muet dans ce pays immense est aujourd'hui encore une entreprise épineuse qui débouche souvent sur échecs et amertume.[1]

(It's easy – and even good form – to make fun of group tours, but for those who neither speak nor read Chinese it's still the only way to be sure of seeing something. To set out into this vast country alone, blind, deaf and dumb, is still today a tricky undertaking that often results in failure and bitterness.)

Nicolas Bouvier acknowledges that he is reluctant to travel with a group, while admitting that it is sometimes a necessity.[2] His fellow tourists rescue him from loneliness, but his 'blindness' and 'deafness' are alleviated by a single individual: his guide. Following a guide goes against the stereotype of the independent traveller – it is something tourists do – but travellers like Bouvier are sometimes forced to admit that without a guide or interpreter their travel experience would be impossible or at least incomplete. Even when they do not follow a paid guide or employ an interpreter, all travellers are obliged to seek the aid of an intermediary at some point. Travellees constantly perform acts of guiding and interpreting, frequently on an unofficial basis, with no money changing hands. They help travellers to cope at a practical level, locating places to eat, drink and sleep, but also to understand their surroundings, to learn about customs and culture, to interact with people whose language they do not speak.

'Guiding' is leading, conducting, directing, but in the context of travel it also means informing and imparting knowledge. 'Interpreting' is translating between two, usually spoken, languages, but also deducing and explaining meaning: the interpreter not only mediates, but also contributes his or her own reading. Ostensibly, guiding and interpreting are different jobs, but both acts may be performed by the same person: guides also translate, interpreters also lead the way. Since guiding and interpreting overlap to such an extent they are treated together in this chapter, and for lexical simplicity I collapse the two into the single term 'guide', unless I refer to a character who is specifically labelled as an interpreter.

The travellee who performs an act of guiding or interpreting may simply be a passer-by who indicates the direction of a restaurant, or a travelling companion who is more familiar with the territory than the protagonist. Travellers also employ professional guides; sometimes for just a few hours, for the tour of a museum for example, at other times for an entire journey, entrusting the organization of their whole trip to the travellee. These mediating travellees are found in every travel book, so potential for research on the subject is great. I therefore limit this chapter to studying guide characters who are officially employed, in order to focus on the particular dynamics that arise from this financial context.

For the traveller in search of authenticity, the guide is a key character and this chapter begins by considering the role that guides play in facilitating the traveller's access to authenticity in the three areas introduced in Chapter 2: information, back regions and encounters. Although guides are well positioned to help travellers, the interplay of different contexts and factors (discussed in Chapter 1) creates tensions that complicate the interaction. Guides must compete with other sources of information, such as guidebooks, and their reliability and motivations are called into question, but trust is also a problem for the guides themselves, who are vulnerable to travellers and writers in their own way. The traveller's encounter with the guide is a potential source of authenticity in itself, but this is threatened by the employer–employee dynamic, an obstacle tackled by both traveller and guide. The important contribution that guides make to journeys is not always reflected in travel books, and the second section of the chapter examines how travel writers represent guides and their work, sometimes crediting them, sometimes rendering them invisible. This in turn raises the dilemma of expressing the travellee's agency and voice, for which the solution may lie with the reader.

Authenticity and Mediation

Guides and guidebooks

One of the main roles of a guide is to provide travellers with information, which is exactly what a travel writer needs to supply a text with detail, but guides have steep competition as information bearers. The travel in travel writing is seemingly always preceded and prepared for by a period of reading, which may date back to the traveller's earliest years. Armchair travel is a common antidote to the forced immobility of childhood and travel writers often explain their impulse to be elsewhere with reference to childhood hours spent reading adventure stories and travel narratives.³ Reading sets high expectations, not only in terms of what to look for when one travels and how to go about it, but also how to process travel experiences.⁴ Reliance on travel texts and guidebooks, as well as sometimes extensive intertextual references, is a common feature of travel writing. Although guidebooks were originally designed to free travellers from their guides and grant them independence, books and people continue to provide competing sources of the information that confers authenticity on objects, places and experiences.⁵ While books provide handy, pocket-size guides, without all the expenses and complications of a guide in the flesh, they also age and can date quickly. The two types of guide represent a confrontation between the present and the absent, and even the living and the dead.

Gianni Celati consults a paper guide and a human guide when visiting Dogon villages in Mali:⁶ Boubacar in the flesh and a book by anthropologist Marcel Griaule, though Boubacar somewhat conflates the two, having read widely, including Griaule.⁷ Celati compares both guides' versions with the reality he observes: the layout of one of the villages appears to reflect Griaule's description, but Boubacar tells him that few villages maintain this pattern (76). Boubacar apparently provides more up-to-date information, but when Celati explores the village he confirms Griaule's version (78). Celati never questions Boubacar's ability to guide him at a practical level, but he does cast doubt on his knowledge of the Dogon. He complains 'Quando torno dovrò dire che di questi villaggi non ho visto quasi niente, tutto quello che posso dire l'ho letto nel libro di Griaule' (86; When I go back I'll have to admit that I've seen almost nothing of these villages, anything I can say I read in Griaule's book), implying that Boubacar has not been as useful a source as Griaule's text. Later Boubacar remarks that Dogon life is impenetrable because of the many dialects and family-kept secrets and Celati concludes that even Boubacar is a stranger among them, further undermining him (90). He endorses Griaule's study instead, though Griaule was no more Dogon than Boubacar; the French anthropologist is endowed with authority by his position in Western academia, another example of the conflict mentioned in Chapter 2 between local and Western sources.

Since texts provide the initial impetus for the journey and set up expectations, it is not surprising if travellers often prefer them to human guides. As Heather Henderson suggests: 'If [the] discrepancy between reality and literature is not to be fatal to their dreams, travelers must find a scapegoat. Clearly Homer and the rest of the Western literary tradition cannot be wrong; questioning them would require travelers to question the whole culture that has produced *them*. It is far easier to grumble about the natives.'⁸ Travel writers have a vested interest in endorsing written sources, since their own texts feed back into the same body of literature. On the other hand, anthropologists Gavin Jack and Alison Phipps suggest that within the context of tourism, 'being guided orally gives higher narrative capital than reliance on a mere written guide'.[9] Although the written guides they refer to are standard guidebooks of the *Lonely Planet* type, which are generally disdained by travel writers in favour of more academic and literary sources (including travel literature), encounters do have considerable narrative capital in travel writing. Local guides are privileged sources of information, especially for the practical aspects of a journey and for their own life experiences. Travel writing has always gained its prestige and authority from the experience of the traveller in the world, as opposed to those who stay at home and read.[10] Travel writing is therefore both marked by and perpetuates a cyclical movement between text and world.[11] There is a tension between, on the one hand, setting text and world in opposition to each other and, on the other, using each to elucidate the other: the text helps to understand the world and experience in the world gives authority to the text. Edward Said describes this as 'a rather complex dialectic of reinforcement by which the experiences of readers in reality are determined by what they have read, and this in turn influences writers to take up subjects defined in advance by readers' experiences'.[12] The travel writer cannot afford to favour one side to the exclusion of the other, but must craft a delicate balance between text and experience, between reading and travelling, between familiar and new sources of information. Guides, as mediators of experience and information, contribute to this balance. During the journey the guide authenticates objects, places and experiences for the traveller, but when writing the text the travel writer exercises the authority to authenticate the guide, or not. Two parallel episodes from Jean-Claude Guillebaud's *La colline des anges* and Corrado Ruggeri's *Farfalle sul Mekong*, describing guided trips to Vietnamese mountain villages, illustrate the tensions in this dynamic. The trips take place only one year apart and bear a close resemblance: each is initiated by the guide and in both cases the villages are found in a state of abject poverty, yet the responses of the two travellers and the textual treatment of the guides could not be more different.

Guillebaud is reluctant to visit the village from the start, criticizing his guide Nguyen T. D. directly: 'L'obscénité paisible avec laquelle le "guide officiel" du Vietnam socialiste nous enjoint de visiter le monde comme un zoo grandeur nature en distribuant des cacahuètes aux tribus locales, est […] révoltante' (*Colline*, 482; The unperturbed, obscene way in which the 'official guide' to socialist Vietnam bids us visit the world as though it were a life-size zoo, handing out peanuts to the local tribes, is […] appalling).[13] Ruggeri, on the other hand, willingly follows his guide Duong, responding to his proposal for the trip with a simple '"Perfetto, andiamo"' ('Perfect, let's go') and later asserting '"ci interessa molto"' ('it really interests us') (212). Guillebaud represents the whole episode as a money-making opportunity for Nguyen T. D. and condemns the commoditization of the village, predicting its exploitation for tourism: 'Dans un an, dans deux ans, des Américaines du troisième âge, par autobus entiers, s'arrêterons [*sic*] ici, sacs de bonbons à la main, devant les "populations primitives du Vietnam dans leur cadre authentique"' (*Colline*, 484; In a year or two, American retirees will stop here by the coachload, bags of sweets in their hands, to view the 'primitive peoples of Vietnam in their authentic setting'). Guillebaud specifically uses the word 'authentique' to criticize the presentation of the village to tourists, sarcastically envisaging a future staging of authenticity while asserting that he is no dupe to the ruse. Ruggeri does not doubt the authenticity of the village, accepting everything as he finds it and trusting Duong's explanations. When he evokes a scene of mass tourism (the scramble at a holiday camp buffet in Italy) he does so precisely to emphasize the contrast with the patient and orderly village children awaiting their treats (214–15). Ruggeri follows Duong's directions for distributing sweets without objecting or contradicting him. Guillebaud subverts Nguyen T. D. both as a traveller during the trip, by disobeying his instructions and rejecting his suggestion of interviews, and as a writer in his text, by explaining that he has already visited this region, having reported on the devastation of the mountain people as a journalist in the early seventies: 'Nguyen T. D. ignore évidemment, que là, *dans cette même région de Khe Sanh*, j'étais venu assister à l'agonie de ces "primitifs"' (*Colline*, 482, emphasis in the original; Nguyen T. D. obviously doesn't know that I came here, *to this same region of Khe Sanh*, to witness the suffering of these 'primitives'). There follow several paragraphs of detailed information on the history and present situation of the mountain people, including an extensive quotation from Guillebaud's earlier article. In this way the travel writer asserts the authority of his own knowledge over his guide's, and by addressing not the guide but the reader, he places the reader and himself in collusion against the guide. Furthermore, Guillebaud presents the reader with an alternative guide, Jean-Baptiste Etcharren, the French missionary who had originally introduced him to the mountain people. In the ensuing chapter he relates some of his experiences with Etcharren, promoting the missionary as a guide, in place of Nguyen T. D., and asserting the authenticity of Etcharren's version. Ruggeri does not share Guillebaud's experience of the region and he accepts Duong's information and instructions. He describes what he observes and deduces, while Duong provides the background, often in long direct quotations. Ruggeri thereby upholds Duong's authority to authenticate.

Whatever the status of the information that guides provide it is assessed and authenticated by travel writers and then presented to readers framed by their endorsement or criticism. Sarga Moussa, writing about the representation of dragomans in nineteenth-century travel writing, suggests that the portrait of the unreliable dragoman was used by writers to assert themselves as reliable mediators. He cites the example of Chateaubriand to show how the writer legitimates his own voice as privileged intermediary between East and West.[14] This is precisely the move made by Guillebaud in the example above. Guillebaud turns the tables on his guides on other occasions, presenting himself as the authority on the history or politics of their countries either because of his own experience, as in Ethiopia, or because of his reading, as in Turkey.[15] In both of these countries he employs young guides and drivers who are principally charged with practicalities and interpretation and, like Celati, he compliments their ability to perform these tasks. Guillebaud suggests that his itineraries introduce them to regions of their own countries with which they are unfamiliar, once more portraying himself as the authority (*Porte*, 712), although he does pay close attention to their reactions and responses: 'Ayberk est aussi curieux que moi et, visiblement, plus surpris encore de vérifier la modernité de son propre pays' (*Croisades*, 596; Ayberk is as curious as I am and is visibly even more surprised to ascertain the modernity of his own country). Ruggeri does not cite literary references as often as other travel writers, such as Guillebaud. He emphasizes his good relationship with Duong and presents him as an authentic source on Vietnam, thereby legitimating his own text as an authentic source by association with the guide.[16]

As Moussa points out, travel writers are also mediators: they mediate for their readers, presenting knowledge and experiences, just as it is presented to them by their guides. They mediate between a body of literature, to which they are committed as both readers and writers, and their experience of travelling out there in the world. In this role guides can be assistants, even colleagues, or they can be rivals. Paradoxically, in both cases they provide a means for travel writers to sanction the authority of their own writing: either by allying themselves with their guides and benefitting from their authority by association, as Ruggeri does, or by discrediting them and claiming authority for themselves, as in the case of Guillebaud.

The gatekeeper

In the quotation opening this chapter Bouvier explains that joining a guided tour is the only way he can be sure 'd'avoir vu quelque chose' (to see something) of China, but this begs the question: what exactly is that 'something' that he believes only a guided tour can provide? Ruggeri expresses a similar opinion of his Vietnamese guide Duong: 'Dipende da questo signore […] il successo del nostro viaggio, sarà lui ad aprirci le porte del paese, a svelarci gli aspetti meno conosciuti, a farci capire cose che nemmeno possiamo immaginare' (149; The success of our journey depends on this man, he will be the one to open up the doors of the country, to unveil its least well-known aspects, to make us understand things that we cannot even imagine). Ruggeri anticipates the unveiling of hidden realities, recalling the tourist's search for authentic back regions. Guides play a key role in mediating such access, which might entail leading the traveller to a place, even a literal backstage, as Ruggeri describes in Ko Pannyi (see Chapter 2), but it could also mean providing access to an event, or an introduction to a particular person or people.[17] The guide is a conduit to more private cultural and social practices and meanings, those reserved for locals, closed to unaccompanied outsiders. In Ruggeri's words, guides open doors for travellers, and lead them through to places, both physical and metaphorical, that might otherwise be out of bounds.

Guides bear considerable responsibility for the success of a journey, but travellers are often reluctant to trust them. Loredana Polezzi argues that distrust characterizes this relationship in travel writing: 'The interpreter [...] is usually depicted as an ambiguous, shadowy character, constantly suspected of plotting multiple, impending betrayals.'[18] As Polezzi implies, distrust between traveller and guide often results from the suspicion of ulterior motives. The friction between Guillebaud and Nguyen T. D. results from a conflict of interests: the guide neglects the travellers' wishes, prioritizing instead the agenda of his employer, the regional tourist agency, as well as his own financial gain. Guides often work for agencies that may dictate what information should be available to tourists. Some require the presentation of particular versions of events to visitors and may also expect guides to keep an eye on their charges.[19] While guides can enable access to authenticity, they are also well placed to prevent it. Travelling around the states of the collapsing USSR, Tiziano Terzani finds that many of his guides do more to hinder than to assist. One employee of the Intourist office in Ashgabat, Turkmenistan is so unhelpful that he disdainfully nicknames her 'la Ragazza col Raffreddore' (the Girl with the Cold).[20] She lies to him about the city's language institute, preventing him from finding a reliable interpreter, and maintains the government's explanation for the disappearance of a Lenin statue (*Buonanotte*, 333 and 338–9). Loyal to her primary employer, she prevents rather than enables access to authenticity, or at least to what Terzani believes to be authentic. Of course, a traveller's expectations of a particular regime will colour their assessment of the information they are given and, as we have seen above, guides must compete with travellers' preconceptions. Part of the problem with the search for authenticity is the nebulous nature of the concept; travellers do not always know exactly what they are looking for, but they may still be suspicious of their guides, or they may have fixed notions about what is authentic, which may differ considerably from their guides' own ideas.

The traveller–guide relationship is not always dominated by distrust, however. Many travellers develop positive relationships with their guides and represent them as reliable and informative characters. Although Bouvier is initially suspicious of Monsieur X, because of unfortunate experiences with guides in Beijing, he is happy to be proved wrong when Monsieur X turns out to be an excellent guide: 'Nous ne le considérions pas comme l'interprète d'une culture mais comme une particule active, vivante, originale de cet ensemble qu'il mettait tant d'ingéniosité à nous faire un peu découvrir, alors que, du fait même de sa fonction, il aurait dû nous en interdire l'accès' (*Journal*, 1035; We didn't think of him as the interpreter of a culture, but as an active, living, original particle of this whole that he was making us discover a little with so much ingenuity, when in fact, because of the nature of his position, he should have been forbidding our access). Bouvier implies that Monsieur X has neglected his official duties, to the travellers' benefit.

Bouvier's comments about Monsieur X are interesting for another reason. Although travellers are sometimes dubious about the authenticity of the back regions and information to which guides provide access, many consider the guides themselves to be authentic representatives of their nation, turning their attention from what lies behind the door to the gatekeeper.[21] In the quotation above, Bouvier presents Monsieur X as a part representing a whole, like a synecdoche for wider Chinese culture and society. Synecdoche is a useful metaphor for this way of representing guides, as well as other interlocutors, in travel writing.[22] The whole represented by the guide may be an entire country or a more specific regional, social or cultural group. Guillebaud, for example, describes the reaction of Vietnamese interpreter Mme D. to a Hanoi nightclub as being 'assez bien l'attitude du Vietnam tout entier' (pretty much the attitude of the whole of Vietnam), but in the following sentence he further defines her as a 'sudiste patriote, anticommuniste fervente' (patriotic southerner, fervent anticommunist), associating her with a particular regional and political identity (*Colline*, 506). Guides often become the focus of attention and travel writers describe their appearance, their comportment, their attitudes to events, even their life stories. The guide as a person thus becomes part of the travel experience.

This use of the guide as a synecdoche raises the question of the guide's actual relationship to the group they are believed to represent. The guide in travel writing recalls the anthropological 'informant', whom James Clifford describes as a 'problematic figure': 'A great many of these interlocutors, complex individuals routinely made to speak for "cultural" knowledge, turn out to have their own "ethnographic" proclivities and interesting histories of travel. Insider-outsiders, good translators and explicators, they've been around.'[23] Guides, like other travellees, are often travellers themselves and, as Clifford implies, their relations to the societies and cultures whose doors they open are not necessarily straightforward. Valene Smith describes how the members of a community who work with tourists are often 'marginal men', although most tourists are unaware of this.[24] As she explains, members of a community who are most able to profit from tourism, because of language skills or cultural contacts, may be marginalized as a result. This is exactly what happened to Nordin, Terzani's guide in Indonesia, who aroused the jealousy of local people because he could use his English to earn money by guiding tourists (*Indovino*, 233–4). While their particular background or knowledge enables guides to act as intermediaries for travellers, it can also distance them from the very communities they represent. Smith asks, 'Is the interpretation about a native culture, when described by a culturally marginal guide, accurate?'[25] This is a concern for anthropologists seeking reliable sources, but also for travel writers seeking authentic experiences. On the other hand, is any individual truly representative of a particular society or culture? Ask a dozen people of the same nationality what authentically represents their country and you will hear a dozen stories that differ from each other, some subtly, some wildly, but they will all differ, reflecting individual experience. This particularity is the richness of travel writing: the anecdote, the individual encounter, the momentary are essential ingredients of the travel book. Travellers pursue the particular in search of the general, but their writing is often strongest when it focuses on the former and weakest when it embraces the latter with too sweeping an ambition.[26] The value of the synecdoche may not lie in its potential for enlightening the whole, but rather in providing an excuse to focus on the part.

So far we have only considered the traveller–guide relationship from the point of view of the traveller, but trust cuts both ways: while the guide's agenda may be detrimental to the traveller, the reverse is also true. The traveller's search for authentic information can put a guide in a risky position, as the mediator who is expected to provide that information. The traveller has the luxury of crossing borders and escaping trouble, while guides may have no choice but to stay and face the consequences. This situation is confronted by many an interpreter during military conflict; Guillebaud tells the stories of Vietnamese 'stringers' who were unable to leave their own war-torn country, while the journalists who employed them went safely home (*Colline*, 440–42).[27] Celia, Sergio Ramazzotti's interpreter in China, is devastated by his casual investigations, which are far more risky for her, as a Chinese citizen, than for him. When the police begin to take an interest in their activities she berates Ramazzotti: '"È facile dare lezioni, quando sai che domani te ne sarai andato.

Tutti cercano di darci lezioni, ma siamo noi che restiamo qui'" (*Birra*, 142; 'It's easy to give lessons, when you know that tomorrow you'll be gone. Everyone tries to give us lessons, but we're the ones who stay here').

From the very beginning of his association with Duong, Ruggeri informs his readers that he hopes to obtain as much information as possible from his guide about his personal experiences of the war and a re-education camp. He is conscious that he must tread carefully and chooses his moment to try to coax Duong to open up: 'È il momento di provare un attacco' (169; It's the moment to try an attack). He asks circumscriptive questions about Duong's relations with people they have met during the day and when the guide answers Ruggeri is triumphant:

> Funziona, si sta aprendo. Guardo Carla con un fremito di soddisfazione, anche se mi rendo conto di essere brutale: ma voglio sapere che cosa succedeva in quei dannati campi di rieducazione. La tattica impone una frenata, a questo punto. Duong si deve sentire compreso, appoggiato, deve essere sicuro che in noi trova solidarietà, soltanto così potrà sfogarsi. (170)
>
> (It's working, he's opening up. I glance at Carla with a shiver of satisfaction, even though I realize I'm being brutal; but I want to know what happened in those damn re-education camps. The strategy requires a pause at this point; Duong must feel understood, supported, he must be certain of our solidarity with him, only then will he be able to unburden himself.)

Ruggeri uses a language of conflict – 'attacco' (attack), 'tattica' (strategy) – to describe his approach to Duong. He is manipulative, planning when and how to broach the subject, trying to put Duong at his ease and exchanging conspiratorial glances and exchanges in Italian, a language Duong does not understand, with his companion Carla. François-Olivier Rousseau attempts a similar approach with his Cambodian guide Sotaï, trying to persuade him to talk about the war, albeit unsuccessfully.[28] Rousseau knows that he is going too far, but explains: 'Mon insistance manque de délicatesse, je le sais, mais je suis comme ça et je m'en justifie par la légitime curiosité historique qui est la mienne' (My insistence lacks sensitivity, I know, but I'm like that and I justify myself with my legitimate historical curiosity).[29] Both Ruggeri and Rousseau admit that their approach is aggressive, but they nevertheless persist. Their actions go beyond taste or manners to raise ethical questions about the traveller–travellee relationship. Both suggest they have a right to the life experiences of their guides, as though the private lives and memories of guides were objects for consumption, part of the travel package. Nor is their pursuit of knowledge merely a question of curiosity, since such juicy material as Duong or Sotaï might impart provides substance for their travel accounts.

Granting space to guides' experiences of personal or collective trauma gives them a voice and brings events to the reader's attention, but we must ask whose interests are being served. In the examples above, neither Duong nor Sotaï offer their stories voluntarily, but are manipulated in the interests of the writer, the text and the reader.

An authentic encounter

Guides not only provide access to authentic knowledge or experiences, but also to interpersonal authenticity, by facilitating encounters between travellers and their interlocutors. In the context of tourism, Nick Kontogeorgopoulos observes that 'Regardless of how or where adventurers travel, feelings of accomplishment and achievement hinge on the quality of the "tour leader", who serves as the vital link mediating interactions between adventurers and Thai hosts.'[30] While guides assist travellers in their relations with others, the guide–traveller interaction can also develop into a friendship, becoming a source of interpersonal authenticity in itself. Travellers often spend considerable time with their guides and they may share significant experiences. Peter Hansen describes the close relations between some climbers and their mountain guides in the Alps and Sherpas in the Himalayas, suggesting that these developed because of the opportunity to escape social hierarchies and bond in the context of shared dangers.[31] A similar example can be found in Guillebaud's *La porte des larmes*, which is haunted by the ghost of Terede, who worked as his interpreter when he was covering the war in Ethiopia. For Guillebaud, Terede was more than a guide, he was 'mon premier compagnon de voyage et de colère' (*Porte*, 657; my first companion in travel and anger), a distinction whose significance will become clearer in Chapter 7, which addresses travelling companions. Bouvier expresses growing esteem for his guide Monsieur X and believes that their friendship is mutual: 'Dès le deuxième jour, il eut à notre égard une attitude de brusquerie amicale […]. Nous lui fîmes savoir – chacun à sa façon – combien nous appréciions son travail et sa compagnie' (*Journal*, 1036; From the second day he treated us with friendly brusqueness […]. We let him know – each in their own way – how much we appreciated his work and his company). The mention of 'travail' (work) along with 'compagnie' (company) implies that a traveller's affection for the guide is not entirely disconnected from his/her assessment of the latter's professional performance.

When the traveller employs a guide, the financial basis of the relationship can become an obstacle to authenticity.[32] Francesco Piccolo parodies the commoditization of tourist relations, describing his disappointment on discovering that his attractive Hong Kong guide has not been flirting with him alone, but with all the men in his tour group (182–6).[33] Piccolo's realization that feigned intimacy is part of the service degrades the traveller–guide relationship. Travel writing is often silent about the economic basis of this relationship, but it is significant, since it creates a dynamic of commercial exchange. In this sense traveller–guide interactions are typical of the majority of interactions between 'hosts' and 'guests': tourists usually come into contact with their hosts in contexts involving some kind of economic relationship: with waiters, hotel staff, tour guides, shop owners, transport staff and even beggars. We have seen above how Guillebaud criticizes the commoditization of the mountain village: genuine contact is not possible with either the villagers or with Nguyen T. D.; authentic encounters do not occur.

Creating the close, intimate relations – or in other words friendships – that are apparently missing from tourism is one way of attempting to transcend the inauthenticity of commoditization. Bernard Ollivier, for example, emphasizes the good-natured relations he establishes with his guide Shoreh in Iran. As they part company he writes: 'Shoreh semble émue de nous quitter; nous, ce n'est rien de dire que nous avons le cœur gros et nous devons nous refréner pour ne pas la serrer dans nos bras. Alors nous enrobons nos mots, par le ton et le regard, de toute l'affection qu'elle nous a inspirée' (Shoreh seems moved to be leaving us; for our part, it's an understatement to say that we have heavy hearts and we have to restrain ourselves from hugging her in our arms. So we embellish our words, through tone and expression, with all the affection she has inspired in us).[34] Through the description of such emotions, Ollivier conveys the sense of a relationship that is genuine and meaningful, transcending its economic basis. Ollivier's attitude towards Shoreh contrasts notably with his disdain for his guide Moussa in Turkmenistan, who is only motivated by money (*Carnets*, 90–91). Although, as Piccolo finds, a guide's friendliness might simply be part of the service, this need not detract from the traveller's perception of authenticity, if the sentiments expressed are considered to be genuine.

The economic basis of the traveller–guide relationship may corrupt its authenticity, but it also creates an unequal power structure, with one employing the other. Whether or not guides cooperate with travellers in their attempts to transcend this dynamic, they also work to subvert it themselves by exercising their own authority over the traveller. Writing about tourism, So-Min Cheong and Marc Miller use Foucault to analyse tourist–host power relations, countering the idea that power is entirely in the hands of the tourist consumer.[35] They suggest that certain 'hosts', including tourist guides, could be considered Foucauldian agents because they control and direct tourists, for example by managing access to places or providing certain types of information.[36]

Cheong and Miller study tourism itself as sociologists, while travel writing is one step removed, being a representation of tourism, but their observations of tourists remain pertinent to travel writing. The veracity of a travel account cannot be ascertained from the text alone, and nor is that the intention here. While it would be unwise to presume that a travel text tells the literal truth, it would be perverse to assume that everything is fictitious. Not only would it be perverse, it would rob travellees entirely of their agency, an agency that is *not* denied them by travel writers. In other words, if we as readers assume that every travellee and every one of their actions and words is a figment of the travel writer's imagination, then *we*, the readers, deny not only the agency but even the very existence of those represented in the text.

Guides are represented controlling the practical aspects of a journey, as well as mediating the information presented to travellers and supervising encounters between travellers and other interlocutors.[37] They not only mediate encounters, they also initiate and manage many of them. Monsieur X, for example, arranges for Bouvier's group to stop at the workshop of a family making traditional shadow puppets (*Journal*, 1034–5). Such an encounter is entirely shaped by the guide's arrangements and his orchestration of the meeting. Guides may also initiate itineraries: in Sri Lanka Nicole-Lise Bernheim's driver Ananda insists that she watch traditional dances and visit an elephant orphanage.[38] Bernheim is reluctant to see the elephants and her write-up is not complimentary, but, like Guillebaud in the mountain village, an event initiated by the guide enables the traveller to experience a new aspect of the country. Travellers are dependent on their guides to make practical arrangements and negotiate on their behalf. Volodja, the journalist who takes charge of Terzani's group in Russia, constantly uses his contacts and language skills to gain access and permits for the travellers (*Buonanotte*, e.g., 23 and 105). Weber and his travelling companions put themselves in the hands of guide Hasan, who makes the complicated arrangements for crossing the Turkish–Iranian border.[39] In all of these ways the guide character subverts the employer–employee dynamic by exerting his/her own authority over the traveller's actions and over the events of the journey. On the other hand, travellers do not always submit willingly to their guides' authority and travel writers may undermine their guides in their texts, as we have seen with Guillebaud's representation of Nguyen T. D.[40] Although guides contribute enormously to the traveller's experience, travel writers do not always acknowledge them. While it is impossible to reconstruct the gaps between event and text, the latter does sometimes reveal its own omissions.

The economics of the traveller–guide relationship have one further implication, which is worth considering briefly. Travel texts often serve as alternatives to guidebooks, advertising particular travel experiences and services, even if this is unwitting on the part of writers. Travel writing feeds into a system of representations that ultimately have an economic outcome.

Although the reader cannot be certain of the real existence of any particular guide in a text, or the correspondence between a character and a real person, guide characters are often, perhaps usually, based on real people encountered by travellers during their wanderings. They earn their living from tourism, and a favourable write-up in a travel book may help them to gain customers, while an unfavourable representation could be detrimental. As early as the 1960s Michel Déon describes how his Greek friend and unofficial guide Spiro used the fame he had acquired from Déon's book to convince tourists to employ him, announcing: '"Vous connaissez Michel Déon? Alors, Spiro c'est moi!"' ('Do you know Michel Déon? Well then, I'm Spiro!').[41] More recently, Ollivier cites several examples of tourists who have read his books, followed his route and encountered his own interlocutors (*Carnets*, 30 and 103).[42] As the readers of travel books become more mobile, they are increasingly likely to encounter the guides portrayed in the books they have read. Writers have a responsibility, assumed or not, in their representations of guides, while the latter have an interest in being represented, without having any means to control that representation other than their actions towards the travellers who are their customers and who become their narrators.

The search for authenticity always stumbles against subjective barriers, unsurprisingly given that it is more conceptual than concrete a notion. The authenticity sought is shaped by a traveller's expectations, the authenticity found is shaped by the guide's expectations and motivations, the authenticity represented is shaped by the implied reader's imagined expectations. It seems appropriate that travel writers often refer to guides themselves as concrete manifestations of something conceptual and frustratingly slippery. As real readers, we are left to wonder what authenticity remains in the events and people recounted in the text. Just as the traveller calls the guide's trustworthiness into question, so we readers scrutinize the text for its reliability, for its apparent excesses and silences and ulterior motives.

The traveller–guide relationship can be envisaged as a negotiation over freedom, an issue we shall return to in the following chapter. The guide is often represented positively when s/he enables the traveller's freedom of movement, even while controlling it, by creating opportunities, guarding the traveller's safety, enabling access. Conversely, when freedom is curtailed by the guide, s/he is more likely to be undermined in the text. In this sense the guide seems trapped in a functional role, as a facilitating force, not an individual, so where does this leave the travellee's own freedom? Attempts to establish authentic relationships with guides are apparently intended to address this, at least in part, but the contradictory expectation that the employer–employee relationship grants certain rights and services continues to commoditize the guide. Guides' own attempts to overcome this, by asserting their knowledge and authority, are limited by travel writers' reluctance to relinquish the freedom of their traveller characters, a move necessary to acknowledge the agency of the travellee. In the following section I examine these issues of representation and agency in more detail.

Translation and Voice

The invisible translator

On a flight between Calcutta and Bangkok Guillebaud is gripped by a sudden panic:

> Sentir le piège se refermer encore une fois, qui vous barricade loin des choses. Comment s'en dégager? Pour cavalcader la conscience en paix sur dix mille kilomètres, il faudrait parler persan, tamoul, hindi, cantonais… minimum! Faute de cela, vous butez sans cesse sur l'opacité infranchissable des langues, des journaux, des enseignes de magasins. Exaspérant![43]
>
> (Feeling the trap close once more, blocking you far from everything. How do you escape it? To travel over ten thousand miles in tranquillity, you would have to speak Persian, Tamil, Hindi, Cantonese… minimum! Failing that, you stumble constantly on the insurmountable impenetrability of languages, newspapers, shop signs. It's exasperating!)

Struggling with the problem of access, inherent to the 'métier de voyageur' (*Asie*, 171; profession of traveller), Guillebaud pinpoints a major obstacle, a matter central to the work of interpreting, but also of guiding: language.

All travellers find themselves short of the necessary language skills at some point. Even the relatively multilingual Terzani curses his ignorance of the local language when he is without a guide in Kirghizstan (*Buonanotte*, 190). Ollivier's linguistic inadequacies are a source of constant woe in China: 'par mon ignorance des langues qu'on y pratique, je suis enfermé dans une solitude profonde' (because of my ignorance of the languages spoken here, I am imprisoned in profound solitude) (*Marche III*, 132). Despite their travels through an impossibly varied linguistic geography, travel writers are often reluctant to admit their failings. Paolo Rumiz hints at his mastery of several Eastern European languages, but never provides enough detail to fully enlighten his readers (*Oriente* and *Uomini*). Weber converses apparently unproblematically with a surprising array of interlocutors, from partisan fighters in Azerbaijan and shopkeepers in Afghanistan to drug addicts on the streets of Bombay (*Russies*, 61–74).[44] He systematically fails to account for language and renders all acts of translation invisible: both his own and those of any other translator. In this he is not alone, although he is a particularly flagrant example.[45] The importance of language and translation to the success of any journey in unfamiliar territory only emphasizes the fundamental and even decisive role of anyone who translates for the traveller. It is therefore a conspicuous omission when travel writers neglect to account for these acts of translation or fail to give credit where credit is due.

Translating translation into a travel text is not a straightforward matter, however. Italians are rarely able to use their mother tongue on their travels, but the same is often true for French travellers; both resort to English as their lingua franca as well as using other languages. Consequently texts undergo multiple translations: from the original language, through the guide (or interpreter) to the traveller, who then operates a further translation into the text. The following example from Ramazzotti shows the many layers of translation, which are made invisible in the text. This three-way conversation takes place between Ramazzotti, Celia and Z. S. Q., a local who had invited the travellers to his father's funeral the previous day. The initials on the left indicate the speaker, words in bold indicate phrases that would have been originally in English, while those underlined would have been in Chinese. The elided acts of translation that Celia would or may have performed are indicated on the right in square brackets:

?	'<u>Ni hao</u>.'	
?	'<u>Ni hao, ni hao</u>.'[46]	
SR	'**È finito il funerale**?' domandai.	[C <u>Translation</u>]
ZSQ	'<u>Oh, sì, stamattina presto. È stata una bella sepoltura</u>' disse. […]	[C **Translation**]
SR	'**Ha subito ripreso il lavoro, vedo**.'	[C <u>Translation</u>]
ZSQ	'<u>Il lavoro non si ferma mai. Ci sono troppi piatti da riempire, a Shaoshan</u>.'	[C **Translation**]
SR	'**Già, viene l'estate**' dissi gettando uno sguardo al cielo color piombo.	[C <u>Translation</u>?]
ZSQ	'<u>Partite presto</u>?' domandò.	[C **Translation**]
SR	'**Non lo sappiamo. Può darsi**.'	[C <u>Translation</u>?]
C	'<u>Perché vuole saperlo</u>?' disse Celia.	[C **Translation**?]
ZSQ	'<u>L'altra sera è venuta la polizia</u>.'	[C **Translation**?]
C	Celia si irrigidì e sbarrò gli occhi. '<u>Dove</u>?' chiese a mezza voce.	[C **Translation**?]
ZSQ	'<u>A casa. Avevamo ancora la bara esposta</u>.' Si rivolse a me. '<u>Hanno chiesto di lei</u>.'	[C **Translation**]
SR	'**Di me? E che diavolo volevano**?'	

C	'**Abbiamo parlato troppo**' disse Celia. '**Lo sapevo che stavamo facendo troppe domande**.'	

(*Birra*, 137–8)

(?	'*Ni hao.*'	
?	'*Ni hao, ni hao.*'	
SR	'**Has the funeral finished?**' I asked.	[C Translation]
ZSQ	'Oh, yes, early this morning. It was a grand burial', he said. […]	[C **Translation**]
SR	'**You've restarted work straightaway, I see.**'	[C Translation]
ZSQ	'Work never ends. There are too many plates to fill in Shaoshan.'	[C **Translation**]
SR	'**Of course, summer's arriving**', I said glancing at the leaden sky.	[C Translation?]
ZSQ	'Are you leaving soon?' he asked.	[C **Translation**]
SR	'**We don't know. Maybe.**'	[C Translation?]
C	'Why do you want to know?' said Celia.	[C **Translation**?]
ZSQ	'The other evening the police came round.'	[C Translation?]
C	Celia froze and her eyes opened wide. 'Where?' she asked quietly.	[C **Translation**?]
ZSQ	'To the house. We still had the coffin on view.' He turned to me. 'They asked about you.'	[C **Translation**]
SR	'**About me? And what the devil did they want?**'	
C	'**We've talked too much**', said Celia. '**I knew that we were asking too many questions**.')	

The intention here is not to reconstruct the conversation as it might have taken place, the written text is unlikely to be an accurate representation of any actual exchange; there is no indication that Ramazzotti is making a recording or taking notes. Besides, a text that reproduced every act of translation would quickly become tedious for the reader. In this short extract, which reads as a straightforward conversation in the text, Celia's many elided acts of translation indicate both how much her presence and activity are made invisible in the text and how the original conversation is transformed. Celia is not merely a mediator for Ramazzotti and Z. S. Q., she also takes part in the conversation, adding her own comments, opinions and explanations. There are moments when Ramazzotti and Z. S. Q. are in conversation through Celia, and moments when one of the two has a private dialogue with Celia, in the relevant language, excluding the other. It is unclear how and when Celia translates her exchange with Z. S. Q. to Ramazzotti, but the author does provide some indication of the languages used: the Chinese greeting opening the conversation suggests that Z. S. Q. does not speak English and indicates that the conversation is carried out in Chinese, which is confirmed later when Celia and Ramazzotti speak together in English while their interlocutor looks on uncomprehending. Celia plays an essential role in enabling and shaping Ramazzotti's dialogue with Z. S. Q., but in the final text barely a few traces remain of her original acts of translation. The elision of translation diminishes the account of the guide's work, as with many other aspects of their activity, giving an impression of greater independence to the central figure of the traveller-writer.[47] Thus the writer uses the text to assert a greater degree of freedom than s/he had during the journey. When travel writers do acknowledge the guide's input, they use various techniques, which I will now examine.

Representation strategies

Just as Ramazzotti inserts a Chinese greeting into his Italian text, other writers include untranslated words or short phrases. This offers a flavour of the original language experience, but rarely more than a taste. Bernheim, for example, introduces a large number of local words in her travel texts, especially *Saisons japonaises* and *Couleur cannelle*, even including glossaries. Once introduced with a translation or explanation the terms are reused, separated from the French with italics. Michael Cronin suggests that travel writers make use of such language items to gain credibility: 'Language is an important source of the detail that confers a plausibility on an account and makes the foreign textually apparent. Words become the souvenirs brought home to the expectant reader. These words often relate to culture-specific items that have no equivalent in the target language of the traveller.'[48] As well as the obvious exoticism, this use of language is another device used by travel writers to create a reality effect.[49]

When interlocutors are quoted in direct speech their words have often been translated, as in the example above from Ramazzotti, but some writers also use the technique of including original pieces of untranslated language when quoting interlocutors. Rousseau and Celati make rare but tactical use of direct speech, for example in conversations with their guides. Rousseau quotes Nepali Sunil directly with short phrases in their original English form: 'Bodnath est […] un lieu de pèlerinage que Sunil a des raisons personnelles de visiter: "I'll pray for my poor mama…"' (47; Bodnath is […] a place of pilgrimage that Sunil has personal reasons for visiting: 'I'll pray for my poor mama…'). Rousseau thus resolves the problem of translation, but conversely he hardly grants any space to Sunil's own voice, only quoting him four times in total. Celati combines translated direct speech with short phrases in the language of enunciation, which is usually French. After some female tourists have been talking with Celati, his companion Jean and Boubacar, he reports,

'A questo punto, commento di Boubacar da comico impassibile: "Si vede che noi tre attiriamo le donne, nonostante ci sia di mezzo un anziano" ("Même avec l'âge")' [90; At this point, Boubacar made a comment like a straight-faced comic: 'You can see that we three attract women, despite having an old man among us' ('Despite age')]. Although Boubacar utters the short quoted phrase, Celati controls the context framing his guide's words, determining the way they are presented to the reader. This is particularly true when single words or short phrases are removed from their wider speech context. Celati (who is the 'anziano') provides his own Italian version of Boubacar's words, in direct speech, interpreting a meaning that is not as clearly expressed in the French original. Celati gives us both versions to compare, but usually the original is replaced by the translation, which is already an interpretation.[50]

The use of direct speech, suggesting word-for-word quotation from the guide's own mouth, thus produces various effects. Direct speech seems to be the most explicit way of giving guides a voice, because it suggests that they are expressing themselves with their own words. On the other hand, by putting the guide's words in inverted commas, by bracketing them off from the rest of the text, the writer distances him/herself from them, and even questions them. As Cronin suggests, samples of original language confer authenticity to the text, they seem to connect directly with the time of enunciation, of travel. Yet, like souvenirs, they are isolated fragments whose meaning is mediated and determined by their new surroundings.[51]

Rousseau and, to a certain extent, Celati avoid translating the words of their guides, but translation is often unavoidable. Fragments of a foreign tongue give a flavour of the original travel experience, but too much of an unknown language alienates the reader and the unfamiliar words remain meaningless.[52] While it is not unreasonable to expect a French reader to understand some English, or an Italian to read some French, the European writer cannot make the same assumptions about languages such as Japanese or Chinese. Unfamiliar languages, as well as extended dialogues in more familiar languages, are therefore rendered into the language of the text and the act of translation is made invisible.

Susan Bassnett examines the credibility of translated dialogues in travel literature, suggesting that as readers 'we collude with the idea that travellers can talk to anyone, anywhere in the world and record their conversations in the form of direct speech'.[53] She notes that authenticity, which she considers to be fundamental to travel writing, is undermined by improbable dialogues, when the reader is expected to suspend disbelief.[54] According to Bassnett then, the authenticity of the travel text is undermined by the reader's uncertainty about the linguistic competence of the traveller. This is certainly the case with a traveller such as Weber, but I would suggest that the same effect results from an overuse of direct speech, whether translated or not. Large sections of Ramazzotti's text are devoted to his conversations with Celia, in direct speech. Ramazzotti gives no indication that he is recording these conversations, unlike Terzani who mentions several times that he takes notes and tape records his meetings with fortune tellers (*Indovino*, 52 and 217). In fact, Ramazzotti tells us that all his material and notes were confiscated by the Chinese police at the end of his trip (*Birra*, 148). The recorded dialogues in Terzani's *Un indovino mi disse* add to the authenticity of his account, while the reader of Ramazzotti's *La birra di Shaoshan* comes to doubt his capacity to remember, undermining the realism of his writing; the reader can only suspend disbelief to a certain extent.

Although direct speech may seem the most obvious way for guides to speak with their own voices, it can be problematic. Other strategies include indirect speech, paraphrasing conversations or reporting their general content in descriptive passages. Terzani and Ruggeri often mix direct and indirect speech with their own elaborations on the topic in question. This technique grants considerable space to guides, attributing long passages of information to them, without always quoting them directly, and therefore maintaining realism. On the other hand, it can become unclear who or what is the source of the information. When a descriptive passage is framed or interrupted by a few sentences of direct speech from the guide, the latter is apparently credited as the source, but it is not always clear. In Istanbul, Weber is guided by Turkish historian Edhem Eldem, who tells him about the city's history. The narrative continues over several chapters, but it quickly becomes unclear whether Eldem is Weber's only source, despite repeated references to him and occasional quotations, suggesting that he is at least a major source (*Festin*, 39–88). Fabrizia Ramondino provides a contrasting example, with her treatment of Ahmed in *Polisario*.[55] Ahmed is not an employed guide, he is a colleague who assumes a guiding role, but he becomes an important source of information for Ramondino. She dedicates a number of pages to reporting and paraphrasing Ahmed's description of fighting the Moroccans, and even reproduces the sketches he drew to illustrate his explanations (66–70). In this way, Ahmed's own account is directly related through Ramondino's text.

Examining the different techniques for masking or revealing translation and for allowing or preventing the guide's voice to enter the text highlights the constructed nature of travel writing and the conscious attribution of agency. Travel writers can treat their guides as privileged interlocutors and sources of authentic knowledge, or they can elide their many acts of translation and render them almost invisible. By so doing, they selectively place characters in the foreground of the text, choosing whether to focus on their own autobiographical protagonists or the travellees who enable their journeys. Diminishing the role of the latter exaggerates the autonomy of the former, conforming to myths of the independent traveller.

Authorship and readership

The representation of travellees in travel writing is limited by two common conventions of the genre, related to the author and the reader. I will discuss these in turn and then consider a possible solution to the dilemma. Most travel books are authored by a single individual who is also the narrator and protagonist of the text, the very traveller to whom and around whom all events happen. While a few travel texts have multiple authors, I focus here on the limitations of single-authored works, since they comprise the majority. Discussing the companion genre reportage, Ryszard Kapuściński acknowledges the contributions of travellees to the final text:

> Each piece of reportage has many authors, and it is only thanks to long-established custom that we sign the text with a single name. In fact it may well be the most collective, co-written literary genre of all, because dozens of people contribute to producing it – the people we meet and talk to on the world's roads, who tell us stories about their lives, the life of their community, events they have taken part in or heard about from others.[56]

While these co-authors provide the material from which the text is constructed, that 'long-established custom' ensures that they are rarely acknowledged. The problems of representation and authority faced by travel writing have been a source of debate and even crisis in another related genre: ethnography.[57] In his introduction to the seminal collection of papers *Writing Culture*, James Clifford encourages a dialogical fragmentary mode, which would bring forward the many voices of the ethnographer's interlocutors: 'Once "informants" begin to be considered as co-authors, and the ethnographer as scribe and archivist as well as interpreting observer, we can ask new, critical questions of all ethnographies. However monological, dialogical, or polyphonic their form, they are hierarchical arrangements of discourses.'[58] *Writing Culture* and the debate surrounding it spurred change in ethnography, and attempts to resolve some of the representational problems of ethnographic authority, such as the single author, have produced texts that self-consciously challenge conventions and experiment with form and style, influenced particularly by literary criticism and postmodernism. The problem of the ethnographer's centrality remains however, as Jack and Phipps admit, referring to *Writing Culture*: 'In practice, the ability to mobilise so many different modes and moods in writing further serves to establish the authority of the ethnographic voice.'[59] Ethnography and travel writing have common historical roots, but the two genres have long since diverged. Although broader understandings of travel literature might encompass ethnographies, the kind of travel writing I examine here lacks the self-reflexivity and methodological rigour of ethnography; it is motivated by different causes and written for a wider, more general audience.

There is rarely any suggestion that the travellees in the texts I examine might become co-authors. Perhaps the only effective way for them to have their own voice is to assume the status of full author and write their own texts, as Celia suggests to Ramazzotti (*Birra*, 137).[60] Even in the age of Internet blogging, authorship is not available to all. Both Bouvier and Guillebaud abbreviate the names of their Chinese guide and Vietnamese interpreter – to Monsieur X and Mme D, respectively.[61] This decision was probably taken to protect their identities for fear that the state authorities might object to something they are reported to have said or done. The need for anonymity highlights the difficulty for some guides to speak with their own voice: Bouvier and Guillebaud both recount Monsieur X and Mme D's opinions, but as a result they cannot attribute them with their real identities. It seems unlikely that either Monsieur X or Mme D would have the opportunity to write their own text freely. In some circumstances, the only way for a guide, or any other interlocutor, to have a voice may be in the text of a passing travel writer. Indeed, interlocutors may even approach travellers in order to broadcast their concerns to an international audience: in Equatorial Guinea Ramazzotti meets Miguel, who welcomes the opportunity to speak to a foreign journalist about the state of his country.[62] This is another reason, along with commercial interests, why guides may be keen to be represented in travel texts.

The second problem relates to the reader: travel writers do not address their texts to travellees, but to readers. The travellee has retreated from second person addressee to an absent third person narratee and has been replaced by an implied reader.[63] In the text, the reader is privy to the traveller's inner thoughts and comments, while travellees are not. We have seen how Guillebaud addresses the reader to undermine his guide Nguyen T. D., likewise Terzani addresses his readers directly to confirm or refute the predictions of his fortune tellers. The following example is taken from a visit Terzani makes to a Chinese clairvoyant in Bangkok who reads his fortune on his body:

'*Le tue orecchie indicano generosità…*' (Una delle solite osservazioni positive tanto per ben disporre il 'paziente', dissi fra me e me.) '… *I tuoi fratelli e le tue sorelle dipendono tutti da te.*'

'Non è vero! Non ho né fratelli, né sorelle', ribattei a voce alta, come per farle dispetto. 'Sono figlio unico.'

Non si scompose. '*Se non sono fratelli, sono allora tuoi parenti. Le tue orecchie dicono che molti tuoi parenti dipendono da te…*' (Sì e no, mi dicevo, già pronto ad altre generalizzazioni, sempre un po' vere e sempre un po' inesatte.)' (*Indovino*, 87, italics in the original)

['*Your ears indicate generosity…*' (One of the usual positive observations to make the 'patient' well disposed, I said to myself.) '… *Your brothers and sisters all depend on you.*'

'That's not true! I have neither brothers nor sisters', I retorted out loud, as though to annoy her. 'I'm an only child.'

She was unruffled. '*If it's not your siblings, then it's your relatives. Your ears say that many of your relatives depend on you…*' (Yes and no, I said to myself, already prepared for other generalizations that would always be a bit true and a bit inaccurate.)]

When Terzani writes 'dissi fra me e me' (I said to myself), he might be describing his thoughts at the time, but he is now addressing his readers. He records his thoughts in brackets for our privilege, allowing us to judge the success or failure of the fortune tellers alongside him (when their readings ring true he mentally congratulates them). Thus the encounter in travel writing is always a three-way (and time-lagged) encounter: travellee–traveller-writer–reader. This is particularly obvious in the example from Terzani, but the same is true for all travel encounters.

Furthermore, it is a convention of the genre that travel writers address, or write back to, a home readership, assuming that their readers more or less share their own cultural background. Travel writing has an informative drive: one of the main *raisons d'être* of the whole genre is to provide readers with information and descriptions of distant places. In order to construct a text that makes sense and hits the right level of assumed knowledge, without patronizing its audience, boring them, or confusing them, a travel writer must have some sense of the assumptions, knowledge and expectations of the readership. A book about India written by a French writer for a French audience will work with a different set of assumed knowledge and expectations to a book about India by an Indian writer for Indian readers.

Yet the readers of travel texts increasingly come from many different backgrounds, not least because travel books themselves travel.[64] This was already a problem for Déon in 1961, when extracts from his book *Le balcon de Spetsai* were translated and published by an Athenian newspaper and then read by Spiro. Spiro's access to Déon's text strained their relationship, though Déon argues that the newspaper embellished his representation (258–9). Travel writers cannot assume that their texts will not be read by those they write about. They should not underestimate the availability of texts and the paths taken by travellees (nor should they overestimate them, by which I mean that we can neither expect a text to be available to someone, nor expect it not to be). Both texts and people seem destined to become more mobile, albeit unevenly. Perhaps this will bring about great changes in the travel writing genre, as audiences become increasingly multicultural and unpredictable. For the time being it seems that travel writers would benefit from Clifford's observation that 'informants' are increasingly readers, and read 'over the ethnographer's shoulder'.[65] A text like Ramazzotti's *Afrozapping*, which carries the subtitle *Breve guida all'Africa per uomini bianchi* (Short guide to Africa for white men), would seem to disregard the travellee reading over the writer's shoulder. On the other hand, a text like Ramondino's *Polisario* receives praise from Polezzi because 'the complex subject positions embodied in it never seem to exclude the possibility that its readers might include Sahrawi people, among many others'.[66] A first step towards polyvocality would be to acknowledge and address multiple readerships.

If the encounter works three ways, it is a triangle with only two sides: one connecting travellee to traveller-writer and the other traveller-writer to reader. The side that would connect the travellee directly to the reader is absent, but perhaps we can imagine ways of compensating for its absence. We have already seen how the travellee determines much of the content of travel texts, in terms of information presented, experiences recounted and encounters narrated.[67] Travel texts often state this directly, and even when they do not, traces of this agency remain, despite the writer selecting or editing, upholding or undermining. Mary Louise Pratt raises this issue in relation to the European production of knowledge about America, pointing out that 'Every travel account has this heteroglossic dimension; its knowledge comes not just out of a traveler's sensibility and powers of observation, but out of interaction and experience usually directed and managed by "travelees", who are working from their own understandings of their world and of what the Europeans are and ought to be doing'.[68] Pratt admits that it is difficult to ascertain the extent to which European knowledge was American in origin; likewise it is impracticable to completely distinguish the word of the writer from that of the guide. Although neat divisions of authorship cannot be drawn, it can be accepted that a travel book is the expression of many voices, and we as readers must not disempower guides ourselves by over-privileging the voice of the writer. Discussing precisely this issue in travel writing about Afghanistan, Corinne Fowler suggests the possibility of developing a 'subversive collaboration between reader and informant', by attending to the gaps and contradictions in the travel writer's text.[69] Fowler goes on to suggest that reading critically is an ethical responsibility.[70] Writers have an ethical responsibility towards those they represent, but so do their readers.

***

All travel writing is a series of translations, in every sense of the word: a rendering into another language, an expression in another artistic medium, an explanation, an interpretation, a transferral, a removal, a transformation, a renovation.[71] Guides and interpreters translate words, experiences and cultural codes for travellers who translate these into their own representations as texts. Travel writers are contained within their own translations; as characters in their narratives they cannot escape the final translation, that of their readers, but they do have a certain control over their self-representation. Similarly, guides and interpreters cannot escape the writers' and readers' translations, but also provide their own representations of themselves. The reader is at the end of a chain of mediation, which begins with a distant reality; at each level of the chain that reality is interpreted, distorted and embellished, beginning with the mediation of the human senses. It is a chain of imprecision, blurred by subjectivity, distrust, poor communication and ulterior motives. At the end of the chain, the reader receives the most mediated representation, but in turn forms for him/herself the final interpretation.

The chain imposes limitations on both experiences and narratives of travel, but travellers are also burdened by their own limitations in the form of expectations and preconceptions that predefine the journey from before the start. Travellers cannot achieve their journeys alone, they depend on those mediating others, but guides are not merely links in a chain; they are individuals with their own agendas, needs and desires. Compromise and collaboration are necessary, but travellers are not always willing to cede the authority of certainty. Travel writers are further limited by the constraints of representation, whether representing themselves as characters or others. The limits of choice are not the same as the limits of ability, and perhaps too often the former is reached before the latter. Too often, that is, because authenticity is also a quality of representation: attributing agency to the travellee also means providing an authentic representation of the journey. As much as a question of authenticity, it is also an ethical choice.

Chapter 4

HOSTING

> Mon alimentation, mon sommeil, ma sécurité ici ne dépendent ni de communications internationales ni de papier monnaie. Ils sont entre les mains des [*sic*] ces frères humains, si semblables et si différents, vers lesquels je marche […]. (Ollivier, *Marche I*, 67)
>
> (My nourishment, my sleep and my safety here depend on neither international communications nor paper money. They are in the hands of these human brothers, so similar and so different, towards whom I walk […].)

The traveller is, by definition, away from home and away from everything that home provides, including food and shelter, making travellers like Bernard Ollivier dependent on the travellees who supply their needs. Locating and using the services that are simple daily necessities, and interacting with those who provide them, consumes much time during any journey. While hospitality has a long history as a duty to strangers, the spread and growth of tourism has hastened the development of the hospitality industry, providing such services in exchange for payment and commercializing the relationship between travelling guests and their hosts.[1] In the age of mass tourism, travellers can only expect to receive hospitality for a price; to be hosted privately, as a stranger, is a rarity. Travellers, like tourists, usually make use of commercial establishments, staying in hotels and eating in restaurants. Such facilities constitute a crucial source of encounters – with staff and other customers – but one of the principal attractions of leaving the beaten track is the possibility of improving contact with people, away from commercial contexts.

When travellees invite travellers into their private homes they offer unique opportunities for authentic experiences and closer personal contact. They also assign the role of guest to the traveller and that of host to themselves, establishing an ancient rapport. Although hospitality is common to societies across the globe, it is culturally varied and expectations differ from one place to the next. Tensions arise from such differences, but are also implicit in the basis of hospitality itself, an ambiguous mixture of generosity and power, of reciprocity and duty.[2] As Émile Benveniste writes, hospitality is etymologically connected to a vocabulary of power: *hospes*, the Latin root, literally means 'le maître de l'hôte' (the master of the guest).[3] As guests, travellers are obliged to submit to their hosts' rules. On the other hand, reciprocity is also inherent in hospitality, which 'est fondée sur l'idée qu'un homme est lié à un autre (*hostis* a toujours une valeur réciproque) par l'obligation de compenser une certaine prestation dont il a été bénéficiaire' [is founded on the idea that a man is bound to another (*hostis* always has a reciprocal value) by the obligation to repay a certain service of which he was the beneficiary].[4] Jacques Derrida explores the implications behind Benveniste's description of hospitality as a pact, in terms of reciprocity: the guest has both rights and duties.[5] Hosts and guests are strangers to each other, yet both take the risk of making themselves vulnerable to the other. The language of hospitality is stretched to apply to both tourists and immigrants, as guests not only of individuals, but also of a host state.[6] The travel in travel writing is closer to tourism than to immigration, but the connecting theme of hospitality reveals tensions between hosts and guests in both contexts, while reminding us that the opportunity to assume the role of either guest or host is not equally available to everyone.[7]

This chapter begins by returning to the theme of authenticity, exploring the parallels between back regions, first introduced in Chapter 2, and the private home of the travellee. It would be entirely consistent with their antitourist stance if travellers favoured invitations into private homes over the inauthentic 'bubble' environment of hotels and the first section puts this hypothesis to the test. I then turn to the tensions inherent in the host–guest encounter, focusing on the contradictions between ideals of freedom and dependency on and submission to travellee-hosts. The final section explores the nature of the travel encounter in terms of two key aspects that are particularly relevant to the hospitality context: reciprocity and duration. As suggested by Benveniste above, hospitality implies or even requires reciprocity, which is often prevented by the mobile status of the traveller, who may seek alternative solutions. This mobility also renders momentary the majority of travel encounters, affecting their potential to develop into relationships and raising the question of their meaningfulness.

Hospitality and Authenticity

Invitation versus reservation

Despite their antitourist rhetoric, travellers use the same facilities as tourists, the same restaurants and hotels – commercial establishments managed by the hospitality industry. As a result, their travel experiences are subject to the same limitations as those of tourists. In his grand hotel in Sri Lanka Francesco

Piccolo feels as though he has hardly left home: 'È come se il mio palazzo fosse rimasto fermo, e il mondo intorno avesse continuato a girare' (86; It's as though my apartment block has stayed still and the world around it has continued to turn). Moving from the air-conditioned hotel to an air-conditioned coach to an air-conditioned restaurant, he is protected from the world he visits, watching it pass by as if on a screen. Tiziano Terzani scathingly describes his luxury hotel in Tbilisi as a 'boll[a] di sapone ad aria condizionata' (air-conditioned soap bubble) (*Buonanotte*, 371). 'Bolla' or bubble is a common metaphor for the controlled spaces created by the tourist industry, which envelop tourists in familiar comforts and cut them off from the authentic outside world and from contact with local people.[8] Within this protected space a modicum of local colour is provided by what Daniel Boorstin calls 'pseudo-events' and Dean MacCannell 'staged authenticity'.[9]

The bubble metaphor recalls MacCannell's use of Erving Goffman's front and back regions: the bubble is equivalent to the staged front region and the desire to leave the bubble echoes the desire to access the back region. Although MacCannell only discusses regions in terms of commercial establishments, in the context of tourism the private home of the travellee is a back region *par excellence*. In his original essay, examining middle-class homes in 1950s America, Goffman describes how homes are divided into a front, where guests are entertained, and a back, consisting of areas such as kitchen, bedroom and bathroom.[10] Goffman acknowledges the possibility of class differences and there are also considerable cultural differences in domestic arrangements around the world, but for a tourist or traveller all private interiors are akin to back regions.[11] With the exception of visits to family, friends or acquaintances (in which circumstances arguably tourists are doing something other than tourism), tourists and travellers are limited to public spaces and only gain access to private homes by invitation. Hospitality in the private home is the antithesis of the inauthentic commercial hotel.

Among the Sahrawi refugees in Algeria, Fabrizia Ramondino spends much of her time visiting people in their tent-homes. These encounters give her important insights into the lives of the Sahrawi and she devotes space in her text to describing them. She pays close attention to the interiors of the tents and the rituals of domesticity and hospitality taking place there (e.g., 47–8 and 50–1). Nicole-Lise Bernheim's Japanese hosts, the Imai family, play a crucial role in her travel experience (Bernheim, *Saisons*); taking her under their wing, they help her with practical problems, guide her in the town and invite her into their home. Similarly, Bernheim's Sri Lankan host Tikiri, who owns the cinnamon plantation where she stays, gives her access to the plantation and the people who live and work there, as well as information that she quotes directly in her text (Bernheim, *Couleur*). In private homes the traveller is privy to domestic habits, learns about social customs and interacts with travellees in an intimate and personal setting, in turn these experiences are given privileged space in travel writing.

When travellers are hosted by the tourist industry their relations with their hosts are principally economic, which, as we have seen in the previous chapter, can interfere with the perceived authenticity of the relationship. A spontaneous invitation from a travellee can provide an opportunity for authentic encounters outside the commercial realm of tourism. Nonetheless, as we have found with guides and interpreters, the financial basis of a relationship can also be transcended by establishing friendly relations, for example when a traveller enjoys more personal contact with hotel owners or staff. Elizabeth Telfer remarks that genuinely hospitable behaviour must have an 'appropriate' motive, but that such hospitality can be found within a commercial context depending on the behaviour and motivations of individual staff.[12] Friendly hotel personnel break the anonymity of the hotel experience and are mentioned favourably in travel texts. In *Chambres d'ailleurs* (1986), Bernheim describes her hotel rooms in detail, but she also takes a particular interest in the hotel owners and staff, who are granted as much textual space as the *chambres* themselves.[13] The tourist industry also compensates with forms of accommodation such as the bed and breakfast, where the tourist stays at the home of the host as a paying guest, enabling a friendlier and more authentic experience.[14] Nicolas Bouvier stays in a bed and breakfast on the isle of Aran and develops a significant relationship with his hosts, using many of their stories in his representation of the island (Bouvier, *Journal*). In Japan the 'homestay' scheme works in a similar way and is designed to give tourists the opportunity to visit an authentic Japanese household. Bernheim makes use of the scheme, but her experience lacks the warmth of Bouvier's and she comments that she feels as though she is staying in a hotel, reminding us that authentic encounters cannot be bought and, as we have seen with guides and interpreters, the success of an encounter depends on the participation of all those concerned (*Chambres*, 21–3). Despite the efforts of the tourist industry, it would appear that private hospitality from travellees provides travellers with more authentic experiences and is therefore more desirable than commercial hospitality.

Back to the bubble

The authenticity of private hospitality also derives from its qualities as a travel experience. Boorstin complains that tourism has made travel easy; it has betrayed the root (*travail*) of the word.[15] The belief persists that being a traveller means taking risks, seeking adventure and bearing hardships. An authentic travel experience should be a challenge, requiring time and effort, and private hospitality meets such requirements. It is elusive, more likely to occur off the beaten track, away from the reach of the tourist industry. The private home of a host can be a minefield of unfamiliar cultural codes and expectations; as guests, travellers are vulnerable to difficult and even dangerous situations. Yet, despite this rich opportunity for authenticity, travellers do not necessarily pursue invitations at every available occasion. This is partly because invitations are not always forthcoming, especially in places where travellers are common and the tourist industry provides for their needs, but it is also because the very qualities that make private hospitality authentic also make it problematic. Entering a private home is not as simple as checking into a hotel; it can entail tensions and misunderstandings between host and guest.

The home in any culture is inscribed with social codes, which vary from one society to the next, increasing the risk of culture clash when a travelling guest accepts an invitation from a host.[16] Travellers are not always conscious of infringing their hosts' customs and such mistakes can cause embarrassment, as Bernheim finds in Sri Lanka when she offers her cook a fish to prepare for dinner, unaware that it is not customary to cook at night: 'Je me sens ignorante, impolie. Je n'oublierai pas' (*Couleur*, 64; I feel ignorant, rude. I won't forget this). On the other hand, such experiences bring new awareness and provide insights into the workings of the visited culture. When setting out from the home of one of his first hosts in Turkey, Ollivier leaves some money to pay for his stay, only to be told later on that he will have seriously offended his host. The error leads to a lesson in Muslim hospitality that the traveller takes to heart (*Marche I*, 60).

Travel is often hard physical work; bodies have their own demands and failings and even the most adventurous minds do not always inhabit cooperative bodies.[17] The physical needs for food and shelter make travellers dependent on their hosts, but the exhaustion of travel is also a mental exhaustion: straining to understand strange languages, adjusting to an unfamiliar environment and undergoing the intensity of new experiences. While hospitality can provide respite, it can also have the opposite effect, forcing the traveller to adapt to another's personal space, to adjust to another's standard of living and comfort. At times, when pressed to accept an invitation, Ramondino finds her tired body resisting, though she pushes herself on: 'Sento che le forze me lo consentiranno, così come ha detto la donna che ha partorito cinque figli in casa.' (101; I feel that my strength will allow me to do it, as said the woman who gave birth to five children at home). Ramondino's analogy suggests necessity, but also overwhelming effort and exhaustion.

For Ollivier, walking alone across Central Asia, often far from the reach of the tourist industry, offers of hospitality are not only a bonus, but a necessity.

He repeatedly emphasizes the importance of these encounters, which give him access to authentic cultural experiences, as well as the pleasure of the encounter itself and the practical assistance of food and shelter. Ollivier tries to avoid hotels as much as he can, invariably lamenting their price, dirtiness and unfriendliness when he does relent. Despite his aversion he finds that commercial establishments have their uses:

> M'arrêter dans les villages signifie que je ne peux, comme dans un hôtel, me laver, me détendre, bien dormir. Je vais, en sortant de Tokat, entamer une marche de dix jours loin des villes, ce qui veut dire dix jours sans repas équilibrés, dix soirées à voir défiler tout un village, dix levers à l'aube, en même temps que mes hôtes, dix jours surtout sans douche, à macérer dans ma sueur. (*Marche I*, 163)
>
> (Stopping in villages means that, unlike in a hotel, I cannot wash myself, relax or sleep well. On leaving Tokat, I'm going to begin a ten day walk far from towns, which means ten days without regular meals, ten evenings watching a whole village parade, ten dawn risings, at the same time as my hosts, and especially ten days without a shower, soaking in my own sweat.)

Given all the social and physical discomforts of being hosted in homes, it is not surprising if travellers opt for the more private and familiar, albeit less authentic, hotel. After all, as Conrad Lashley points out: 'The commercial and market driven relationship which allows the customer a freedom of action that individuals would not dream of demanding in a domestic setting is one of the benefits claimed for the "hospitality industry".'[18] The exchange of money may be a regrettable sign of inauthentic commercialization, but it does remove the pressures of mutual obligation that private hospitality entails.[19] It is also the price of greater personal liberty and privacy. A strategic return to the tourist bubble is perhaps an inevitable part of any journey, if only to restore one's forces for a new foray into the unknown.

The more acute the cultural differences, the more eventful the experience of private hospitality and therefore the more worthy of a written narrative, but also the more potentially stressful and tiring. On the other hand, when host and guest share cultural roots, private hospitality can provide a break in the journey, offering an opportunity to relax in recognizable surroundings, converse fluently and eat familiar food. Sergio Ramazzotti's journey through Africa is punctuated by invitations, mostly from other Italians or Westerners who live and work there. In Gabon, for example, he meets three American Peace Corps workers and decides to make *melanzane alla parmigiana*. '[L]'Africa per stasera rimane fuori, lontana mille anni luce' (*Vado*, 151; For tonight Africa stays outside, a thousand light years away) he remarks, suggesting that among Americans, eating Italian food, he feels as though he is physically elsewhere, perhaps in another kind of bubble. Such an occasion remains an event because of the unusual juxtaposition of the familiar and the unfamiliar: the travel experience is not the *melanzane alla parmigiana*, but the fact of baking one in Gabon.

Accounts of hospitality in travel writing suggest that, in practice, travellers do not always prefer private to commercial hospitality and are often grateful to retreat to the tourist bubble. The everyday embodiedness of travel can outweigh desires for encounter and authenticity, which are then put aside in favour of comfort and rest. The contrast between commercial and private hospitality and the sometimes contradictory attitudes towards them reflect the tension between ideals of travel and the practical realities of the journey. Travel writing reveals the tension between what one wants to do, or thinks one should do, and what one is actually able to do, physically, mentally, practically. The journey is always a compromise between the ideal and the reality and the text bears the traces of these limitations.

Freedom

Hospitality as control

When travellers accept invitations into private homes they enter the domain of their hosts, entrusting them with their safety and submitting to their rules. For all Ollivier's enthusiasm about the hospitality he receives, he also has some unpleasant and even perilous experiences. In Eastern Turkey, where the conflict between Kurds and Turks makes the rural population wary of strangers, he finds himself greeted with suspicion and sometimes hostility. In the village of Alihadjeu, he is given the food and shelter he seeks, but the villagers are so suspicious that they keep watch on him and eventually summon the army to arrest him. The event is an ordeal for Ollivier: at one point the building where he is staying is surrounded by all the men of the village, including one armed with a gun (*Marche I*, 188). When the soldiers insist on taking him away he is furious, since their intervention ruins his itinerary, but the episode frightens him, despite his indignation, and he refers back to it several times, including the following year (e.g., *Marche II*, 17–18).

As Ollivier's experience demonstrates, hospitality itself is used to control the traveller. Tom Selwyn remarks that 'while the essence of hospitality lies in sharing (food, lodging, entertainment), the very process of sharing may involve dominating too'.[20] In Kirghizstan Terzani visits the town of Uzgen, hoping to learn about the recent conflict between Kirghiz and Uzbeks, but his visit is carefully managed to prevent him from meeting any residents of the town. One of his hosts' principal tactics involves a series of formal meals, using their hospitality to control his movements. Terzani is angry when he realizes what is happening:

> Esasperato, mangio e mi sento ancora più male. Mi rendo conto che, a forza di banchetti, ho passato una mezza giornata a Uzghen senza parlare con qualcuno che non fosse un funzionario governativo, senza vedere la città, senza farmi un'idea di quel che vi è successo e tanto meno di quel che vi succede adesso. (*Buonanotte*, 197)
>
> (Exasperated, I eat and I feel even worse. I realize that because of these banquets I have spent half a day in Uzgen without speaking to anyone who is not a government official, without seeing the city, without getting any idea of what happened here and even less what is happening now.)

Terzani's hosts, like Ollivier's, disguise their intentions to control his movements behind a facade of hospitality. In both cases the hosts' ulterior motives undermine the authenticity of their welcome, but what concerns the travellers most is the constraint on their freedom of movement. Their own powerlessness frightens Ollivier and irritates them both, yet travellers who are hosted are always subject to the travellee's will. They are both surprised and angered to find their hosts exercising the power over their guests that is their privilege as hosts.

The shared etymological root of hospitality and hostility is often evoked to highlight the close relationship between these two concepts that are not as distinct as they might seem in language today.[21] Selwyn suggests that the two belong on the same continuum: 'both are expressions of the existence, rather than the negation, of a relationship'.[22] Some of the experiences of being controlled while being hosted, described by travel writers, occur in the blurred line where the two meet. Travellers arrive as strangers in others' lands and as such face a choice described by Eric Leed: 'The first option presented to the arriving strangers is that of "friend" or "enemy", potential help or potential harm.'[23] The host has the power to ascribe either identity to the traveller, but travellers are not powerless. In Yugoslavia Bouvier and his companion Thierry enter a hut where a group of gypsies are enjoying their evening with drink and song. 'Lorsqu'on apparut sur la porte, la musique s'arrêta net. Ils avaient posé leurs instruments et nous fixaient, stupéfaits et méfiants' (When we appeared at the door, the music stopped dead. They had put down their instruments and were staring at us, stunned and suspicious). As Bouvier recognizes, 'Nous étions nouveaux venus dans ces campagnes où rien n'arrive; il fallait montrer patte blanche' (We were newcomers in these rural parts where nothing happens; we had to show our credentials). The travellers make an effort to appease their hosts: 'On s'assit à leur table qu'on fit regarnir de vin, de poisson fumé, de cigarettes' (*Usage*, 105; We sat down at their table, and had it replenished with wine, smoked fish and cigarettes). The atmosphere improves and the two stay to enjoy and record the gypsies' music, to the delight of the players. The two travellers accept their role as strangers and act to alleviate the gypsies' apprehension. By so doing they succeed in making themselves welcome where Ollivier failed. Hospitality is a negotiation, as Mireille Rosello explains: 'Hospitable exchanges often create situations in which one party must second-guess the other's desires or needs. And not knowing what the other expects, or wants, will create moments of malaise and discomfort, as well as moments of pleasure and joy. Hospitality is also about resigning oneself to friction, approximations, gradually altered protocols.'[24] This discomfort is an inevitable ingredient in the travel encounter, but it is also the price to pay for the pleasure of connection.

Although hosts are ostensibly in control, guests are not the only ones who take risks when they enter a host's home or territory; the host is also vulnerable.[25] Apart from possible physical threat, hosts are susceptible to criticism from their guests, as Jane Darke and Craig Gurney suggest: 'The hosts' performance is only occasionally secure, and may be judged inadequate by the guest (or vice versa) due to different expectations of gender roles, of the functions of home and of generation and social classes.'[26] This is particularly true when those guests are travel writers who represent their hosts in their texts. Corrado Ruggeri, for example, is scathing about the food offered to him at a wedding in Vietnam: 'Siamo giovanotti d'appetito, almeno normalmente, ma qui c'è davvero da farsi coraggio perché non c'è nulla che sia, non dico invitante, ma che appaia commestibile' (211; We have healthy appetites, at least usually, but here we really need some courage because there is nothing that is, not just appetizing, but that even appears edible), he complains, before verbally demolishing each dish in turn. Travel writers address readers whom they presume share their own cultural values, so when cultural differences lead to discrepancies in expectations between host and guest, the traveller-guest can appeal to the reader's sympathies, to the detriment of the host.

For all the power exerted over the guest by the host during the journey, the writer is able to recover and undermine the host in the text. This is demonstrated by Ollivier's representation of the people of Alihadjeu. Although the text only provides the traveller's perspective, we can imagine the rationality of the villagers: they live in a poor, rural, isolated village; Ollivier is a complete stranger who can barely communicate with them and, walking alone with a rucksack of mysterious contents, he is also a complete anomaly; the head of the village is away and yet Ollivier refuses to show his passport or the contents of his bag to anyone else, only conceding to do so after being repeatedly asked. In such circumstances it is hardly surprising that he causes alarm, yet he repeatedly uses derogatory language to describe the villagers: they are 'cons' (bloody idiots), a 'petit peuple de misérables' (little gang of wretches) (*Marche I*, 189). He laments 'leur folie collective, la convoitise [...] et l'ignorance' (207; their collective madness, their greed [...] and ignorance). Once his initial fears have subsided he is most riled by the hypocrisy of their hospitality, as he makes clear when he describes his departure from the village: 'J'ai la toute petite satisfaction de leur lancer d'une voix de stentor – je connais la phrase par cœur – en traversant cette populace assoiffée de vengeance: "Merci pour votre hospitalité." J'ai, ainsi, le sentiment de quitter les lieux la tête haute' (190; Passing through this mob, who are thirsty for vengeance, I have the tiny satisfaction of throwing at them in a booming voice (I know the phrase by heart): 'Thank you for your hospitality.' That way, I feel I am leaving the place with my head high). Thus the travel writer appeals to the reader in order to recover lost authority from hosts who exercise control over the traveller's journey.

The world is my playground

Leisured travel is synonymous with freedom and mobility. The authors of *Pour une littérature voyageuse*, for example, accumulate images of distance, exoticism, adventure, and escape, all implying an ideal of free movement. Freedom is implicit in Alain Borer's suggestion that 'Un carnet d'adresses et une carte de crédit suffisent pour faire le tour du monde' (An address book and a credit card are enough to complete a tour of the world);[27] in Michel Le Bris' description of a world full of promise: 'Le cri du monde! Certains soirs, c'est comme une déchirure, une promesse chuchotée de mondes à conquérir' (The call of the world! Some evenings, it's like a tearing, a whispered promise of worlds to conquer);[28] in Michel Chaillou's insistence that adventure requires travel: 'Quand on reste à l'intérieur des maisons, il ne peut pas y avoir d'aventure, il faut qu'il y ait de l'espace, que ça respire, qu'on soit vent debout, qu'on soit fouetté par le mystère…' (When you stay inside the house, there is no possibility of adventure, there has to be space, room to breathe, you must head into the wind, you must be whipped by mystery…).[29] Freedom is not only an ideal in travel writing; it is taken for granted as a fact, as a natural characteristic of travel.

This presumed right to free movement manifests itself most obviously when it is threatened. On entering China from Kirghizstan Ollivier's pledge to travel by foot is blighted by the Chinese authorities, who force him to take a car for one hundred kilometres, ignoring his considerable efforts to obtain permission to walk, which include a letter from the French ambassador to China. He has no power to resist, but emphasizes his anger and disappointment, and the lack of sympathy from the customs officers (*Marche III*, 98). Ramazzotti, who travels by public transport from Algiers to Cape Town, goes one step further when he is returned to Algeria by the guards at the Niger border: he accepts help from a taxi driver to cross the border in secret, but the plan backfires when the Niger police catch him and send him back (*Vado*, 78–87). Ramazzotti is more resigned than Ollivier, but he is also inconvenienced and his itinerary is disrupted by the interventions of travellees.

The travellers' frustrations are easy to understand, but their expectations of freedom are almost perverse given the inequalities of international mobility. The tourists who leave Europe do not move under the same restrictions as the immigrants who seek entry into Europe and both writers know that the hospitality they demand of others would rarely be reciprocated in their own countries. Ollivier himself compares French hospitality unfavourably with the kindness he receives on his journey (e.g., *Marche II*, 90). Ramazzotti crosses paths with Africans hoping to migrate to Italy and is well aware of the welcome that awaits them (e.g., *Vado*, 89–90). Yet the rights of others to govern their own territory, to decide who should enter it and how, to manage the movement of foreign travellers within their borders, are put into question. It is as though the whole world were a playground for the European traveller to move in freely, to access at leisure regardless of the ownership of territory. This implies colonial nostalgia, but it also fails to acknowledge the unilateral realities of mobility.

Free movement may be an ideal, but it is not even a right under the United Nations' Universal Declaration of Human Rights, which only grants, in Article 13, that '1) Everyone has the right to freedom of movement and residence *within* the borders of each state' and '2) Everyone has the right to *leave* any country, including his own, and to *return to his country*.'[30] Zygmunt Bauman identifies mobility as the most coveted value in our newly globalized world, but also as the source of new social divisions: 'The freedom to move, perpetually a scarce and unequally distributed commodity, fast becomes the main stratifying factor of our late-modern or postmodern times.'[31] The unequal distribution of wealth is one reason for the relativity of the freedom to travel, especially at leisure, but the very right to movement is not equal either: for many, restrictions on travel are strict and borders are impermeable. Bauman describes the elite at the top of the mobility hierarchy as 'tourists', regardless of purpose, while those at the bottom are 'vagabonds': 'The tourists stay or move at their hearts' desire. They abandon a site when new untried opportunities beckon elsewhere. The vagabonds know that they won't stay in a place for long, however strongly they wish to, since nowhere they stop are they likely to be welcome. […] The tourists travel because *they want to*; the vagabonds because *they have no other bearable choice*.'[32] The metaphor of hospitality is applied to both tourism and immigration, yet in the latter case it describes a power relation that prevents the immigrant from being at home in the host nation: 'It is the native who is empowered to feel at home and to assume the position of the host. If the immigrant is imagined as "the guest", the "host nation" maintains its historical position of power and privilege in determining who is or is not welcome to enter the country, but also under what conditions of entry.'[33] What happens if we replace the word 'immigrant' in this quotation with 'tourist'? In an ideal world everyone would move freely, but since reality is far from such an ideal we might turn the problem on its head and ask whether tourists and other leisured travellers have the right to move as freely as they assume. Travel books certainly represent encounters with hosts who exercise 'power and privilege in determining who is or is not welcome to enter the country'.

Travellers' assumptions about their freedom recall what Shannon Sullivan describes as 'ontological expansiveness' in her study of white privilege:

> As ontologically expansive, white people tend to act and think as if all spaces – whether geographical, psychical, linguistic, economic, spiritual, bodily, or otherwise – are or should be available for them to move in and out of as they wish. Ontological expansiveness is a particular co-constitutive relationship between self and environment in which the self assumes that it can and should have total mastery over its environment.[34]

Sullivan is writing about race, while the inequalities of international movement are determined by wealth and nationality, rather than race as such, but her analysis remains pertinent to this context. Sullivan goes on to examine ways in which white people can combat white privilege themselves, even from a position of privilege, suggesting that: 'White people must curb the expansive, ubiquitous way in which they often transact, including the way that they transact as if no one else of significance does or should inhabit the world.'[35] In her novel about Senegalese immigration to France, Fatou Diome expresses a similar sentiment:

> Le prix du visa que les Sénégalais payent pour venir en France équivaut à un salaire mensuel local, alors que n'importe quel Français peut se rendre au Sénégal à loisir, sans aucune formalité. Celui qui ne m'aime pas assez, ou ne me fait pas assez confiance pour me laisser venir chez lui à ma guise, doit apprendre à frapper à la porte lorsqu'il veut entrer chez moi.[36]
>
> (The price of the visa that Senegalese pay to come to France is equivalent to a month's salary locally, while any French person can travel to Senegal at leisure, without any formalities. Someone who does not like me enough, or does not trust

me enough to let me come to his home as I please, must learn to knock at the door when he wants to enter my home.)

Sullivan appeals to white people, or travellers in this case, to restrain their expansiveness, while Diome calls on travellees to assert their rights as hosts. We have already seen evidence of the latter, but there are also times when travellers demonstrate their willingness to curtail their own privileges. Bouvier and Thierry, for example, come across Turkish villagers dancing to music, but the atmosphere is tense and their greetings are met with silence. The travellers refrain from recording the music on this occasion and soon leave. Bouvier follows the account with a reflection on the role of fear in preserving the traveller's safety:

> … on renonce alors à entrer dans *cette* rue, dans *cette* mosquée, ou à prendre *cette* photo. Le lendemain, on se le reproche romantiquement et bien à tort. La moitié au moins de ces malaises sont – on le comprend plus tard – une levée de l'instinct contre un danger sérieux. Il ne faut pas se moquer de ces avertissements. (*Usage*, 155, emphasis in the original)
>
>   (… so you give up on entering *this* street, *this* mosque, or taking *this* photo. The next day, you reproach yourself romantically and certainly wrongly. At least half the time this uneasiness, as you later understand, is instinct reacting to a serious danger. Such warnings are not to be mocked.)

With self-preservation in mind, the travellers obey the interdiction of their hosts and do not insist on imposing their presence. Stefano Liberti provides another example in *A Sud di Lampedusa* (2008), which recounts five years of pursuing and meeting African emigrants on their way to Europe.[37] In Tangiers he ignores the strict division in accommodation between Africans and tourists, insisting on checking into a hotel reserved for Africans. He senses immediately that he is not welcome and spends an uncomfortable few nights, locked up in his tiny room alone, watched but never addressed by the other occupants. He is afraid for his safety because of his relative wealth, constantly fearing attack: 'Temevo quel momento anche perché sapevo che, se fosse arrivato, sarebbe stata unicamente colpa mia, che avevo voluto così ostinatamente invadere quello spazio che non mi apparteneva' (Liberti, 158; I also feared that moment because I knew that, if it happened, it would be my fault alone, having wanted so obstinately to invade space that was not mine). After failing to make himself welcome, Liberti leaves. In both of these cases the travellers are made to feel profoundly uneasy by travellees whose territory they have entered uninvited. Sullivan explains the importance of recognizing such situations: 'Complementing the realization that there are some spaces that white people should not enter and do not have legitimate authority to enter, fighting whiteness vis-à-vis space also means that white people must recognize that it is not inappropriate or unjust for them to feel uncomfortable when they do enter spaces that are predominantly non-white.'[38] It is natural for travellers like Bouvier and Liberti to make mistakes in their negotiation of territory, and even to attempt to push the boundaries, but it is important that they acknowledge them as mistakes and recognize the right of their hosts to make them unwelcome.

All of these episodes, where hospitality is requested and refused, are also encounters. The commanding border guards, the hostile villagers, the unfriendly migrants: all are individual travellees who come into contact with the travellers and direct or control their movements. Confrontational encounters are particularly common at border crossings. Ramazzotti opens *Vado verso il Capo* with the description of a recurring dream that haunts him on his return from Africa. An African official asks to see his passport and he hands it over but screams his objections, imagining a litany of problems:

> ... *bloccato, ritardo, sguardo sospettoso, interrogatorio, sequestro pellicole/macchina fotografica, costretto a tornare a casa, prezzolare (finiti i soldi), il viaggio continua, sono sempre più povero, povero come la gente che ho incontrato finora, perché un altro problema?* (problème, problem), *i miei visti sono regolari, regolari, regolari.* (*Vado*, 7, italics in the original)
>
> (... blocked, delayed, suspicious stare, interrogation, confiscation of film/camera, forced to return home, to pay bribes (running out of money), the journey continues, I'm always getting poorer, as poor as the people I have met so far, why is there another problem? (problème, problem), my visas are in order, in order, in order.)

Such conflicts arise more frequently with the trend for decelerated modes of travel, which take travellers on unconventional journeys to places where their presence is an anomaly. When Paolo Rumiz crosses the Hungary–Ukraine border by train he is met with suspicion: 'La polizia ucraina non capisce cosa ci faccia lì. Due agenti bestemmiano, mi aprono il sacco con aria cupa. [...] Mi guardano come una bestia rara. Succede così tutte le volte che di lì passa un semplice viaggiatore' (*Oriente*, 46; The Ukrainian police don't understand what I'm doing there. Two officers curse, opening up my bag with a sullen air. [...] They look at me like I'm a rare species. This happens every time a simple traveller passes through). They let him cross, but the reactions of the individual police officers emphasize the unusual nature of Rumiz's journey. The figure of the official represents the blurred line between hospitality offered by individuals and hospitality from the state.[39] They act on behalf of the state, whose hospitality or hostility they enact, but remain individuals in direct contact with the state's potential guests. These encounters are often characterized by a tension between this official role and the human individuality of the two interlocutors. As with guides and interpreters, the host's response to the traveller is determined by multiple factors and tensions, including both personal and wider community attitudes. These are not always in harmony, but nor are encounters with border officials antagonistic by necessity, as Bernheim finds when she and her companion are stuck at the Pakistan–India border one night: 'Un douanier compatissant nous invite chez lui pour la nuit, sa courtoisie excusera son pays' (*Chambres*, 215; A sympathetic customs officer invites us to his home for the night, his courtesy will excuse his country). Here the hospitality of the individual travellee compensates for the inhospitality of his state.

The European traveller's ideal of freedom is constantly questioned by encounters.[40] The ideal is in tension with the reality of travel described in the texts, where host travellees curtail the traveller's mobility. Put another way, the ideal of freedom disguises and denies the traveller's dependence on the travellee. Arguably, hospitality is by nature in contradiction with freedom, because it implies reciprocity and obligation: hosts have duties, but guests also have responsibilities. The guest is not free to come and go at will, but is subject to the host's rule, whether that host is an individual travellee, or a nation state. International travel has become so commonplace that it is easy for tourists and travellers to forget that they, as much as immigrants, are always someone's guest. Their travellee hosts actively remind them of this.

The Nature of Encounters

Reciprocity

Ideally hospitality is a reciprocal arrangement: today's host should be tomorrow's guest.[41] In reality, the host's invitation to a traveller often highlights the inequality of travel; there may be no prospect that the traveller will ever be called upon to reciprocate. Travellers' hosts may never become their guests because of a lack of financial means, different cultures of travel and unequal rights to free movement. Franck Michel is pessimistic, arguing that the relationship between host and guest in tourism can never be equal because these circumstances define its inequality from the start.[42] Since this is the case, travellers seem to benefit unfairly from invitations, not only do they receive food and shelter for free, but they also gain experiences that are valuable material for their narratives. So how do travel writers address this imbalance? How do they reciprocate the hospitality they receive? And is this even possible?

Remuneration is sometimes feasible and acceptable, but, as Ollivier quickly learns in Turkey, attempting to pay a host may be inappropriate and even cause offense. Some travellers look for other ways of compensating their hosts. Ramondino, for example, performs small services: posting a letter, translating a medical report (73 and 79). Ollivier himself is especially keen to demonstrate his desire to repay the many hosts on whom his journey depends. He uses the traditional traveller role of entertaining them with the tale of his journey and carries a bag of lapel pins for the children. He develops a ritual of taking photographs of his hosts to post back to them, insisting on the importance of this small act of reciprocity and the care he takes to record his hosts' names and addresses (e.g., *Marche I*, 63–4).[43] Nonmaterial reciprocity is also inherent to hospitality itself, which constitutes an event for host and traveller alike. Ruggeri describes how he and his partner Carla are the 'ospiti "importanti"' (210; 'important' guests) at the wedding they attend in Vietnam; the bridal couple and their families are all keen to be photographed alongside them. Terzani's presence at a circumcision party in Bukhara is apparently considered by the children's parents to be a great gift (*Buonanotte*, 304). This mutual exoticism suggests that the hosting experience is more reciprocal than it may seem; particularly in places where tourists and other visitors are rare, a passing stranger is a welcome novelty. Paul Lynch, Maria Laura Di Domenico and Majella Sweeney suggest that engaging with guests can 'permit the host to indulge in vicarious mobility that transcends the reality of physical immobility'.[44] Hosts may end up as characters in travel texts, but travellers also become characters in their travellees' own tales. Since we are focusing on the perspective of the travel writer, it is impossible to draw conclusions about the real reciprocity of hospitality, but we can identify a desire on the part of some travellers to demonstrate reciprocity towards their hosts. Particularly when accepting food and accommodation from hosts with limited means, as Ollivier or Ruggeri do, writers exhibit their desire to compensate for apparently inequitable situations, by asserting that their hosts do benefit in some small way at least. Once more, these travel writers are addressing their readers as people who share their own cultural expectations and their expressions of giving are directed as much towards these readers as any act that preceded them may have been addressed to their hosts.

The chance to play host to a travellee is rare, but we might ask just how willing travellers would be if such reciprocity were a real possibility. Bernheim, who so benefits from the welcome she received from the Imai, confesses that she is alarmed when they suggest that their daughter Ikuyo move to Paris. 'Je proteste […]. Je n'ai pas eu envie d'avoir des enfants. Pourquoi, même si elle est exquise, adopterais-je une Japonaise de vingt-cinq ans?' (I protest […]. I didn't want to have children. Why then would I adopt a twenty-five year old Japanese woman, even if she is delightful?). Ikuyo does move to Paris and Bernheim admits: 'Que je le veuille ou non, elle est devenue ma fille japonaise.

Retournement de situation. L'arroseur arrosé. Le mangeur mangé. Feux croisés' (*Saisons*, 149; Whether I like it or not, she has become my Japanese daughter. Reversal of the situation. The biter is bitten. The eater is eaten. Crossfire). In this case, the possibility of a more equal exchange is helped by the greater equality of economic circumstances.

The flow of tourists from Europe out into the rest of the world is paralleled by a reverse movement of migrants coming to Europe. These two paths cross constantly, invisibly, yet tourists and migrants rarely come into direct contact with each other. Ramazzotti and Liberti provide two interesting examples of travellers who do encounter migrants, by chance in one case and by design in the other, and both face the prospect of having their hospitality called upon. In Algeria Ramazzotti shares a lorry with a group of men hoping to leave Africa for Italy. He takes their photograph and they request his address in order to send him theirs and receive a copy of the picture:

> Per un attimo, con malignità, ho pensato che mi avrebbero bombardato di lettere chiedendomi di aiutarli a procurarsi un visto d'ingresso o un permesso di soggiorno per l'Italia, di garantire per loro presso qualche ambasciata italiana del Nordafrica o di mandare loro dei soldi. (*Vado*, 98)
>
> (In a moment of malice I thought they would bombard me with letters asking me to help them obtain an entry visa or residence permit for Italy, to act as guarantor for them at some Italian embassy in North Africa or to send them money).

Repenting, Ramazzotti provides his address, but he receives only one forlorn letter giving a little news and asking for nothing in return.

Ramazzotti and Bernheim both acquiesce to their travellees' requests, but their reluctance suggests that travellers do not necessarily expect travellees to invade their own lives and personal spaces once their journey is complete. To what extent then do encounters, which are so valuable to travel, continue into the traveller's life beyond the journey? Travellers may eagerly seek encounters while they are travelling, but an invisible boundary seems to separate journey from home and the suggestion that a travellee might breach that boundary by intruding into the traveller's home life seems surprising and even threatening. Travellers regularly invade others' private spaces, but are protective of their own. The division between home and away is reinforced in travel writing by the boundaries of the text, which separate the experiences narrated from the writer's life at home.[45]

In his encounters with African emigrants, Liberti is conscious of his position of privilege; on one occasion when he gives out his phone number he admits that he does it 'più per alleviare la mia cattiva coscienza di europeo libero di viaggiare a piacimento che per mantenere veramente un contatto' (36; more to alleviate my bad conscience as a European who is free to travel at leisure than to really maintain contact). The Italian journalist meets dozens of migrants during his journeys and follows some of them by phone, e-mail and text message, reporting their successes and failures. One travellee, Sindou from the Ivory Coast, whom he first meets in Istanbul, eventually becomes his guest in Rome. Liberti receives phone calls from Sindou in Athens, asking for his assistance to reach Italy illegally, a request that throws him into indecision. Eventually Sindou makes his own way to Italy and Liberti, although initially reluctant, then helps him out, hosting him for a few weeks, showing him round and teaching him about the country. A friendship develops, 'strana ma intensa' (169; strange but intense), but Liberti questions its authenticity, conscious of his own professional interests and the asymmetries between them (179). He decides that there is genuine reciprocity in their relationship: he helps Sindou to settle in Italy, while Sindou provides him with valuable information about the immigration routes and even takes care of arrangements when Liberti returns to Africa. Greater reciprocity enables a more trusting relationship: 'Ormai Sindou si fidava. Ai suoi occhi, non ero più il giornalista invadente che cercava di estorcergli informazioni su come avveniva il passaggio. Ero colui che doveva consigliarlo nella permanenza in Europa, il suo tutore' (171; By then Sindou was trustful. In his eyes I was no longer the invasive journalist trying to extort information from him about how the crossing worked. I was the one who had to advise him during his stay in Europe, his guardian). Liberti's journey creates continuity between home and away: those whom he encounters abroad are travelling towards and eventually reach his home, where he meets them again, on his return. His experience is unusual, since travellers rarely deliberately seek encounters with migrants. As long as travel writing maintains strict borders between home and away, life and journey, tourism and migration, it leaves little space for genuine reciprocity, only for the expression of a vague desire, the acknowledgement of guilt. It is also a limitation of the genre in its current form: because travel books narrate the traveller's journey away and rarely their return home, anything brought back vanishes with the end of the text. Reciprocal hospitality may well take place outside the travel book's borders, suggesting that it does not belong with the narration of the journey.

So far I have only considered reciprocity as a like-for-like exchange of hospitality for hospitality, or at the very least for some practical favour, between travellee-host and traveller-guest characters within the text. Writing about an episode in François Maspero's *Les passagers du Roissy-Express*, Rosello suggests that the text itself can host the travellee: 'Just as Madame Zineb welcomes Anaïk into her home, the story welcomes Madame Zineb into this multifaceted history of the Paris *banlieue*, where she becomes an important character.'[46] In this way, the hospitality provided to the traveller is reciprocated by the text 'hosting' the travellee. Travel books are like metaphorical homes belonging to writers, within which they can offer hospitality to their own hosts in exchange for the literal hospitality they received as travellers. Travellees may appreciate such metaphorical reciprocity, particularly when portraits are flattering. Ollivier reads sections of his travelogue to Sabira Tchoukourov, who had hosted him the previous year, reporting that she is moved to tears because none of the many writers who had passed through her house had ever written her first name before (*Marche III*, 16). Sabira clearly appreciates the acknowledgement, at least according to Ollivier, but we have already seen how Spiro was perturbed by Michel Déon's characterization of him (see Chapter 3) and he is likely not the only travellee to feel indignant. In a sense, travellees as guests in books submit to the control of their writer-hosts, just as those writers submitted to their own rules when they were traveller-guests. There is an important difference, however: travellers are able to terminate hospitality arrangements, they can choose to leave, to move on, to forget the experience and seek out others. Travellees as guests in travel books have no such choice; they rarely have the chance to withdraw their presence, their representation, from the printed text.

Time and friendships

By definition the traveller is on the move, crossing paths with dozens of travellees, but rarely spending long with any individual. This raises questions about the duration and meaningfulness of the travel encounter. Hospitality interrupts the traveller's movement, creating time for the relationship between travellee-host and traveller-guest to develop, so it is pertinent to address this question here. Marco Aime is critical of the kinds of encounters arranged within the context of even ethical tourism, because they do not allow for personal connections and are especially short on time.[47] He focuses on organized tours, so what he says about individual contact does not necessarily apply to travellers; however, what he writes about time is relevant to travel writing.

> Come spesso avviene nella vita di tutti noi, il tempo trasforma gli incontri in amicizia, oppure in semplice conoscenza formale, o ancora fa sì che ogni tipo di rapporto si interrompa. Il tempo può chiarire le perplessità e le ambiguità iniziali, appianare le differenze o solo accantonarle, spostando la relazione su altri binari. In ogni caso, solo il tempo può rivelarci se da un incontro può nascere un legame.[48]

(As often happens in all of our lives, time transforms encounters into friendships, or into simple formal acquaintances, or it ensures that any kind of contact is broken. Time can clarify the initial perplexities and ambiguities, even out differences or simply put them aside, shifting relations onto other tracks. In each case, only time can reveal if an encounter can develop into a relationship.)

In the light of Aime's comments and given the lack of time at the disposal of moving travellers, we might ask how travel writers handle the evolution of encounters, within the restricted time of a journey and the narrative time of a text. Ollivier's *Longue marche* series and Bernheim's *Saisons japonaises* make a suitable comparison, given the different natures of their journeys: the one moving rapidly between many places and encounters, the other spending a long time in one place and with one family.

Ollivier constantly pushes forward with his journey, often walking further in a day than he had intended. His desire to keep moving means that he must decline invitations or that he cannot spend as much time with people as either they or he would like (e.g., *Marche II*, 245). He rarely spends more than one night with his hosts, which is ironic given that he explicitly emphasizes that his travel experiences are superior to those of other tourists because he is walking and is therefore taking more time (e.g., *Marche I*, 262). Despite spending so little time with the people he meets, he insists upon the intensity of these encounters:

> Amitiés d'un jour, et pourtant fortes et solides comme si le temps les avait affermies. Je n'avais jamais éprouvé cela auparavant: que l'amitié, l'amour, ne sont pas affaire de temps mais le résultat d'une secrète alchimie, et que l'éternité, non plus, n'est pas une affaire de durée. (*Marche I*, 283–4)
>
> (Day-long friendships, and yet as strong and solid as if time had consolidated them. I had never experienced this before: that friendship and love are not a matter of time but the result of a secret alchemy, and that eternity itself is not a matter of duration).

Ollivier therefore contradicts Aime, by asserting that a genuine friendship can emerge in a short space of time. It is not possible to ascertain the extent to which Ollivier's friendships are mutual, although he does receive some repeat invitations (e.g., Monir and Mehdi in Iran, *Marche II*). Several years later Ollivier repeats his journey, this time by car, as described in *Carnets d'une longue marche*, with the explicit purpose of meeting up with his hosts and other interlocutors. He writes that he has exchanged a few letters with some, but has apparently not maintained contact with most. Nonetheless, he reports that he is greeted with great warmth by many of those whom he successfully locates, suggesting that his initial impressions about his encounters were not illusory. Perhaps the most interesting aspect is his own conviction about these relationships: it is important to him to assert that his encounters generate friendships.

In contrast with Ollivier, Bernheim more or less stays put in Koya in *Saisons japonaises*. She develops a friendship with her hosts, the Imai family, emphasizing the importance of taking time and of her own efforts:

> Les échanges avec les Imai se sont faits avec lenteur, il a fallu que je prouve mon intérêt, ma sincérité […]. J'ai dû montrer ma vérité. Ils savent désormais qu'ils peuvent compter sur moi, que je fais ce que je promets de faire. À partir de là, je ne l'ignore pas, les portes que j'ai ouvertes le resteront pour la vie. (*Saisons*, 99)
>
> (Exchanges with the Imai were established slowly, I had to prove my interest, my sincerity […]. I had to show my truthfulness. They know from now on that they can count on me, that I do what I promise to do. From this point on, I am aware of the fact that the doors I have opened will stay open for life).

Towards the end of the book she describes their close relationship, in a section entitled '*Imai Nicole*', which implies that she has become part of the family:

> J'aime les Imai, ma famille japonaise. Je m'en vais, je pense à eux. Le soir, […] je vais parfois partager leur repas, à la fortune du pot. Petit à petit, j'ai appris à participer à leur intimité, à leur gaieté. […] Bientôt, ou dans une autre vie, lorsque j'aurai changé de moi, les Imai m'adopteront. (*Saisons*, 224–5)
>
> (I love the Imai, my Japanese family. When I go away, I think of them. In the evening […] I sometimes go and share their meal, pot luck. Little by little, I have learned to participate in their private lives, in their joys. […] Soon, or in another life, when I will have changed self, the Imai will adopt me.)

Bernheim also states that her relationship with the Imai defies claims that foreigners cannot create connections with the Japanese (*Saisons*, 225). The friendship continues after she leaves Japan, particularly through Ikuyo, who moves to Paris. In *Couleur cannelle* Bernheim buys cinnamon to send to the Imai, whom she calls 'ma *famille japonaise* de Koyasan' (161, emphasis in the original; my *Japanese family* from Koyasan). Bernheim's friendship with the Imai better reflects Aime's ideas, but she might be considered to be exploiting the relationship by writing about it.[49] Ollivier's multiple fragmentary encounters are more typical of travel writing, especially when the traveller is constantly on the move, though he is more sentimental than most.[50]

Michael Cronin makes an interesting distinction between what he calls horizontal and vertical travel: 'Horizontal travel is the more conventional understanding of travel as a linear progression from place to place. Vertical travel is temporary dwelling in a location for a period of time where the traveller begins to travel down into the particulars of place either in space (botany, studies of microclimate, exhaustive exploration of local landscape) or in time (local history, archaeology, folklore).'[51] These two ways of travelling could be applied to travel encounters, particularly the examples of Ollivier and Bernheim. Ollivier, the horizontal traveller, accumulates a large number of brief but often intense encounters, while Bernheim, the vertical traveller, takes the time to develop more sustained relationships with a small number of people. Although horizontal travel is more conventional, this kind of journey is subject to criticism from antitourists when taken to extremes of speed and superficiality. Vertical travel is not exactly synonymous with deceleration, but does stem from a similar motivation; calls for vertical or slow travel reflect the perception that too much travel is horizontal. Nonetheless, both types of travel enable encounters that are special in their own different ways. The merits of sustained, meaningful relationships are perhaps more obvious, but brief intense encounters can also be significant. Travelling is a special and temporary state of being, so it is not surprising that most travel encounters share these qualities.[52] Although Ollivier highlights particular individuals, overall his encounters have a cumulative, collective value. The relationships between Bernheim and the Imai develop between individuals, while Ollivier's many encounters describe the relationship between one man, Ollivier, and a wider humanity. This recalls other travel writers and their collections of encounters, such as Ramazzotti and his beer labels, or Terzani and his fortune tellers.

Sustained relationships, such as those Bernheim develops with the Imai, exceed the travel text, while Ollivier's brief encounters are events within and limited to the text, just as the personal life of the writer exceeds the text, while the journey usually does not. Yet brief encounters may be more significant to the narrative than long-lasting relationships that remain in the background. Real time is not the same as textual space: an encounter that lasts only a brief time in reality may be granted considerable significance in a text and conversely a long-lasting relationship may receive little textual space, spilling into the life of the writer and out of the reader's sight. We will continue to examine the nature of encounters in the following chapters, through closer consideration of brief encounters in Chapters 5 and 6, and long-term relationships in Chapter 7. The themes of reciprocity and duration reflect the desire of many travel writers to bestow significance on their encounters, no matter what nature they take. Nonetheless, an encounter involves two people, each with their own motivations and expectations. The following description of the anthropological encounter applies to other kinds of travel: 'Quite apart from what research project one designs in advance, the reality is very much more that what one does in the field is determined by what other people allow one to be. In other words, the anthropological self is significantly shaped by the interests, attitudes and understandings of the other.'[53] What travellers are allowed to be, and what encounters they are allowed to have, are likewise shaped by travellees.

***

The encounters in this chapter expose the tensions between ideals and the practical experience of travel. Authenticity is one ideal, a nebulous concept that travellers and tourists aspire to achieve, but whose very vagueness makes it impossible for anyone to be confident that they identify it correctly. The apparently authentic experience of receiving hospitality at the private home of a travellee is threatened by the distractions of physical and mental exhaustion that are elemental to travel and hindered by the misunderstandings and tensions that arise from dissimilar host and guest expectations. Ultimately, authenticity is often abandoned for the comfort and reassurance of the inauthentic tourist bubble. Freedom is another ideal of travellers, who imagine their journeys as an escape, an adventure, a flight into the unknown: images that embody liberty. Freedom is a precious value, but it is not a reality shared by all, it is not even a universal right. European travellers, who take their right to mobility for granted, are often surprised and even angry to find that assumed right restricted and obstructed by their travellee hosts. If travellers are not as free as their imaginations it is because they are always someone else's guests and their freedom sometimes conflicts with the rights and the freedoms of their hosts. Encounter is the third ideal addressed in this chapter: they are the wealth of many journeys, the aim of many travellers, the material of many travel narratives. Encounters are not as collectable as beer labels, however, they are often troublesome events, confronting travellers with their own limitations – their inflexibilities, prejudices, failings – as well as the limitations of their journeys – their brevity, lack of reciprocity, transience. The journey is always a compromise, between ideals and practicalities, but the process of compromising requires interaction with travellees and it is this process and these interactions that give travellers a story to narrate.

Chapter 5

STARING

Viaggiare non serve molto a capire [...] ma serve a riattivare per un momento l'uso degli occhi, la lettura visiva del mondo.[1]
  (Travel doesn't help [us] much to understand [...], but it helps to stimulate the use of [our] eyes for a time, [our] visual reading of the world)

Sightseeing and its accompanying activity photography have long been central to tourism. European elites of the early sixteenth century used to travel for conversation, to encounter and speak with learned men. But the eye soon gained precedence, initially as a tool for acquiring knowledge through fledgling scientific observation and later gazing at art and beauty, in pursuit of the picturesque.[2] Despite Italo Calvino's assertion in the quotation above, the visual remains crucial to the way travellers and tourists both experience *and* understand the places they visit.[3] John Urry uses Michel Foucault's analysis of the medical gaze to describe the 'tourist gaze': a number of socially constructed gazes, practiced by different social groups in different settings and historical periods.[4] Urry and Carol Crawshaw have also highlighted how tourist expectations, experiences and memories are predetermined and structured by the visual.[5]

Travel writers are addicted to the visual as much as tourists and the cult of the eye described by Adler and Urry structures both their approach to travel and the resulting texts.[6] Like tourists, they seek famous sights and are obliged to navigate images that have become clichés through overdescription and over-representation in ubiquitous photographs. In terms of encounters, travel writers constantly observe and describe travellees' appearance: their physique, gestures, actions and clothes. Problematically, such observation alone sometimes forms the basis of cultural and social analysis.[7]

Tourism and photography have a long association, both originating in the first half of the nineteenth century and developing in parallel.[8] Today their union is so fixed in the cultural imagination that the camera has become the archetypal symbol of the tourist. Photographs are the ultimate proof of travel experiences and taking a photograph has become the tourist's natural response to events.[9] The camera shapes preconceptions: the photographic images viewed before the journey teach the tourist what to expect, and it also shapes travel practices: tourist itineraries are planned around photo opportunities.[10] The camera is the source of some of the most enduring and common criticisms of tourism: that tourists are more interested in taking photographs than in the things and people photographed. This would suggest that photography is detrimental to travel encounters and that the camera erects a barrier between traveller and travellee; but this is not always the case, as we shall see in the second part of this chapter.

The emphasis on the visual in travel and travel writing leaves the other senses somewhat neglected, yet interpersonal encounter engages more than vision alone.[11] Hearing is vital to communication – to listen to and understand the words of guides and interpreters, for example. Taste serves the traveller who is invited by a host to share a meal. Smells are perhaps the least pleasant or expected sensory element of encounter, but travellers sometimes find their sweaty unwashed bodies offending the noses of travellees. Touch is reserved for more intimate encounters, some of which will be addressed in the following chapters. Nevertheless, I reserve this chapter for vision and I justify the choice by turning the tables on the traveller. We usually think of the traveller as the observer, as the eye that gazes, but travellers are also observed or stared at by travellees and the first part of this chapter focuses on this reverse dynamic. The focus is not so much the travellee's actual perception of the traveller, since traveller's writings are my primary material, but rather the represented experience of being the object of another's look, or stare. I examine how the travellee's stare affects the traveller's self-perception, but also how travellers resist the imposed stare. In the second part of the chapter I turn to photography, considering how travellees respond to the camera, but also how the traveller can use it as a tool to facilitate encounters, rather than a means of appropriation, as it is often described.

The Stare of the Travellee

The gaze, the stare and the travel encounter

> Si un Européen est interrogé à son retour des Indes, il n'hésite pas, il répond: 'J'ai vu Madras, j'ai vu ceci, j'ai vu cela.' Mais non, il a été vu, beaucoup plus qu'il n'a vu.[12]
>
> (If a European is questioned on his return from the Indies, he doesn't hesitate, he replies: 'I saw Madras, I saw this, I saw that.' But really he was seen, far more than he saw.)

Travellers are accustomed to being spectators, absorbing the sight of travellees in their landscapes and cityscapes with an all-encompassing gaze. Analysis of the visual in travel writing tends to focus on the traveller as observer, but, as Michaux points out, travellers are seen by others as much as they see others. They are not television viewers, protected from the world by a screen, but play an active role in the spectacle and become objects of vision themselves. It is often forgotten that travellers, who place so much importance on seeing, on viewing, on photographing, on consuming visually, are visually consumed in turn.

So-Min Cheong and Marc Miller question the tendency to always identify power with the tourist, arguing that power is multidirectional and is also exercised over tourists by their hosts.[13] Using Foucault's language of agents and targets, they criticize Urry's emphasis on the tourist as agent, suggesting that tourists are targets of the host's power, operated specifically through their gaze. Cheong and Miller describe separate groups of what I would call travellees: brokers, including travel agents and guides, and locals, who may not have any direct commercial contact with tourists. We have already seen how guides and hosts exercise power over travellers, but the same is true for other travellees, even in the absence of verbal or prolonged contact. 'A major reason tourists are the primary objects of the gaze of brokers and locals has to do with their very visibility, hence targetability. They are not only conspicuous in organized tours and through processes of registration and documentation, they are also physically distinguishable from locals. Their style of dress, language, accent, and possessions contrasts with those of the residents of the destination.'[14] Cheong and Miller propose rethinking power in tourism to acknowledge hosts' power over tourists. Darya Maoz extends this idea to examine the 'mutual gaze', where tourist and local gazes meet.[15] She emphasizes that 'the gaze is not necessarily ocular and is not concerned only with spectacle [...], but relies on mental perceptions'.[16]

Cheong and Miller and Maoz use the vocabulary of the gaze, inherited from Foucault to describe a socially constructed, disciplining, normalizing look. In *Staring: How We Look*, Rosemarie Garland-Thomson introduces the stare: 'The stare is distinct from the gaze, which has been extensively defined as an oppressive act of disciplinary looking that subordinates its victim.'[17] The stare is useful because it covers a broader range of looks than the gaze: Garland-Thomson identifies the elemental qualities of staring as being physical response, cultural history, social relationship, and knowledge gathering.[18] This is an intriguing combination: although the stare, like the gaze, is socially and culturally constructed, it also incorporates the instinctual biological response to something attention grabbing, as well as emphasizing the stare as an encounter. Staring is a natural reaction to things that interest us, particularly to novelty; it is an attempt to integrate the new into the known in order to minimize uncertainty.[19] This makes the stare particularly relevant to travel and Garland-Thomson even suggests that 'the middle-class value of traveling, seeking a diverse environment, [...] can be seen as forms of deliberate, and therefore controlled, stimulation through novelty'.[20] Travellers travel to stare, but as Michaux reminds us, they also become objects of the travellee's stare. While the deliberate stare of the traveller is also the tourist gaze, the look of the travellee is perhaps closer to Garland-Thomson's stare, since it is usually a natural or instinctual response to the unexpected sight of the traveller. While the gaze has the advantage of emphasizing the operation of power through a look, this is also incorporated by Garland-Thomson in her analysis of 'staring as dominance'.[21] The gaze is implicitly a one-way action, necessitating such problematic terms as the 'reverse gaze', which only reinforces the notion that gazes are normally unidirectional, while staring is an interaction between starer and staree.

> An encounter between a starer and a staree sets in motion an interpersonal relationship, however momentary, that has consequences. This intense visual engagement creates a circuit of communication and meaning-making. Staring bespeaks involvement, and being stared at demands a response. A staring encounter is a dynamic struggle – starers inquire, starees lock eyes or flee, and starers advance or retreat; one moves forward and the other moves back. A staring interchange can tickle or alienate, persist or evolve.[22]

Although I focus on the stare of the travellee, I examine the point of view of the traveller, emphasizing interaction from the start. I choose to use Garland-Thomson's vocabulary of staring in this chapter, but this is not to suggest that the gaze is irrelevant. Looks are enormously varied, a fact reflected by the breadth of the English vocabulary of the visual, and neither staring nor gazing is entirely adequate to describe every kind of look that passes between traveller and travellee, while the two also overlap considerably.[23] In the following sections I examine firstly how the travellee's stare operates as a channel for controlling and managing travellers and secondly how the latter respond to such scrutiny, how travellers withstand the stare.

The travellee as starer

Travellees who stare at travellers are represented demonstrating the same emotional responses that travellers are accustomed to operate themselves. When far from the beaten track, where travellers are an uncommon sight, their mere appearance can become the object of eager curiosity, as Nicolas Bouvier reports in Tabriz: 'Il y avait peu d'étrangers dans la ville. C'est étonnant un étranger. À travers le jardin, par-dessus le mur des courettes, du haut des toits en terrasse, nos voisins arméniens nous observaient. Gentiment' (*Usage*, 184; There were few foreigners in the town. A foreigner is an amazing thing. Across the garden, over the courtyard wall, from high on the terraced rooftops, our Armenian neighbours watched us. Kindly). Travellers may seek diversity and exoticism in other places and other people, but they are also different and exotic in the eyes of those others. In Siberia, Tiziano Terzani and his companions attract the attention of local children, some of whom attempt a little English, while others 'vogliono semplicemente guardare le nostre facce, le nostre scarpe, le cinture, le camicie. Siamo la cosa più esotica che si siano mai trovata davanti' (*Buonanotte*, 32; simply want to stare at our faces, our shoes, belts, shirts. We are the most exotic thing that they have ever encountered). Travellers are amused and bemused by the people they see, but they also find themselves to be sources of entertainment for travellees. Christine Jordis describes how villagers in Bali sometimes laugh at her and her companion and wonders if this is a reaction to the comic sight of white faces with their 'nez pointus' (pointy noses).[24] Male travellers are usually cast as the voyeurs, but travellees are not averse to a little voyeurism of their own. At Nicole-Lise Bernheim's hotel in Delhi she catches both the hotel owner and the maid's teenage son spying on her and her companion (*Chambres*, 190 and 194).[25] All of these stares unsettle the traveller: seeing themselves reflected in the eyes of travellees makes them conscious of their own novelty. Travellees draw attention to travellers' behaviour and identity, to their appearance and their presence, in ways that they may find surprising or disconcerting. Accustomed to examining others' strangeness, travellers suddenly find their own is writ large in the travellees' stare.

The sight of the traveller elicits a range of responses from travellees, but it also arouses interest for different reasons. As outsiders, travellers are conspicuous because their appearance or behaviour is unusual. Even the fact of travelling, the means and the manner, can attract unexpected interest, as Bernard Ollivier discovers: 'Il ne doit pas y avoir beaucoup de marcheurs en Turquie, [...]: je suis regardé comme une véritable curiosité, une rareté, un phénomène national' (*Marche I*, 99; There can't be many walkers in Turkey, [...]: I am viewed as a real curiosity, a rarity, a national phenomenon). Travellers on decelerated journeys are particularly visible, but travel writers also come under scrutiny for the other half of their profession: writing, as Gianni Celati finds when taking notes on a train in Senegal: 'La mia compagna nella cuccetta di fronte mi osserva scrivere molto intenta, a occhi fissi, delle volte anche per cinque minuti' (113; My neighbour in the opposite bunk watches me write very intently, with a fixed stare, sometimes for as much as five minutes). Celati's emphasis on the duration of the stare suggests that it disconcerts him. He expresses his surprise at being an object of interest for an apparently commonplace activity. Such constant scrutiny can be a wearisome burden, as Ollivier experiences in villages in China, where his ignorance of the language impedes more fulfilling communication: 'Je continue de remonter la grand-rue, imperturbable, vrillé par mille paires d'yeux épatés. Au vrai j'éprouve un certain malaise malgré l'habitude que j'ai prise, ici, d'être observé avec tant d'insistance et de curiosité' (*Marche III*, 264; I continue to climb the main street, imperturbable, pierced by a thousand pairs of startled eyes. In truth I suffer some uneasiness, despite being accustomed to being observed here with such insistence and curiosity). During his journey from Algiers to Cape Town, Sergio Ramazzotti discovers that rumours are circulating along his route about a white man with a red bag travelling by public transport and he is shocked to realize that everywhere he goes he is watched, or 'spied on' ('spiato') as he puts it (*Vado*, 116–17). The travellers clearly do not expect to be the object of such persistent attention: they travel to see, and find themselves seen.

The traveller's behaviour and appearance are not the only things that activate the travellee's stare, but also their identity, their very existence. In many parts of the world, white travellers are in a racial minority and are consequently conspicuous. Francesco Piccolo opens *Allegro occidentale* with a long account of a scene in Hong Kong where a travellee's stare leads his alter ego Mister Piccolo to a revelation about identity. Mister Piccolo shares a lift with a Chinese man who 'mi guarda con un'espressione stupita, quasi sgrana gli occhi, come se non avesse mai visto un essere umano europeo, o per qualche altro motivo che non capisco' (9; looks at me with an expression of astonishment, almost opening his eyes wide, as though he has never seen a European human being before, or for some other reason that I don't understand). Piccolo is troubled by the attention but is even more disturbed when it turns out that he is being mistaken for Nicolas Cage. The scene is played out comically: the more Mister Piccolo insists that he is not the actor, the more his interlocutor is convinced that he is. Finally, he realizes 'che non è vero soltanto che per gli occidentali i cinesi sono tutti uguali, ma è vero anche il contrario. Anche per i cinesi gli occidentali sono tutti uguali' (12; that it is not only true that for Westerners the Chinese all look the same, but that the reverse is also true. For the Chinese too, Westerners all look the same). Mister Piccolo is shocked to find that a racist stereotype applied by white people to other races is applicable in reverse. The stare of the Chinese travellee both emphasizes his racial identity and robs him of his individual identity: he is just another white man and may as well be some actor whom he does not remotely resemble. The traveller's race, a simple fact taken for granted at home, suddenly becomes a defining feature of his/her identity. Likewise, in his introduction to *Afrozapping*, Ramazzotti states, 'Se c'è una cosa che devo all'Africa, è la consapevolezza di essere bianco' (11; If there is one thing that I owe to Africa, it's the knowledge that I am white). This comment follows an anecdote about a bus driver who silences the traveller's complaining with the cutting remark: '"Il problema di voi bianchi è che siete troppo bianchi per adattarvi a come vanno le cose dalle nostre parti"' (11; 'The problem with you white people is that you're too white to adapt to how things work in our part of the world'). Further on Ramazzotti lists the names that African travellees use to address him: '"*Masara!*", "*Yovo!*", "*M'zungu!*" […] "*Homme blanc!*", "*White man!*"' (202). These labels, he explains, all share the same meaning and greet him continuously in any African city. Individual Africans, rather than the continent itself, have made the traveller conscious of his racial identity: with their stare they single him out as an outsider and vocally label him with his race. He sees his whiteness reflected in their eyes and hears himself named as a white man from their lips.

Arriving in Mali, Celati experiences a similar moment of realization: 'più di tutto ci prende alla sprovvista il fatto d'essere bianchi' (11; more than anything else, the fact of being white takes us by surprise). He goes on to explain the implications of this newly highlighted identity: 'Perché siamo qui a rappresentare non quello che siamo o crediamo d'essere, ma quello che dovremmo essere in quanto bianchi (ricchi, potenti, moderni, compratori di tutto)' [11; Because we are here to represent not what we are, or think we are, but what we should be as white people (rich, powerful, modern, buying everything)]. The travellee's stare does not simply fix on aspects of the traveller's physical appearance, but also imposes identities on the traveller. Travellers may not usually think of themselves as white, but the travellee's stare forces them to assume both this knowledge and the burden of expectations that go with it, such as the stereotypes about wealth mentioned by Celati.[26] Travellers are obliged to negotiate with the identities imposed on them by travellees, even when these are mistaken, as Paolo Rumiz finds on a train in Ukraine. 'A Vasilkiv il treno si è riempito di pendolari. Gente dura, taciturna. Dopo un po' realizzo che mi guardano, tutto lo scompartimento mi guarda. Anche la donna che ho accanto' (*Oriente*, 55; At Vasylkiv the train filled up with commuters. Tough, taciturn people. After a while I realize that they are staring at me, the whole compartment is staring at me, even the woman next to me). Rumiz is wearing a small hat and realizes that the passengers think he is Jewish, which is confirmed by his neighbour, who ushers him out of the compartment and gently removes the hat, then takes him to another part of the train. Rumiz, like Ollivier in China, is unable to diffuse the attention with verbal explanations.

The crowd eyeballing Ollivier are most likely curious, but Rumiz implies that his onlookers have something more serious in mind. As well as highlighting travellers' unusual behaviour and imposing constructed identities on them, the travellee's stare can also control or direct. 'The power of the local gaze on tourists […] can lead tourists to quickly understand where they might go and what they might do.'[27] This is aptly demonstrated in this episode, where the travellee commuters make Rumiz unwelcome by staring at him. The commuters neither utter a word nor make any gestures, but through the simple act of persistent staring they destabilize Rumiz's sense of security and force him to leave their space. His neighbour, perhaps a local herself, quickly interprets these stares and comes to his rescue. Such use of the stare recalls the host's control over the traveller's movement; Cheong and Miller connect hospitality and the gaze: 'The local gaze has drawn tourists into homes and into the private spaces of locals, while it has also prohibited the same.'[28] In both of the episodes from Bouvier and Liberti that we encountered in Chapter 4, the hosts who reject the travellers do so through their stare. In the village in Turkey, Bouvier and Thierry are cold-shouldered and ignored, chased away by the travellees' refusal to engage in eye contact with them (*Usage*, 154–5). Liberti, on the other hand, becomes the object of a disconcerting collective stare in the hotel in Tangiers. When he climbs to the roof of the hotel he can hear shouting and laughing: 'Ma quando entrai, calò il silenzio. Decine di sguardi si posarono su di me. Chi ero? Un poliziotto? Una spia? Nessuno osò chiedermi nulla. Ma quel tacere improvviso era più eloquente di qualsiasi parola.' (156; But when I arrived, silence fell. Dozens of looks settled on me. Who was I? A policeman? A spy? No one dared ask me anything, but that sudden silence was more eloquent than any words). Again, in both of these examples, no words are spoken, but the 'eloquent silence' of the travellees' stare controls the travellers' movements and forbids them access. Travellees can erect barriers between themselves and travellers, or they can use the stare to initiate encounters and create connections.

The travellee's stare is received but also interpreted by the traveller and this interpretation is presented to us as readers. When the stare is not accompanied by any other gesture or verbal message travellers may understand it in different ways, even misinterpreting travellees' intentions. When Liberti meets the eyes of the hotel guests he specifies that they say nothing, yet he imagines the questions they are thinking. Alex Gillespie examines this problem in his study of tourists photographing Ladakhis, arguing that the effect of the Ladakhis' gaze is determined not so much by the intention of the gazer, but rather by the meaning understood by the tourist.[29] He finds that tourists often misinterpret the Ladakhis' gazes, reading into them their own anxieties about tourist photography. Gillespie's analysis suggests that the Ladakhis do not exercise power themselves; they are only a 'vehicle' for the power of the gaze.[30]

The problem with this reading, as Gillespie himself acknowledges, is that it robs the travellee of agency, verging on solipsism. Misinterpretation, particularly because of cultural differences, is a hazard incurred by both traveller and travellee, but it does not divest starers of their agency. The thoughts that Liberti writes into his travellees' minds might be incorrect, but he probably correctly perceives that he is the object of a powerful stare. Once more, as with guiding and hosting, staring is another way that travellees control and limit the traveller's freedom, and this agency is manifest in the travel text despite its one-sided perspective.

The traveller as staree

Ollivier, who attracts so much interest from travellees, is encouraged to reflect on his chosen journey:

> Est-ce donc si incongru, si extravagant et inconcevable qu'un homme aujourd'hui puisse avoir la simple envie de parcourir le monde à pied? J'ai l'impression de faire là quelque chose somme toute d'assez banal, mais l'on me renvoie si régulièrement de mon aventure l'image d'une entreprise insensée que je vais finir par en douter… (*Marche II*, 33)
>
> (Is it really so incongruous, so extravagant and inconceivable that a man today could have the simple desire to travel the world on foot? I have the impression that I am doing something really quite banal here, but others so frequently reflect back at me the image of my adventure as an insane undertaking that I am going to end up having my doubts…)

Some travellers buckle under pressure from the stare and desist from whatever activity is attracting attention, as in the cases of Liberti in the hotel, Bouvier in the village and Rumiz on the train. Others tackle the travellee's stare in different ways: resisting it, deflecting it, bouncing it back.

Alexandre Kauffmann demonstrates how travel writers deflect the travellee's stare, redirecting it onto other travellers.[31] He describes young Thais gathering to people-watch in Bangkok's tourist district: 'Ils s'installent sur les terrasses comme au théâtre. Ils observent la faune de ce quartier où les Thaïlandais ne sont qu'une minorité' (They settle on the terraces as though at the theatre. They observe the fauna of this neighbourhood where Thais are only a minority).[32] Here Kauffmann dissociates himself from the 'faune', the tourists who are the objects of the stare, suggesting that he evades the looks of the Thai travellees, and creates a third position for himself, observing both starers and starees. Similar moves are used by travellers keen to dissociate themselves from tourists: the traveller-narrator assumes the vantage point of invisible observer. This is a difficult position to maintain, however, when the traveller is pinned down by the travellee's stare.

Travellers also bounce the stare back, using it as a source of information about the travellee. Bernheim, for example, learns a lesson about Sri Lankan culture through the way her own behaviour is regarded by the staff in the house where she is staying: 'Lampe de poche à la main, les trois serviteurs viendront m'observer, allongée près du chien. Je fais spectacle' (*Couleur*, 37; Torch in hand, the three attendants come to watch me, lying beside the dog. I am on show). The owner of the house explains that '"pour eux, un chien est la mauvaise réincarnation d'un être humain"' (37; 'for them, a dog is the bad reincarnation of a human being'). Although the travellees' curiosity focuses on Bernheim, it is their own beliefs that are unusual enough to require explanation in her text. To the reader, the traveller is the norm, while the travellee's stare is unusual or exotic. Stares are bounced back in this way in many of the examples already cited: Rumiz uses his experience on the train to discuss anti-Semitism in Ukraine and Piccolo narrates the episode in Hong Kong to illustrate Chinese perceptions of Europeans.

When travellees wish to proceed from visual to verbal communication with travellers, they address them with a variety of names and labels, often referring to their race or nationality, as Ramazzotti describes in Africa. Travel writers report and repeat words such as *gaijin* in Japan, *farendj* in Eastern Africa and *farang* in Thailand, using them in their texts for different effects.[33] Sometimes they simply refer to other tourists, but travel writers also apply them to their autobiographical characters, acknowledging that they are perceived as different by others. When Bernheim reflects on the nature of her journey around Asia, she uses travellee labels to define her own identity as a traveller: 'En pays tamoul, on appelle "pandas" ceux qui voyagent longtemps avec peu d'argent. Panda je suis. Le terme "dharma bum" inventé par Kerouac et souvent utilisé à Kathmandou, désigne les Occidentaux saisis par le bouddhisme. Dharma bum je ne suis pas' (*Chambres*, 78; In Tamil country they call those who travel for a long time with little money 'Pandas'. I am a Panda. The term 'Dharma Bum', invented by Kerouac and often used in Kathmandu, refers to the Westerners gripped by Buddhism. I am not a Dharma Bum). Such labels also emphasize the divisions between travellers and travellees. On a train in Ethiopia Jean-Claude Guillebaud writes, 'Trois jeunes filles oromos, dont les châles flamboient sous l'effet de la vitesse, rivalisent de chatteries, sourires appuyés, plaisanteries incompréhensibles aux *farendj*' (*Porte*, 674; Three young Oromo girls, whose shawls flicker with the speed, rival each other in playfulness, emphatic smiles, jokes that are incomprehensible to the *farendj*). '*Farendj*' underlines the distance already implied by 'incompréhensibles' and highlights the divide between the French travellers and the Ethiopian girls.

Reappropriation implies a degree of defiance; assuming the other's term for oneself is a form of control, a way of exercising power over how one is designated by others. Labelling the traveller with the travellee's terms can also, paradoxically, be a way of refusing an imposed identity. Travel writers distance themselves from such terms by setting them apart in italics or inverted commas, or by using them ironically. In Iran Ollivier is hosted by the owners of a restaurant, who initially let him sleep in a prayer room, but then make him swap rooms with their waiter. Ollivier concludes that 'un *katolik* dans ce lieu dédié au culte musulman, sans doute que cela faisait désordre' (*Marche II*, 44–5; no doubt it didn't look good to have a *katolik* in this place devoted to Islam). Ollivier refers to himself as *katolik* when travellees perceive him as other because he is not Muslim, but the use of the non-French spelling and italics suggests that he does not necessarily identify himself as a Catholic. Ollivier makes ample use of such terms, both reappropriating in order to reassert control over his own self-image and using sarcasm to distance himself from the labels. The reappropriation of these words in travel texts reflects ambivalence on the part of travellers about finding themselves reflected in the travellee's stare.

Marc Boulet offers an unusual example of a traveller who circumvents the stare of the travellee, by disguising himself as one.[34] He lives for several months imitating an untouchable beggar on the streets of Benares, India, both as an experiment in travel and in the hope of gaining an inside view of such a life.[35] He is apparently successful in disguising his identity as a French traveller: learning Hindi, dressing appropriately and even dying his skin to fit the part. He describes his new invisibility: 'Les autres Indiens vont et viennent autour de moi, personne ne me regarde. […] Ce soir, pour la première fois en Inde, je suis anonyme. Je me fonds dans le décor' (85; The other Indians come and go around me, no one looks at me. […] This evening, for the first time in India, I am anonymous. I melt into the background). With his disguise he removes himself from the stare of the travellee and is free to operate his own stare, on all who pass before him: Indians and foreign tourists alike. He maintains an ambiguous position between the two, sometimes identifying with one group, sometimes with the other, but never entirely at home with either. At the same time, he lives in constant fear that his disguise will be found out, that his constructed invisibility will melt away and he will enter all too clearly into the local stare for the imposter that he is. Although Boulet no longer stands out as a European tourist, his assumed position in the Indian caste system essentially disrupts or minimizes his contact with travellees. He finds occasional companions, but fails to develop any sustained relationships while he is living as a beggar and is often miserable and lonely: 'Je n'ai lié aucune amitié. Je m'enlise dans la solitude et j'ai eu plusieurs fois envie de pleurer' (132; I have formed no friendships.

I am mired in loneliness and several times I have wanted to cry). Ironically, Boulet's most sustained interactions with travellees occur while he is living in Benares as a French traveller, preparing to assume his disguise.

Boulet's unusual experience demonstrates the central role of eye contact in any interaction: no matter how unwanted, hostile, mistaken or offensive the travellee's stare might be, it is also a precondition of encounter: the traveller must enter the travellee's field of vision for interaction to take place. The stare of the travellee is an acknowledgement: the traveller-staree is the focus of attention, not lost and overlooked, like Boulet in his disguise. Garland-Thomson describes staring as a natural response to curiosity, and when the travellee's curiosity about the traveller mirrors the traveller's curiosity about the travellee, an encounter occurs. 'Between strangers, staring is uncomfortable, especially the intense, prohibited, baroque staring that does not disguise itself. That discomfort can be positive, however, rather than oppressive. A stare is a response to someone's distinctiveness, and a staring exchange can thus beget mutual recognition, however fleeting.'[36] Like the discomfort of hospitality, the discomfort of staring is a necessary ingredient in travel encounters. The mutual recognition Garland-Thomson mentions is often lacking in travel writing, but there are moments when the staring traveller catches themselves being stared at by the travellee. Bernheim is particularly conscious of mutual looks, describing moments when she and travellees watch each other in all three of her travel books. In the public baths in Japan, for example: 'Des villageoises de Ryushi ou quelques touristes japonaises m'accompagnent parfois, évaluant d'un œil discret mes seins, mes cuisses. Je fais de même. Égalité de la nudité, nous sommes semblables devant la vie, la mort' (*Chambres*, 71–2; Village women from Ryushi or a few Japanese tourists accompany me sometimes, discreetly evaluating my breasts, my thighs. I do the same. Equality in nudity, we are similar in the face of life and death). Bernheim emphasizes the common ground between traveller and travellee as equally starer and staree, subject and object. To travel is also to submit oneself to such discomforts as the travellee's stare. To accept the stare, to acknowledge the travellee's right to stare is to open oneself to the possibilities of encounter.

Photography and Encounter

Tourists and cameras

Tourist photography is often the focus of criticism and its impact on those targeted by the lens makes it particularly dubious in the eyes of its critics. Susan Sontag describes photography as an appropriation, or even an aggression, and the camera as predatory: 'To photograph people is to violate them, by seeing them as they never see themselves, by having knowledge of them they can never have; it turns people into objects that can be symbolically possessed.'[37] Her criticisms are picked up and elaborated in the context of travel by both Marco Aime and Franck Michel. Aime also laments the reification of the individuals photographed by tourists: 'l'individuo inquadrato diventa un'immagine di sé: perde la sua personalità per acquistare quella che il fotografo intende assegnargli: mistica, esotica, pittoresca, selvaggia, ma soprattutto statica' (the individual in the frame becomes an image of him/herself: losing his/her personality to acquire that which the photograph assigns him/her: mystical, exotic, picturesque, wild, but above all inert).[38] Aime's description of the photograph imposing a constructed identity on the photographee recalls the stare, reminding us that the photograph is an extension or a permanent freezing of the stare. Michel evokes the theme of encounters, suggesting that they are undermined by the tourist's obsession with collecting photographs: 'Nul doute qu'une telle relation de voyage dépersonnalise froidement les rencontres humaines, elle fige le temps en le fixant et ne voit plus, ne sent plus, ne réagit plus à la vie autour' (There is no doubt that such a travel encounter coldly depersonalizes human relations, it freezes time by fixing it and no longer sees, no longer feels, no longer reacts to life around).[39] He wonders what tourists would think of themselves if they could see themselves from the other's perspective since, as we know, 'l'observateur est toujours un observé' (the observer is always observed).[40] Sontag, Michel and Aime all agree that, especially in the context of travel, the camera distances traveller and travellee by dehumanizing the latter and preventing human interaction.[41] At worst the camera becomes the means by which the traveller violates the travellee.

In travel writing, criticism of tourist photography is a common expression of antitourism. Jordis, for example, complains that tourists unthinkingly photograph everything:

> Le touriste n'a pas le temps d'écouter, à peine de voir: il photographie. Il ne fait pas travailler son cerveau: il manie son appareil, on lui a fait croire que c'était plus sûr. La mécanique a remplacé l'organe visuel, une photo au lieu d'un souvenir, la solidité du papier contre l'image évanescente. (92)
>
> (The tourist has no time to listen, and hardly even to look: he takes photographs. He does not make his brain work: he uses his camera, he has been made to believe that it is more reliable. Mechanics have replaced the visual organ, a photo in place of a memory, the solidity of paper versus the fleeting image.)

Clearly Jordis does not identify herself with 'le touriste', although she does mention that her husband takes photographs (79 and 98). She associates the tourist's dependence on the camera with insecurities about control: the camera promises a lasting physical appropriation that is impossible in the mind alone. Terzani explains that some people in Asia try to avoid being photographed, believing that the image robs them of something precious: 'E non ha[nno] forse ragione? Non è anche nell'usura di decine di migliaia di foto, scattate da turisti distratti, che le nostre chiese hanno perso la loro sacralità, che i nostri monumenti hanno perso la loro patina di grandezza?' (*Indovino*, 31; And [aren't they] perhaps right? Isn't it also through the wear and tear of tens of thousands of photographs, taken by distracted tourists, that our churches have lost their sanctity, that our monuments have lost their patina of greatness?). Despite their disapproval travellers do not necessarily refuse to participate in this image-seeking mania. Terzani's belief that the photograph degrades its subject does not prevent him from taking photographs himself. In fact travel writers often refer to the photographic practices of their autobiographical protagonists or their travelling companions. The fact of continuing to practice photography while criticizing it demonstrates a degree of self-consciousness about using a camera, suggesting that it need not be rejected altogether, but that there is an ethics of travel photography.

The following sections will explore the dual nature of the traveller's camera: as something both intrusive, a source of antagonism between traveller and travellee, and interactive, providing a tool to create and sustain encounters. Some travel texts contain accompanying photographs, taken either by the traveller-writer, some of whom double up as professional photographers, or by a photographer companion. I maintain my focus here, however, on the textual description of photography and the camera, rather than analysing any images that accompany the texts. My interest is in the encounter as narrated in the text rather than the image, which is in fact often absent from the text.

Photography as intrusion

Travellers are often guilty of the same indiscretions as tourists in their use of the camera. Ollivier, for example, receives an angry response in rural Turkey when he photographs a horse-drawn cart passing him on the road, to the irritation of one of its occupants:

> Furieuse, la femme qui n'a pas eu le temps de se voiler le visage crache lorsqu'ils arrivent à ma hauteur. Son image lui appartient et je l'ai volée, je tâcherai d'y penser par la suite. Mais ceux qui me sollicitent et ceux qui ressentent cela comme un vol – ou un viol –, comment les distinguer? Voilà ce qu'il me faut encore, entre autres, apprendre. (*Marche I*, 226)

(The woman, who has not had time to veil her face, is furious and spits when they draw level with me. Her image belongs to her and I have stolen it, I will try to remember this in the future. But how can I tell the difference between those who request [photographs] and those who experience it as a theft – or a rape? This is something I still need to learn, among other things).

Ollivier acknowledges that he is at fault, but he also suggests that his camera provokes diverse reactions, not all of them negative. In Paris Anaïk Frantz, travelling with François Maspero, is challenged when she photographs a group of Malians from afar (Maspero, 127–8).[42] They are affronted because she did not ask their permission and Frantz receives a thorough telling off, but she is also angry with herself and concerned that the journey is corrupting her practices: 'Jamais je n'ai pris des photos aussi vite [...]. Les Africains du foyer ont raison: il faut prendre le temps de respecter les autres. Je ne veux pas finir comme les touristes dingues de la photo, trop pressés pour regarder ce qu'ils prennent' (134; I have never taken photos so quickly [...]. The Africans at the hostel are right: it's important to take time to respect others. I don't want to end up like tourists, crazy about photos, too rushed to look at what they are photographing). Frantz evokes tourists to represent exactly the kind of photographic practices she rejects. Photographees express various reasons for not wanting to be photographed, such as religious taboos or political fears, but they are also wary of the photographer's intentions, since they have no control over the use of the photograph.[43] As with the stare, the travellee's response to photography is bounced back to reflect their attitudes. Nonetheless, while the travellers in both examples are shown photographing with the same disregard as tourists, they justify and excuse themselves: a lesson is learned, the error will not be repeated. These brief scenes – where the traveller errs, is admonished by the travellee and is then redeemed in the eyes of the reader by suitable humility or reflection – serve as moral lessons in the etiquette of travel photography. Photography is a direct act of appropriation, but the travellers are keen to demonstrate their awareness and to represent their efforts to use this power responsibly.

On these occasions Ollivier and Frantz admit their guilt and accept the other's right to object, but this is not always the case. Ramazzotti, for example, is less sympathetic when he is forbidden from taking unflattering photographs in Cameroon. He claims to be a tourist, not a journalist, but the officials who arrest him are suspicious, recalling previous experiences with backpackers:

'Ti raccontano sempre le stesse cose, voglio fare una foto ricordo, voglio solo una foto ricordo, poi chissà come mai nei giornali dei loro paesi vengono fuori queste foto e sotto alle foto si scrive: ecco le strade del Camerun, ecco come sono ridotti i mezzi di trasporto, ecco in che condizioni si viaggia in Camerun.' (*Vado*, 140)

('They always tell you the same things, I want to take a souvenir photo, I only want a souvenir photo, then who knows how in their country's newspapers these photos come out and underneath it's written: these are the streets of Cameroon, this is the state of the transport, these are the conditions in which people travel in Cameroon'.)

Ramazzotti parodies what he identifies as propaganda and overzealous censorship by Cameroonian citizens, while doing his best to sneak his photographs out of the country. He plays the role of the daring journalist whose photographs expose the truths behind the government's lies. Unlike the other travellers, who prioritize the relationship over the photograph, at least in retrospect, Ramazzotti upholds his representation over that of the travellees.

Travellers conscious of the intrusive nature of photography and keen to avoid offending the travellee-photographee tackle the problem in different ways. One solution brings us back to a theme already addressed in the chapters on guiding and hosting above: financial compensation. When there is little opportunity for lasting contact, as in busy tourist spots, a financial or material exchange can compensate for the objectifying act of photographing. The encounter is then defined by money, which resets the balance of power between photographer and photographee and creates a form of exchange: payment for a pose. Guillebaud and his companion, photographer Raymond Depardon, are confronted with indignation in a street in Djibouti: 'Les passants s'irritent de notre curiosité, des hommes et des femmes tendent le poing vers l'objectif du Leica. J'entends des phrases murmurées sur notre passage: "Regarde! Ils profitent de nous. En France, ils gagneront du fric avec ça"' (*Porte*, 663; The passers-by are annoyed by our curiosity, men and women shake their fists at the Leica's lens. I hear comments murmured as we pass: 'Look! They are taking advantage of us. In France they'll earn cash with that'). When he later pays a woman they have photographed he admits, 'Ce n'est pas glorieux, peut-être obscène, comment savoir?' (688; It's not honourable, maybe obscene, how can we know?). The sentiments surrounding such transactions seem to be invariably negative: money corrupts and cannot compensate for genuine contact. Photographees are in their rights to ask for payment, however, especially given that a professional photographer like Depardon does earn his living with his images. Duccio Canestrini exhorts tourists to take the time to establish relations with their photographic subjects, and to accept gracefully if asked to pay.[44]

Another solution adopted by the traveller conscious of the aggressive potential of the camera is simply not to photograph. This may be a generalized antitourist gesture, maintained throughout the journey, a common move among certain types of tourist, particularly backpackers.[45] It also reflects the belief that travellers write, while tourists take photographs.[46] The refusal to photograph may be a response to specific scenes, when the choice not to take a picture is an ethical one. This is demonstrated by Depardon, packing away his camera on the way to the mountain village in Vietnam in protest against their guide Nguyen T. D. (Guillebaud, *Colline*, 482). Bouvier and his companions refuse to photograph a funeral procession in China, although their guide suggests that it would be an honour for the mourners if they did. Bouvier justifies their reluctance with the taboo of death in the West, but also 'parce qu'en voyage il ne faut jamais se dire "je tiens là quelque chose" et vouloir à tout moment faire feu de tout bois' (*Journal*, 1037; because on a journey you must never say 'I've got something there' and want to exploit every means all the time). Like Jordis, Bouvier criticizes the desire to appropriate everything, again implying that the camera is often used – inappropriately – to this end. Once more the traveller's self-awareness about the use of the camera in the context of travel imparts a minor moral lesson, defining an ethics of travel photography.

An interesting twist on the issue is presented by the gap between image and text, in the sense that the photographs whose creation is described, or at least mentioned, in the text are not always reproduced for the reader. In *Vado verso il Capo*, for example, Ramazzotti discusses his photography, and especially the problems it causes, and he even describes certain photographs, but the reader has no access to them. The photographs themselves exist completely outside the text, so all we are left with is the textual representation of the action of taking photographs. When the image is absent, the textual representation of the photographic act, particularly the interaction between photographer and photographee, takes precedence. While the act of taking the photograph can still be considered an appropriation from the point of view of the photographer, the reader is not complicit, since the reader cannot appropriate the image. Anything it might represent or signify is meaningless; it literally does not exist.[47] This readjusts the balance, drawing significance away from the image and conferring it on the events and interactions surrounding the creation of the image, the encounter itself.

Photography as interaction

So far, I have repeated the general consensus that photography violates the travellee and that the camera is a barrier between traveller and travellee, but it need not always be thus. Photographs are accepted and even solicited by travellees as often as they are refused. The gypsies whose music Bouvier records in Yugoslavia are keen to be photographed: 'Il fallut bien sûr photographier tout ce monde. Les filles surtout. Chacune voulait être seule sur l'image. Elles se poussaient et se pinçaient. Une bagarre rapide s'ensuivit – ongles, malédictions, gifles, lèvres fendues – qui se termina dans une gaieté tournoyante et dans le sang' (*Usage*, 110; Of course we had to photograph everyone, especially the girls. Each one wanted to be alone in the picture. They pushed and pinched. A fight quickly followed – nails, curses, slaps, split lips – which ended in a whirl of gaiety and blood). Ramazzotti finds that taking a photograph earns him privileged treatment from the photographee: the driver of his lorry in Algeria requests a portrait and in return invites him to travel in the relative comfort of the cabin (*Vado*, 98–9). These examples suggest that photography is not necessarily an affront to the travellee; the subjects do not always perceive it as a violation or an appropriation. After all, as Sontag herself writes, 'To photograph is to confer importance.'[48] Anthropological studies reveal varying attitudes to tourist photography, depending on a range of criteria, such as the photographee's understanding of the functioning of a camera, their understanding of the tourists' motivations and intentions, cultural or religious attitudes to images, the density of tourism and consequent level of intrusion, regional pride, or the nature of the encounter with tourists.[49] Travellers may be unaware of prevailing expectations and, as Gillespie suggests, can only follow their instincts about appropriate behaviour, or, as Ramazzotti does in Cameroon, choose to ignore the other's objections. Nonetheless, the behaviour of the photographer, especially in terms of motivations or perceived motivations, is often decisive in generating particular responses.[50] Taking a photograph need not be a theft or a violation; it can also initiate positive interaction and even exchange. The camera can be reimagined in positive ways and used as a mediating tool to create or fortify connections between people and to facilitate encounters.

Bouvier describes how the family photo album is a social tool in Japan:

> En visite, je suis à peine installé qu'on m'en pose un sur les genoux pour conjurer les premières minutes d'embarras et dans l'espoir de me fournir un sujet de conversation sans épines: les biches de Nara, le volcan Aso, les temples de Nikko.[51]
>
> (On visits, I have hardly sat down when they place one on my knees to conjure away the first minutes of embarrassment and in the hope of supplying me with a safe topic of conversation: the does of Nara, the Aso volcano, the temples of Nikko.)

The album not only eases interaction between hosts and guest, but also provides the traveller with another perspective on the country, via the content of the album, the discussions around them and the social interactions that Bouvier describes. His neighbours in Tokyo have their own cameras, but they ask him to take photographs for them because his equipment is of a superior quality, in exchange for which they give him small gifts. Photography therefore becomes a channel for contact and exchange and, as Bouvier acknowledges, it begins to open doors for him (*Chronique*, 586).[52] It is often said that tourists do not experience their journeys when they are travelling, but rather later, when they return home, when the photographic souvenirs of the journey are viewed and shared with friends. Tim Edensor describes photography, along with other memory-collecting activities, as future-orientated tourist work.[53] Jordis parodies Japanese tourists taking photographs of paintings in the complete darkness of a church: 'les peintures, si elles existaient, ils les verraient chez eux, entre amis, calés dans leurs fauteuils' (94; they will see the paintings, if they exist, back home, among friends, settled comfortably in their sofas).[54] Photographs as objects therefore become the focal point of an interaction, not with the travellee subjects of the photographs, but with an already established social network back home. Bouvier's example demonstrates that by sharing photographs, traveller and travellee include each other in their social networks. Similarly Ollivier describes a couple of cyclists who use their digital camera to share their photographs with their photographees (*Marche III*, 61). Digital cameras, like Polaroids before them, make an immediate exchange more feasible.[55] In this way, traveller and travellee share the socially important moment of viewing.

Both Ollivier and Frantz make systematic use of their cameras as a means to encounter. Ollivier uses photography to repay his many hosts, and he describes the role his camera acquires during his journey:

> Aussitôt qu'ils aperçoivent mon appareil, les paysans veulent que je photographie leur grange ou eux-mêmes. Dans ces villages, un appareil photo est une rareté et être pris en photo un événement unique. C'est pourquoi d'ailleurs je me suis promis d'envoyer leur portrait aux personnes qui m'ont reçu. C'est le seul moyen que j'ai trouvé pour les remercier de leur accueil, puisqu'elles n'acceptent pas d'argent et que le poids de mon sac m'interdit de transporter des présents. (*Marche I*, 63–4)
>
> (As soon as they catch sight of my camera, the farmers want me to photograph their barn or themselves. In these villages a camera is a rarity and being photographed is a unique event. Besides, this is why I have promised myself that I will send the people who host me their portraits. It is the only way I have found to thank them for their welcome, since they won't accept any money and the weight of my bag prevents me from carrying presents.)

Ollivier emphasizes the positive reactions of his photographic subjects: 'Il faut voir d'ailleurs avec quel plaisir ils posent et veillent à ce que je note bien leur adresse' (*Marche II*, 122; Besides, you should see their pleasure in posing and how they watch to see that I note their addresses correctly). Throughout his journeys he makes a point of offering to take photographs and carefully noting addresses, telling us that on his return to Paris after his first trip he posted out 120 letters with 200 photographs to those he had met (122). Significantly, Ollivier does not publish the pictures; they remain a private memento of his encounters and a private item of exchange between himself and the travellee. He reports that he received a stream of letters from readers demanding images of the people he met (*Carnets*, 12). He chose to fulfil these requests by repeating his journey in the company of illustrator François Dermaut, who drew and painted portraits of their travellees, old and new, as well as watercolours of landscapes and buildings, published as *Carnets d'une longue marche*. Dermaut's careful portraits are the antithesis of casually snapped photographs. Furthermore, they are all named, linking the travellees depicted to their stories in the text and including the reader in the encounter. Ollivier's camera is a tool that serves his encounters and his photographs are items of exchange that create reciprocity between traveller and travellee.

Ollivier is an amateur photographer and, he claims, a poor one; but Frantz makes at least part of her living from her photography, which Maspero describes in detail at the beginning of *Les passagers du Roissy-Express*:

> Les photos d'Anaïk avaient chacune une longue histoire. Elles n'étaient pas faites par surprises, elles n'étaient jamais agression. Ni images à la sauvette ni images-viol. Pas de mise en scène, non plus. Les visages n'y sortaient pas de l'inconnu pour retourner à l'anonymat: chacun y portait un nom, chacun était relié à des souvenirs, des confidences, des repas, un peu de chaleur partagée, des heures vécues ensemble. L'histoire qu'elle racontait était toujours une histoire *à suivre*. [...] C'étaient des photos qui prenaient leur temps. (18)
>
> (Anaïk's photos each had a long story. They were not taken by surprise, they were never an assault. Neither images taken on the sly, nor raped images. There was no staging either. The faces did not emerge from the unknown to return to anonymity: each one carried a name, each one was connected to memories, to little secrets, to meals, some shared warmth, a few hours spent together. The story she told was always to be continued. [...] These were photos that took their time.)

Once more, the emphasis is on encounter and the photograph is the souvenir of the encounter. Maspero adds that Frantz always sends her photographs to the people in them (48), so they also acquire an exchange value, enabling reciprocity between traveller-photographer and travellee-photographee, as Jean-Xavier Ridon explains: 'L'échange se construit en ces termes: je te donne ta photo – où tu pourras te reconnaître, mais aussi reconnaître que tu es reconnu, et tu me donnes ton histoire comme une clef possible du paysage traversé à travers ta parole' (The exchange is constructed in these terms: I give you your photo – in which you can recognize yourself, but also recognize that you are recognized, and you give me your story as a possible key to the landscape crossed through your words).[56] As well as hosting the travellees by recounting their stories, the text hosts them in their photographs.[57] The photographs in *Les Passagers du Roissy-Express* either have no captions, or only the place name is indicated. Significantly, only two captions give the name of the photographee: those of Gilles and Gérard, who are two of the travellers' more prominent guides (102 and 301). Elsewhere the reader is left to guess at connections between the people described in Maspero's text and those portrayed in Frantz's photographs, which is not always easy. This lack of correspondence between images and text sometimes leaves the figures in the photographs anonymous and unidentifiable, seemingly undermining the purported intentions of photographer and writer, but Maspero's textual representation of most of the encounters is consistent with the way he initially describes Frantz's photography. Besides, Frantz's photographs are not simply illustrations for Maspero's text; the book is an artistic collaboration and the photographs tell their own story, reflecting the 'co-equality' of text and image that W. J. T. Mitchell praises as a quality of the photographic essay.[58] Writing specifically about *Les passagers*, Kathryn Jones comments positively on how Frantz's photographs contribute to the book's 'collective conversation'.[59] These are two independent travel accounts, one in prose and the other in photographs, sometimes coinciding, but each telling its own story.

Guillebaud and Depardon have collaborated on two travel texts: *La colline des anges* and *La porte des larmes*, large format books that give text and image equal space and attention. Guillebaud describes Depardon's photographic practices, emphasizing his patience when capturing street scenes and the people in them. Depardon slowly places himself in front of people and aims his camera at them, to which they respond by freezing or smiling, but he rejects such posed photographs and lowering his camera he waits.

> Il sourit aux gens, comme s'il s'agissait de les rassurer, d'obtenir un consentement silencieux. Ce face-à-face peut durer de longues minutes et n'aboutit pas toujours. Raymond s'éloigne alors sans avoir pris de photo. Quelque chose, ne s'est pas produit; une rencontre n'a pas eu lieu. (*Colline*, 496)

(He smiles at people, as though to reassure them, to obtain silent consent. This face-to-face exchange can last long moments and doesn't always succeed. Raymond then moves away without taking any photos. Something did not work out; an encounter did not take place).

Although these interactions do not involve any verbal communication or any prolonged contact, Guillebaud calls them encounters ('rencontres') nonetheless. Depardon uses a visual language of smiles and gestures to gain consent, but does not encroach further on his subjects (*Porte*, 716). This is a different approach to Ollivier and Frantz: Depardon is patient and gentle, but also seeks to minimize the intrusion and does not attempt to establish more prolonged relations. While he does take his photographs, his desire not to disrupt is another way of showing respect for his photographees.

Ollivier, Frantz and Depardon's use of photography is what Aime calls bilateral, where photographer and photographee have communicated and the latter has consented to the photograph, as opposed to a unilateral approach where the photographer takes no account of the subject.[60] The first two often go beyond a simple gesture to gain consent, establishing a meaningful relationship with their photographic subjects long before the photograph is taken.[61] The image then becomes a souvenir of the encounter and even an object of exchange. As we have seen in the previous section, both Ollivier and Frantz make mistakes and misjudge their subjects, but they both demonstrate self-awareness and willingness to be corrected and learn. Camera ownership is not universal and if there is often a discrepancy between the way travellers and travellees view photography, it is because the camera is almost always in the hands of the former. It remains to be seen how the dynamics of encounters will evolve when the travellee turns not only a stare but also a lens on the traveller.[62] Nonetheless, when travellers are conscious of this privilege and take the ethics of travel photography seriously, the camera can become a catalyst for shared encounters.

***

Discomfort is an enduring condition of travel, whether physical, psychological or social. The first is perhaps overemphasized as the 'travail' that makes 'real' travel: the glamour and heroism of overcoming geographical barriers and physical limitations that supposedly separate travellers from tourists. Discomfort is often less sensational, however; it characterizes tiny moments that occur and recur throughout a journey, particularly during encounters: the tensions of hospitality that we have seen in the previous chapter, the clash of cultural expectations, the unpleasantness of being the object of a stare, the awkward negotiation over taking a photograph. Discomfort forces travellers to stop and seek its cause; it puts things into question: assumptions, behaviour, desires. Social unease is part of the journey as much as physical exhaustion, and although the latter is more expected and accepted, the former is perhaps ultimately more valuable. Being open to the discomforting potential of encounter means being open to submitting to the actions of travellees: accepting the stare, acknowledging their right to control, admitting fault and failure. Travellers might expect travel to challenge them, but they cannot always choose their challenges; if the journey is to be a real test, then it must be unpredictable, it must confront the traveller unprepared. Perhaps the real traveller, if there is one, is the one who submits to the unpredictable, who accepts discomfort, who allows it to unbalance them.

The discomfort of encounter necessitates negotiation, it forces reassessment and compromise. Travellers must navigate between their own expectations and desires, and those of their travellees. They are not free to move and act at will, their freedom constantly collides with that of their travellees and the two must negotiate with each other. The encounters in this chapter initiated by the camera illustrate this necessity, but also the fruits that are borne of willing cooperation, in the form of encounters and even relationships established. The ethics of travel photography expressed in the travel writing examined above suggests that travel itself could likewise be re-envisioned as collaboration, rather than appropriation.

Chapter 6

CHALLENGING

> Un simple détail, parfois, suffit à notre honte. Il est certains malaises qui font partie du voyage. Les taire serait mensonge, les exagérer serait complaisance. Je n'ai jamais très bien su que faire de ces péripéties infimes qui, de loin en loin, viennent bousculer le train-train d'un récit et poser des questions sans réponse. (Guillebaud, *Porte*, 735)
>
> (Sometimes a simple detail is enough to shame us. Certain moments of unease are part of the journey. To suppress them would be a lie, to exaggerate them would be an indulgence. I have never known very well what to do with these miniature episodes that disrupt the humdrum routine of a tale every now and then and pose questions without answers.)

The chapters above have addressed some of the most typical encounters between travellers and travellees, all defined by actions carried out by one for or to the other. This chapter focuses on encounters that are not so easy to label with a verb or classify as an action. They can be loosely described as challenging encounters: when the travellee presents the traveller with a challenging situation or decision, or challenges the traveller's expectations or beliefs. Such encounters do not always occupy a significant amount of time or textual space, but they are invested with emotional or moral significance. As Jean-Claude Guillebaud suggests in the quotation above, these encounters are often characterized by discomfort or even shame, by doubts about how to act and how to represent them in writing. Guillebaud's final observation, that they throw up questions without answers, is particularly relevant: challenging encounters present travellers with dilemmas, with moral choices. The travellee acts on the traveller by forcing the latter to choose to act, or not to act. In order to clarify, I will begin with two examples, from Muriel Cerf's *L'antivoyage* and Sergio Ramazzotti's *Vado verso il Capo*.[1]

Arriving at Borivli station near Bombay, Cerf and her companion Rita are met by a crowd of beggars and lepers. Cerf describes their feelings 'de pitié exacerbée, d'énervement, de fureur même contre ces pauvres cons détestables et décourageants de misère et les salauds qui les font se traîner le ventre par terre pour une pièce de monnaie' (52; of intense pity, irritation, even fury against these wretched idiots, who are detestable and discouraging in their misery, and the bastards who make them crawl on the ground for a coin). She and Rita desperately give away all their money in a 'rage folle' (mad fury). They are stunned by the scene: 'on s'en va les yeux flous, perdues, sans savoir ni quoi dire, ni quoi faire, ni quoi penser' (52; we leave with our eyes blurred, lost, not knowing what to say, or what to do, or what to think). As suggested by Guillebaud, the challenging encounter fills the travellers with doubt, uncertain what to think or do, how to respond. Cerf goes on to describe its ethical significance: 'Merde, est-ce qu'on serait vraiment capables de s'en foutre complètement [...]. Donc être ignoble, s'habituer à vivre dans cet hôpital, ou crever. La misère à ce degré donne un tel vertige d'impuissance que la raison y chavire et l'estomac avec' (52; Shit, would we really be capable of not giving a damn at all [...]. Be contemptible, then, get used to living in this hospital, or die. Misery to this degree causes such vertigo of impotence that reason founders and your stomach heaves). Cerf describes conflicting and contradictory emotions of pity and anger. The beggars' very presence imposes these feelings and demands an impossible choice between 'être ignoble' (be contemptible) or 'crever' (die). They challenge her notions of justice and appropriate action by placing her in an unfamiliar and bewildering position.

Ramazzotti opens a new section with a dramatic statement: 'Il nome dell'uomo è Destiny O'Kere e io cambierò la sua vita' (*Vado*, 118; The man's name is Destiny O'Kere and I will change his life). Destiny is a charismatic and pious character, who drives Ramazzotti's bus in Nigeria and later writes to him in Italy. He requests a financial contribution to help him set up a recording studio and Ramazzotti recounts that without much reflection he sent him 50 dollars. The account of the bus journey is interspersed with Destiny's letters, creating suspense by delaying the conclusion of the story. Another letter arrives, thanking Ramazzotti for the money and enclosing photographs of the new studio. Ramazzotti is amazed: 'Ancora non capisco come cinquanta dollari abbiano potuto costruire tutto questo. [...] La banconota americana che spedii a Destiny non ha cambiato soltanto la sua vita. Credo che abbia cambiato soprattutto la mia' (*Vado*, 125–6; I still don't understand how 50 dollars could have built all of this. [...] The American banknote I sent to Destiny has not only changed his life, I believe that above all it has changed mine). Ramazzotti's meeting with Destiny is granted special attention and space in the text, emphasizing the power of the brief encounter. Ramazzotti admits that he told no one about his gift to Destiny, fearing that others would believe he was the victim of a scam.

The two episodes from Cerf and Ramazzotti share the common themes of an emotionally powerful encounter and a moral dilemma. As their different natures suggest, such encounters take diverse forms, but here I limit myself to meetings with travellees playing three specific roles: rickshaw riders, prostitutes and beggars, because these encounters recur often enough to provide a range of examples for comparison. Challenging encounters confront travellers with unfamiliar situations, forcing them to examine their own ethics, but also requiring on-the-spot decisions. The representation of such encounters in travel writing stages the ethical dilemma within its specific context, exposing the traveller and his/her choice to the scrutiny of the reader. As we have seen in Chapter 2, economic inequality underlies many of the ethical dilemmas faced by travellers and tourists, particularly in the context of encounter, so it is pertinent to begin by examining some of the ways that economic issues emerge, or are concealed, in travel writing.

Economic Power

At home in Europe it is easy to feel detached from wider global inequalities, but when Europeans travel they often come face to face with those who live in very different circumstances to themselves. Travel brings together people from disparate cultures, but also with disparate standards of living. The example from Cerf above suggests that this young traveller encounters extreme poverty for the first time when she visits India, while the more experienced Ramazzotti is nonetheless amazed by the buying power of his 50 dollars. Relative wealth affords travellers a great deal of power, yet this topic is rarely discussed in travel texts.

Travel writing has traditionally provided a means for writers to fund their travels, but travel writers rarely divulge their finances or budgets.[2] In Jean Lacouture's introduction to Guillebaud's *Un voyage vers l'Asie*, for example, we learn that the book was originally commissioned as articles for *Le Monde*, but Guillebaud only alludes vaguely to this: 'on m'envoie vers l'Orient avec quelques dollars et deux gros cahiers à ressorts' (*Asie*, 96 and 98; they are sending me East with a few dollars and two large spiral notebooks). Francesco Piccolo acknowledges *Marie Claire*, which 'ci ha permesso di andare in giro per il mondo' (241; enabled us to travel around the world), another vague reference to funds. Nicole-Lise Bernheim mentions that her journey in *Chambres d'ailleurs* was financed with an inheritance from an aunt, but we only learn this in the later *Saisons japonaises* (11). Travel writing rarely reveals more than these few details about the financing of journeys and of course it discloses even less about any earnings from publication. Perhaps such details would seem tasteless or superfluous, but their absence fuels a myth of leisure and freedom, masking the conditions that enable travel. Nicolas Bouvier is a notable exception, often referring to his money problems in the texts that describe his long journey across Asia (e.g., *Usage*, 141–6 and *Chronique*, 588–92). He and his companion Thierry Vernet set out with little, planning to earn their way with Bouvier's pen and Vernet's paintbrush, a venture that is not always successful and penury becomes a characteristic of their journey. Marc Boulet's budget also plays an important role when he disguises himself as an untouchable in India. Living solely on his begging earnings is part of his challenge and he gives the reader detailed accounts of his income and expenses (e.g., 107 and 132). Travel writing seems to be more forthcoming on money issues when the traveller's finances match, at least temporarily, those of the travellee, indicating a general uneasiness about the wealth gap.

Wealth is the condition that enables leisured international travel; it buys the freedom to treat the world as one's playground. Even for professionals, who pay their way with their writing, travel is an expensive enterprise. As Marco Aime points out, the fact of being able to afford a long-distance plane ticket is an indication for many travellees of the traveller's wealth.[3] Wealth is an enabling condition in more subtle ways as well: Bernard Ollivier is able to walk 12,000 kilometres across Asia in his early sixties because he enjoys the health and free retirement that are benefits of a life of relative comfort. Whether or not travellers consider themselves to be affluent at home, they often find that they are when they travel. 'La misère de l'Éthiopie fait de nous des milliardaires, voilà la vérité' (*Porte*, 691; Ethiopia's poverty makes us billionaires, that's the truth) declares Guillebaud, opening a chapter addressing the issue of money. The wad of dollars he carries 'magically' frees him from the problems faced by locals. Dollars open doors, as Tiziano Terzani finds in Samarkand (*Buonanotte*, 219, 221 and 222); they also open border gates, as Olivier Weber reports crossing from Turkey to Iran (*Festin*, 205–6). Sometimes the disparity in buying power is so great that it goes to the traveller's head, as Corrado Ruggeri suggests, bemoaning tourists who haggle persistently over discounts that mean nothing to them, but everything to the vendor (49–50). When something is a trivial cost to one and a significant benefit to the other, the interpersonal encounter is bound to suffer.

Travellers' wealth grants them power but conversely it also makes them vulnerable. Guillebaud confesses that he and Raymond share the fear of finding themselves suddenly stripped of their money in the middle of nowhere, 'plus pauvres que les plus pauvres' (*Porte*, 692; poorer than the poorest). He wonders what compassion, or cruelty, they would meet then. Ollivier, who is particularly vulnerable on his lone walk, suffers the threat of theft several times (e.g., *Marche I*, 164–5, 177–9, 271–6 and *Marche II*, 263) and the reality once (*Marche II*, 118–122). Aside from the menace of literal robbery, travellers are easy targets for excessive price hikes and bribe requests. In Mali and Senegal, Gianni Celati is constantly assailed by street sellers and must negotiate the price of services arduously (e.g., 16, 45, 95, 154–5). As we have seen in Chapter 4, Ramazzotti has frequent confrontations with border guards who often demand bribes. When he crosses from Gabon into Congo, a fellow traveller comments: 'Non c'è bianco che passi di qua, e sono pochissimi, le assicuro, che non venga derubato in un modo o nell'altro' (*Vado*, 166; Not a single white person who passes through here, and there are very few I assure you, does not get robbed in one way or another). This observation indicates expectations about wealth associated with the traveller's race. European travellers find themselves preceded by images of wealth, imposed on them by the stare of the travellee, as we have seen in the previous chapter. Celati is the object of assumptions about wealth in Mali; Ollivier discovers similar beliefs, to his cost, in the village of Alihadjeu, discussed in Chapter 4. As he puts it later: 'Je représente l'Europe et sa richesse, ses voitures et ses bijoux, ses MacDo et ses starlettes' (*Marche I*, 260; I represent Europe and its riches, its cars and its jewels, its McDonalds and its celebrities). Wealth erects barriers between travellers and travellees: Guillebaud calls it 'la frontière invisible de l'argent' (*Porte*, 691; money's invisible border), which exiles him from ordinary life and from the very people whom he hopes to meet. Conversely, Bouvier finds that his Japanese neighbours open up to him when they discover that, contrary to their expectations of a foreigner, he is not at all wealthy (*Chronique*, 587). Money enables encounters, because it enables the journey, but also disrupts them, contaminates them. Economic inequality not only contributes to the encounters in this chapter, but causes them to happen in the first place: the relationship between the traveller and the rickshaw rider, beggar or prostitute is defined by the wealth of the former and the poverty of the latter.

Previous chapters have already addressed some of the implications of economic relations for encounters. I identified a desire among travellers to transcend the financial basis of relations with their guides and hosts, by establishing authentic relationships or friendships based on genuine sentiments rather than material exchange. The disparity in wealth between traveller and travellee disrupts encounters, but it also raises ethical issues, which I will examine more closely in the following sections.[4] Duccio Canestrini connects economic inequality and tourism candidly: 'La mano tesa dell'indiano di Calcutta non è […] una spiacevole parentesi nella giornata del turista, ma il presupposto stesso della sua vacanza in India' (The outstretched hand of the Indian in Calcutta is not an unpleasant parenthesis in the tourist's day, but the very precondition of his/her holiday in India).[5] How does the tourist respond to that outstretched hand? How should one travel as a rich man or woman in a poor country? How should one deal with everyday encounters in this context? Celati puts the traveller's dilemma in cynical terms: 'Il bianco è un mammifero destinato all'incessante assalto di piccole menadi nere, ma spesso vuole credersi un uomo giusto e caritatevole, proprio per mettersi al di sopra di questa nemesi della giustizia distributiva' (160; The white man is a mammal destined for the incessant assault of little black maenads, but he often wants to believe himself to be a fair and charitable man, precisely to place himself above this nemesis of distributive justice). This desire to appear fair and charitable is evident in the travel narrative, though it is debatable whether the target audience is the travellee or the reader.

Justification: Rickshaw Riders

The hand-pulled rickshaw was first used in Japan in the 1870s and soon spread to other parts of Asia, reaching its peak of usage in the 1920s.[6] The development of cycle rickshaws followed shortly after the invention of the bicycle, but they were slower to catch on, only beginning to be used on a large scale in Asia from the 1930s.[7] Hand-pulled rickshaws disappeared from most Asian countries after the Second World War; Calcutta is the only place where they are still employed on any significant scale today.[8] The cycle rickshaws that replaced them remain in use in a variety of forms in different parts of Asia.[9] The *sai kaa* of Rangoon, the Vietnamese *cyclo* and the *becaks* of Yogyakarta all function on the same principle of a manually powered vehicle.[10] Recently small numbers of cycle rickshaws have been introduced to some European and North American cities, but these remain a novelty aimed at tourists.[11] The Western tourist in Asia encounters the rickshaw, or equivalent, as a culturally unfamiliar and even exotic form of transport.

The rickshaw represents more than an antiquated or exotic curiosity; it is often the most practical way to move about, but the tourist is confronted with the fact that the rider must haul vehicle and passenger himself.[12] The encounter with a rickshaw is therefore also an encounter with its rider. Rob Gallagher suggests that 'Nowadays, we think of the hand-pulled rickshaws as a cruel and anachronistic form of transport.'[13] The cycle rickshaw could be considered less gruelling since movement is aided by the bicycle, but it is still propelled by the effort of the rider. When considering whether rickshaws should be banned on humanitarian grounds, Gallagher points out that 'there are many other trades "which compare with rickshaw pulling in the intensity of manual effort they require: however, these are hidden in the docks, factories or the countryside, whereas the sweat of pulling is easy to observe"'.[14] Travellers rarely access docks or factories, and although they do encounter agricultural labourers, the latter are often treated as an ingredient in the picturesque of rural scenery.[15] Rickshaw riders are a conspicuous manifestation of the hard manual labour that is usually replaced by machinery in Europe, and as such they represent wider inequalities.

The traveller's encounter with the rickshaw rider often begins with a statement about the ethical dubiousness of this means of transport. As soon as the rickshaw is mentioned, Ruggeri affirms, 'Ho sempre un grave scrupolo di coscienza quando mi trovo davanti ai risciò' (153; I always have serious qualms of guilt when I find myself faced with a rickshaw). When accepting a ride Guillebaud admits, 'Pas très fier de lui, le petit Français, traîné ainsi par un Indien aux cheveux blancs qui court pieds nus entre les brancards, comme un cheval' (*Asie*, 155–6; He's not very proud of himself, the little Frenchman; pulled along by an Indian with white hair who runs barefoot between the shafts, like a horse). Christine Jordis opens her chapter on *becaks* with: 'Tout d'abord nous avions refusé de monter dans ces lourdes caisses propulsées par la seule force de deux maigres mollets pédalant sans relâche' (213; At first we had refused to ride in these heavy boxes powered only by the force of two thin calves pedalling without rest). All three accept rickshaw rides, while inserting an appropriate pause for reflection. When weighing up the disadvantages of the rickshaw, they focus on the physical cost to the rider, whose vulnerability is emphasized through details such as 'pieds nus' (barefoot) and 'maigres mollets' (thin calves). The rider is pitied because his body seems unequal to the effort required, never admired for proving himself equal to the task. Ruggeri points to the health risks for rickshaw riders (153), while Jordis finds the vehicle anachronistic and decadent: 'C'était renouer avec le temps des litières, ou des chaises à porteurs; après tout, nous n'étions pas malades, nous pouvions bien marcher' (213; It meant returning to the era of litters, or sedan chairs; after all, we weren't sick, we could perfectly well walk). The rickshaw is also an encounter with cultural difference and several travellers compare their own 'Western' attitudes to those of locals, who are less perturbed. For Jordis, this observation eases her own reluctance, while Ruggeri and François-Olivier Rousseau both claim that Western attitudes reflect a greater respect for the humanity of the riders (Jordis, 213; Ruggeri, 153; Rousseau, 48). Differences are also established between forms of rickshaw: the cycle-powered vehicle is considered less exhausting and more dignified than those powered by running pullers. Ruggeri tells us that he refused to use such a vehicle in Calcutta (153), while Bernheim reasons: 'Louer les muscles des bras ou ceux des jambes d'un autre, revient au même mais le vélo est moins humiliant pour le tireur et son client, et moins fatigant pour le corps entier du coolie' (*Chambres*, 144; Hiring the arm or leg muscles of another comes down to the same thing, but the bicycle is less humiliating for the puller and his client, and less tiring for the coolie's whole body). At this early stage in the encounter the rider is an extension of his vehicle, he is the arms and legs that power movement, not yet a person, though it is his personhood that causes the ethical quandary.

When it comes to actually using a rickshaw, travellers almost always make a point of justifying their choice, or attempt to alleviate the rider's burden in some way.[16] Ruggeri's traveller-protagonist is persuaded to accept a rickshaw ride by his companion Carla, who points out that the riders are earning their living and that refusing a ride does nothing to improve their situation (153). After describing his own hesitation, Guillebaud reports a similar reflection: '"Ça te gêne peut-être, mais en allant à pied par scrupule de conscience, tu prives un rickshaw de son gagne-pain." Cette réflexion m'a décidé' (*Asie*, 156; 'It bothers you perhaps, but if you went on foot because of an uneasy conscience, you would deprive a rickshaw rider of his source of income.' These thoughts persuaded me). Thus the problem is turned on its head: the traveller is not exploiting the rider, but doing him a favour. This is further established by emphasizing the poverty of the riders: Ruggeri tells us that some riders eat and sleep in their vehicles, which may be their sole possession (153), while Jordis reports that her rider talks of a family to feed and a lack of customers (216). Bernheim, who tells us that she avoids using rickshaws in Calcutta (*Chambres*, 144), takes a different approach when the moment to choose a ride arises: 'Rickshaw pour rentrer à l'hôtel. Tu en choisis soigneusement le tireur qui doit être fort, adroit, posséder un bon équilibre et connaître les rues autorisées' (149–50; Rickshaw to return to the hotel. You carefully choose the puller, who must be strong, skilful, have good balance and know the authorized streets). The rickshaw is more acceptable if the rider is deemed physically capable of withstanding the effort. Rousseau and Pier Paolo Pasolini take their scruples even further, both dismounting to relieve their riders of the burden of their weight for all or part of the journey (Rousseau, 48).[17] Far from being redundant, the rickshaw rider in Pasolini's account becomes his guide and interlocutor. Like Ruggeri and Jordis, Pasolini engages his rider in conversation, learning his name and telling the reader something of his life story: Josef used to be a sailor who travelled the world, now he is sick and has eight children to feed. He is not merely a human horse, but was once a traveller himself.

The apparent need for justification when travellers employ rickshaw riders is indicative of their expectations about the ethics of their readership. They self-consciously justify themselves to their readers, not to the riders, reinforcing the impression that these ethical dilemmas are considered more relevant to their readers than to the encountered riders. The travellers who engage with their riders as people, albeit in different ways, resolve their dilemmas, or at least defend their chosen courses of action, through this interaction. Their decisions also reveal negotiations between cultural and moral norms and the very specific context of encountering a particular rider and undertaking a particular journey.

Distancing: Prostitutes

The economic power of the traveller can disrupt and corrupt encounters, but it can also purchase them. Ian Littlewood connects sex tourism to wealth: 'The economic power of the tourist remains at the centre of the web of threads that link travel and sex. However resolutely this economic superiority is displaced into other, non-commercial kinds of assistance, its reality seeps back into the marrow of the relationship.'[18] Franck Michel identifies sex tourism as a new form of colonialism and warns of its increasing democratization and emergence as a mass movement, like tourism before it.[19] Despite the growth of the sex tourist industry and the seemingly increasing association between sex and tourism, much travel writing is remarkably consistent in steering its protagonist-travellers away from such activities. The encounter with the prostitute is not a rare occurrence, but it is striking how rarely travellers are represented accepting sexual services and how often they resolutely reject such offers. In *Sultry Climates*, Littlewood's study of sex tourism from the eighteenth to the mid-twentieth centuries, he identifies a discrepancy between the public presentation of tourism as a cultural venture and the private practices of sex tourism. He asserts that sex has been neglected in the study of the history of tourism, but recognizes that this is 'both because the tourists themselves have presented their travels as a cultural narrative rather than a sexual one – letters home commonly tell of the churches visited, not the brothels – and also because tourism is an approved social activity that needs to guard its own respectability'.[20] Littlewood deliberately unearths accounts of sex tourism, while I am responding to the presence, or absence, of encounters with prostitutes in a more general selection of writing. But the texts I consider do suggest continuity consistent with Littlewood's analysis, in the desire to represent travel as a cultural, and not a sexual, adventure. The encounter with the prostitute entails similar moral issues to that with the rickshaw rider, but travellers demonstrate a more clear-cut sense of where to draw the line in their interactions with the former. While the prostitute's offers are almost always rejected, different tactics are employed, to different effect. Ollivier explains himself in the simplest terms: 'Depuis l'adolescence, j'ai toujours refusé toute relation avec une prostituée. Je ne vais pas commencer à soixante-quatre ans' (*Marche III*, 203; Since adolescence, I have always refused any relation with a prostitute. I am not going to start at 64). Others create more elaborate ruses.

Rousseau and Ramazzotti both portray the women who approach them as piteous creatures, focusing on unattractive details of their physical appearance and character. Rousseau is scathing about the Nepalese masseuse who offers him extra services: 'Elle penche vers moi un mufle chiffonné d'épagneul et entrouvre, dans un sourire, une bouche prématurément démeublée.

Le massage est mou, sans technique et sans conviction, je ne donnerais même pas trois sur dix à la masseuse' (59; She leans towards me with a worn-out muzzle like a spaniel's and opens her prematurely unfurnished mouth in a smile. The massage is weak, lacking technique and conviction, I wouldn't even give three out of ten to the masseuse). Ramazzotti describes an unsuccessful attempt to seduce him in a bar in Gabon:

> Due oscene puttane truccate con diversi ettogrammi di rossetti e ombretti, languono stravaccate sul bancone del bar. Una di esse tenta di abbordarmi mostrandomi dei graffi sui polsi. 'Ieri sera mi sono quasi uccisa in una delle stanze di sopra,' mi dice. 'Non lasciarmi dormire da sola stanotte, ti prego.' La respingo per concentrarmi sul liquore. (*Vado*, 155)
>
> (Two obscene whores, made up with hundreds of grams of lipstick and eye shadow, languish sprawled out on the bar counter. One of them tries to chat me up, showing me scratches on her wrists. 'Yesterday evening I almost killed myself in one of the rooms upstairs', she says. 'Don't leave me to sleep alone tonight, please.' I reject her and focus on my drink)

Both texts express a kind of horrified urgency to dissociate the travellers from the prostitutes, suggesting that the women are threatening. These encounters show that, even in the most unexpected circumstances, travellees pose a challenge to travellers. In an interesting contrast Ramazzotti interviews a Cameroonian prostitute, Kathryn, about an HIV 'vaccine' scandal of which she was a victim (*Afrozapping*, 108–10). The encounter is purely in the nature of investigative journalism; there is no implication that Ramazzotti might become Kathryn's client. The writer treats the prostitute with sympathy: she is granted a name and a story and he quotes her at length. This different treatment reflects the fact that Kathryn represents less of a threat to Ramazzotti than the prostitutes who accost him for business, because she allows him to assume the worthy persona of the journalist uncovering corruption, rather than the less honourable role of the sex client.

Humour or self-parody is another distancing tactic, used by both Celati and Bouvier. Celati describes his companion Jean barricading himself in his hotel room with earplugs to escape the seductions of the hotel prostitute (23 and 27). Celati confronts her himself, but remarks that 'In quanto essendo vecchio e anche un po' sordo, sono immune da ogni seduzione' (27; Being old and also a little deaf, I am immune to every seduction). He acknowledges her charms and reflects that 'Come bianco incantato devo stare attento' (27; As an enchanted white man I must be careful). In Sri Lanka, a dubious Bouvier agrees to join his neighbour for a visit to a brothel, but they lose their way, are caught in a rainstorm, their car breaks down and when they return to the hotel, soaked, they are mocked.²¹ Here the focus is on the travellers, rather than the prostitutes, and humour undermines the image of the predatory male tourist: Celati and Bouvier are too bumbling and incompetent to be threatening. As Patrick Holland and Graham Huggan point out, however, self-parody is also a means used in travel writing to exonerate travellers of responsibility.²² Whatever strategy is adopted, the end result is the same: the prostitutes are turned away and the travellers maintain their integrity.

The question here is not whether travellers purchase the services of prostitutes during their travels, but rather how these encounters are represented in travel texts. The events that happen during a journey and those narrated in a text are two separate things. In his interviews with Irène Lichtenstein-Fall, Bouvier talks of visiting brothels in Japan, but when asked why the prostitutes he met do not feature in his books, he replies: 'En grande partie, à cause du vocabulaire. Également parce que, dans le domaine des expériences amoureuses, je ne prétends rien apprendre à personne' (*Routes*, 1292; For the most part because of the vocabulary. Equally because, in the field of romantic experiences, I don't claim to have anything to teach anyone). Bouvier's reference to 'vocabulaire' (vocabulary) implies that his coyness is also motivated by the requirements of genre: that sexual exploits do not belong in travel books. The resolute distancing between travellers and prostitutes (at least when exercising their profession) contributes to the creation of the traveller persona and is a comment on the ethics of travel. This is reinforced by the representation of others, particularly other tourists, participating in sex tourism. Guillebaud, for example, describes a noisy crowd of Chinese revellers taking over a hotel in Hue, Vietnam, dressing up in costumes and partying with local prostitutes on a junk on the river. His Vietnamese guide, Mme D., reacts with indignation, and the hotel staff 'affiche un dégoût aussi désolé qu'impuissant' (*Colline*, 494; display distaste that is as sorrowful as it is impotent). The disapproval, which implies moral judgment, is reinforced because it is represented as the hosts' opinion. Alexandre Kauffmann travels to Bangkok for the explicit purpose of tourist watching, which inevitably includes sex tourist watching: backpackers using massage parlours (73–4) and older Western men with their young Thai boyfriends (85–7). Although Kauffmann avoids taking a moral stance, the sex tourists disappoint him because they do not live up to the myth of the 'real' traveller that brought him to Thailand, once more reflecting differences between travel practices. Celati is assailed by 'bambine prostitute' (prostitute children) in Dakar, whom he turns away only to find them warmly greeting an Italian man, who then tells Celati about his annual African sex tourism (172–3). Celati dryly lists this episode as another 'caso esemplare di turismo africano' (172; exemplary case of African tourism) to add to his collection of appalling or idiotic behaviour on the part of tourists. Again, he avoids any explicit expressions of disapproval, but clearly distances himself from the Italian and his activities. As we found in Chapter 5, observing others serves to set travellers apart from the crowd and, in this case, dissociates them from sex tourists. This is another manifestation of antitourism: the tourists' misbehaviour is highlighted and the comparison reflects favourably on the traveller. Thus travel writing expresses its ethics: by example and counterexample.

Doubt and deliberation are absent from the examples cited above, suggesting that views on prostitution are more clear-cut than views on rickshaws. Ruggeri provides an example of a more ambiguous attitude to sex tourism, taking his observation of tourists to the level of voyeurism although, like the other travellers, he also draws the line at active participation. He and his partner Carla are guided by various Western initiates around the nightlife of Patong Beach and Bangkok (126–37 and 231–9). Ruggeri describes the shows they watch and the massage parlours they visit in detail, evaluating the female workers and enjoying the spectacle of other Western tourists participating in the shows. He and Carla harass Filippo, their Italian guide, into divulging a detailed account of his own experiences with masseuses, but as soon as Filippo suggests that they might want to try for themselves they shift the conversation onto another topic (233–5). The chapter concludes with Ruggeri convincing Peter, another guide, to allow him to spy on a prostitute and client, but at the final moment, in front of the open door, he announces 'Grazie, ma non mi interessa vedere quello che succede' (239; Thanks, but I'm not interested in seeing what's happening), to Peter's irritation. There is an awkward tension in these episodes between the desire of the voyeur and the limits of what Ruggeri seems to deem acceptable. Ruggeri wavers between representing his autobiographical protagonist as a sex tourist, unselfconsciously assessing the bodies of the women on display, and a more serious traveller, examining the sociological implications of sex tourism and distancing himself from sex tourists. His portrayal of Carla is equally inconsistent: she is sometimes described enjoying the show and flirting happily with the prostitutes, and at another time she announces '"Non ho voglia di vedere schifezze"' (233; I don't want to see filth). By limiting his own participation to voyeurism, Ruggeri suggests that there is a moral line to be drawn, but his indecisiveness may also be symptomatic of changing attitudes to sex tourism which, as Michel laments, is increasingly accepted, at least in certain forms.[23]

Ruggeri introduces another interconnection between travel and prostitution that is worth considering briefly. Prostitutes are frequently objects of the traveller's stare and are represented as both spectacle and scenery. As Ruggeri suggests, prostitution holds a fascination that makes it a tourist attraction in itself.

Cerf visits the red light district of Bombay as a tourist, explaining: 'La vraie porte de l'Inde, ce n'est pas l'arc de triomphe planté en face du Taj Mahal Hotel, mais la rue des putes. La rue initiatrice, la célébrité de Bombay avec le Crawford Market et les tours du Silence' (48; The real gate of India is not the triumphal arch planted opposite the Taj Mahal Hotel, but the street of whores. The street of initiation, the fame of Bombay along with Crawford Market and the Towers of Silence). Thus the red light district and its inhabitants are tourist sights like any commemorative monument or famous museum. They provide a spectacle for tourists to visually consume, without being compelled to engage with the women on any more personal level. On the other hand, the less glamorous side of prostitution is often evident in urban scenes. Guillebaud, for example, describes his arrival in Addis Ababa:

> L'accueil est rude et la ville est glauque. Restons-en là... Des groupes de jeunes gens sont postés aux carrefours; des prostituées peintes comme des matrones de Fellini jaillissent dans la lumière des phares et agitent les bras quand nous passons; sur la plupart des avenues, les lampadaires sont éteints. (Guillebaud, *Porte*, 698)
>
> (The welcome is rough and the town is shabby. Let's leave it at that... Groups of young people are stationed at the crossroads; prostitutes, painted like Fellini's matrons, appear suddenly in the headlights and wave their arms as we pass; the streetlamps on most of the streets are out).

Here, prostitutes become part of the scenery, part of the shabbiness, along with the unlit streetlamps; their presence is shorthand for urban poverty.

By distancing their traveller-protagonists from the prostitutes who approach them, travel writers express a fairly clear-cut sense of ethics in relation to sex tourism, revealing expectations about the travel genre and its readership. Voyeurism is a more morally nebulous area, but perhaps this is not surprising, given the ascendency of visual consumption as a travel practice. Travellers rarely engage with prostitutes as individuals and the lack of contact and communication between the two is striking for this absence. Intercourse at any level, whether sexual or simply verbal, is avoided at all costs.

Dilemma: Beggars

Like prostitutes, beggars also blend into the scenery, often catalogued as a symptom of poverty and hardship. Terzani, for example, describes the scene around the airport in Nikolayevsk, Russia: 'La piazza è piena di buche. Tre bambini sporchi e pezzenti vengono a chiedere l'elemosina' (*Buonanotte*, 112; The square is full of potholes. Three dirty children in rags come to beg).

Such descriptions are particularly common in writing about India, where poverty is one of the stereotypical images that travellers anticipate. John Hutnyk condemns Western 'rumours' of Calcutta that constantly portray it as 'an overcrowded place of poverty and despair, of desperation and decline'.[24] Guillebaud begins his description of a scene in Calcutta by drawing attention to the clichés associated with the city, listing in the same sentence begging lepers and crumbling imperial façades (*Asie*, 163). He then redirects our interest to the less stereotypical elements, such as fervent business activities: 'comptez non pas les mendiants mais les "démarcheurs" qui vous houspillent dans un anglais bricolé' (*Asie*, 164; don't count the beggars but the 'salesmen' who hustle you in self-assembled English). The beggars then, like the decaying signs of empire, are just part of the mundane background. Like prostitutes, they are granted no context, no lives or stories or names, only a physical appearance and social condition.

Beggars are not as passive as their description suggests, however. The children whom Terzani describes alongside the potholes approach him purposely. Unlike many of the encounters in previous chapters, where travellers requiring a service initiate encounters, beggars actively seek the attention of travellers. Canestrini describes the lepers begging in Puri, India: 'è difficile dimenticare quel sorriso, al contempo supplichevole e accattivante, ma anche di soddisfazione e quasi di vendetta. Come a dire: "Adesso voglio vedere come fai a tirarti indietro, di fronte a una simile disgrazia"' (it is difficult to forget that smile, at the same time imploring and engaging, but also one of satisfaction and almost of revenge. As if to say: 'Now I want to see how you manage to back out of this, confronted with such a scandal').[25] These travellees turn their stare on the traveller, fully conscious of the challenge they pose. As Canestrini describes, they confront the tourist and demand, 'So what will you do now?' but also, to the travel writer, 'What will you write?' As he argues, there is no easy answer as to whether or not to give money to beggars, and travellers are faced with the dilemma of choice.[26] Not all of the travellees in this section ask travellers directly for money, so not all can be labelled as beggars, but they do all present travellers with challenging dilemmas framed by inequality.

Immediately following Ramazzotti's description of Destiny O'Kere and his contribution to Destiny's recording studio he describes another encounter. On his way to the Nigeria-Cameroon border he meets Joseph, a Liberian refugee who has lost his family and fled his war-torn country, hoping to reach his brother in Yaoundé. Ramazzotti reports Joseph's story at length, quoting him directly and portraying his situation as a refugee sympathetically. At the border the Nigerian guards demand a 50-dollar bribe from Joseph, an enormous sum, which he is unable to pay. Although Joseph does not ask

Ramazzotti directly for the money, the traveller feels a sense of responsibility towards him, knowing that he is the only person present who would be willing or able to help him out. He initially decides to pay for Joseph, though he is loath to reinforce the rule of corruption. However, he only has unbroken 100 dollar notes, which he cannot change and which he refuses to give to the guards. Instead he leaves, full of anger and self-disgust. 'Joseph è rimasto sulla riva a fissarmi come l'attrice di un vecchio film. Manca solo che si metta a piangere con una colonna sonora adatta' (Joseph stayed on the riverbank staring at me, like an actress in an old film. The only thing missing was for him to start crying with a suitable soundtrack) (Ramazzotti, *Vado*, 133). Once more we encounter the power of the travellee's stare. Ramazzotti uses humour to make light of the scene, comparing Joseph to an actress, and tries to console himself, reflecting that it is not his duty to eradicate corruption in Nigeria and that Joseph will find a solution. He realizes that his justifications are nonsense:

> Sono stato egoista, eccome. Sapevo di avere già speso molto e di essere rimasto con pochi dollari, e avevo paura di rimanere *io* senza soldi, nella condizione di profugo-non profugo [...]. Ho avuto paura di diventare un profugo. E me ne pento, me ne pento, non finirò mai di pentirmene. (*Vado*, 133).
>
> (I was selfish, that's what I was. I knew that I had already spent a lot and that I had only a few dollars left; I was afraid of being left without money myself, in the condition of refugee-non refugee [...]. I was afraid of becoming a refugee. And I regret it, I regret it, I will never stop regretting it.)

Ramazzotti's action might well seem selfish – what is 100 dollars to an Italian who is able to spend weeks travelling the length of Africa? As he says himself, 'Quante volte ho speso cento dollari per una stanza d'albergo?' (*Vado*, 135; How many times have I spent 100 dollars on a hotel room?). Although Ramazzotti feels some responsibility towards Joseph he is able to detach and move on and despite his regret he does not return. He is conscious of his power as a Western tourist, but that same fact also enables him to pursue his journey and leave Joseph behind. The story does not flatter his autobiographical protagonist, though it does illustrate the complexity of his decision, setting it within a particular context and taking into account the different factors bearing on his choice: the constant scourge of bribery, the scarcity of banks and frequent encounters with those in need. Within *Vado verso il Capo*, this episode offsets Ramazzotti's account of his generosity to Destiny: although the writer does not acknowledge it, the 50 dollars sent to the Nigerian is also the 50 dollars denied to the Liberian.

Guillebaud is particularly sensitive to challenging encounters, describing several in *La colline des anges* and *La porte des larmes*. The lines quoted at the beginning of this chapter open the narration of such an encounter in Ethiopia. He describes the shame and discomfort of certain moments that pose questions without answers, but are an integral part of any journey. There follows the account of a brief but intense encounter, when Guillebaud and Raymond spy a perfect photo opportunity: a barefoot girl struggling to carry a pair of heavy water cans. They both leap out of their car and rush towards her, but she screams with fright, drops her load and flees in terror. The travellers are immediately ashamed of themselves, but uncertain how to repair the situation, not wanting to follow her, lest they scare her more. Her fear and flight is a slap in the face for them, forcefully revealing the damage of their mere presence.

> Nous sommes condamnés, par notre fait, à vivre un petit désastre jusqu'à son terme. L'incident n'est pas si anodin. Il fait instantanément affleurer ce qu'en temps ordinaire, vaille que vaille, nous feignons d'oublier: la brutalité inattentive du tourisme, l'ontologique sottise de toute curiosité 'exotique'. (*Porte*, 735–6)
>
> (We are condemned, by our actions, to live out a small disaster to its end. The incident is not so harmless. It instantly brings to the surface that which, under normal circumstances, we somehow pretend to forget: the careless brutality of tourism, the ontological stupidity of all 'exotic' curiosity).

The encounter is barely more than an exchange of eye contact, but merits its own chapter in Guillebaud's account, as he recognizes that no matter one's intentions, all travel is disruptive. Here the traveller acknowledges his responsibility for the girl's distress, the unexpected happenings of a journey, its unintended consequences. He also confronts his powerlessness to repair the damage he and Raymond have caused. There is no neat solution, no ethically correct response.

In *La colline des anges* Guillebaud concludes a chapter about how he and Raymond cope with their exposure to poverty in Vietnam with a salient encounter with a begging child. He describes how the travellers suppress their emotions with forced humour, but they surface in silences or bursts of anger. Begging girls surround Guillebaud on a boat, attempting to sell him their petty wares of chewing gum, coke and cigarettes. The traveller resists, following his usual policy, but under the girls' persistent barrage and the gaze of Raymond and other passengers, he finally yields and buys from one child, turning the rest away. At this point the smallest girl, rejected, bursts into tears, 'des larmes fortes et graves, comme un désespoir qui, soudain, ne se cache plus et n'appelle pas l'ironie' (*Colline*, 510; strong serious tears, as of desperation that is suddenly no longer hidden and doesn't call for irony). Guillebaud offers to buy all her goods, but it is too late, the child no longer even cares: 'Il n'y a que le désespoir inconsolable d'un enfant pauvre et *immensément* malheureux. | J'achète tout, de force, et je caresse ses cheveux. | Piteux.' (*Colline*, 510, emphasis in the original; There is only the inconsolable despair of a poor and *immensely* unhappy child. | I buy everything, forcibly, and I stroke her hair. | Pitiful). This is not one of the knowing adults described by Canestrini, but the child still confronts Guillebaud with her poverty. She is no longer just another pestering street seller but a suffering individual; her tears hold Guillebaud responsible, at least for the duration of their encounter.

The examples from Ramazzotti and Guillebaud illustrate many of the qualities that Martha Nussbaum identifies in novels: the priority of the particular in terms of attention to individual travellees, the role of emotions in the traveller's personal responses to situations, contingency in the unexpectedness of these encounters and finally the contextualizing details that bear on the traveller's ethical choices.[27] Both Ramazzotti and Guillebaud dramatize the moral dilemmas faced by tourists. Each has a readymade policy: not to pay bribes or not to buy from street children, but when confronted with a particular individual and a particular context a policy is not sufficient. These encounters throw up questions without answers, as Guillebaud recognizes, but at the same time the traveller faces the responsibility of making choices. This is an unexpected consequence of the journey; these encounters and the dilemmas they entail are not part of the itinerary, yet perhaps every traveller should expect them, as Guillebaud says: 'Il est certains malaises qui font partie du voyage' (*Porte*, 735; Certain moments of uneasiness are part of the journey). Malaise is precisely the quality of challenging encounters; it captures their unpleasantness, their awkwardness. Travellers suffer malaise because they are unprepared and they respond to the dilemmas they present provisionally, inadequately.

Neither Ramazzotti nor Guillebaud represent their protagonists in a flattering light, but they do attempt to justify their choices. In *Allegro occidentale* Piccolo takes a more brutal look at tourism. He expands from the particular experience of encountering begging children in Sri Lanka to explore the reasoning, conscious or not, behind tourists' choices to give money and gifts, and to whom, presenting the attitudes of tourists to the poor in a critical and cynical light:

> Noi scegliamo. Selezioniamo, indaghiamo. Non regaliamo school pen e bon bon a chi capita, al primo che ce li chiede. No. Poiché riceviamo molte richieste, diventa per noi automaticamente naturale scegliere chi è che riceverà un dono e chi no, con un criterio tutto nostro di selezione. (146)
>
> (We choose. We select, we investigate. We don't give a school pen and a sweet to whoever happens to be there, to the first who asks for one, no. Since we receive

many requests, it becomes automatic and natural to choose who will receive a gift and who won't, with selection criteria all of our own).

The tourist has the power to choose and enjoys exercising it, but as Piccolo points out his/her selection criteria are not necessarily logical and there are always some who lose out while others gain, as Guillebaud discovers to his cost.[28] Piccolo argues that the tourist's encounter with poverty is not an unplanned drawback of the journey, but a key motivation, suggesting that tourists are disappointed when recipients of gifts do not show sufficient gratitude (147). He highlights the contradiction between tourists' desire to travel to poorer countries in order to do good and their irritation at the constant assault of poverty, which quickly becomes insufferable (151–2). Like Ramazzotti and Guillebaud, then, he also explores the tension between expectation and experience, between a theoretical sense of morality and a practical context, which is always less straightforward than the theory.

While others focus on the ethical choice itself, Piccolo criticizes the fact of placing oneself in a situation where one has such a choice to make, since it means assuming a position of power. Responsibility is thrust on Ramazzotti and Guillebaud by their unexpected encounters with travellees, but Piccolo argues that this situation is not a surprise for travellers, but rather confirms their expectations and even desires. This is a radical but thought-provoking suggestion. While many travellers and tourists might disagree with Piccolo's view, it is undeniable that both come face-to-face with inequality with increasing frequency. Furthermore, Piccolo connects European tourism with the reverse journey – immigration to Europe – ending the chapter by returning to Italy: 'Eppure non c'è bisogno di compiere il nostro esotico-filantropico-compassionevole-sociologico viaggio in Sri Lanka o in India o in Africa. Non c'è bisogno di andare noi da loro, perché sono loro che vengono da noi. Tutto quello che cerchiamo è arrivato sotto casa' (155; Yet there is no need to undertake our exotic-philanthropic-compassionate-sociological journey in Sri Lanka or India or Africa. There is no need for us to go to them, because they come to us. Everything that we want has arrived on our doorstep). He cites the example of the gas pump attendant: 'Per non farti fare tre metri, lui è venuto da un paese lontano migliaia di chilometri' (155; So that you don't have to move three metres, he has come over from a country thousands of kilometres away). The roles are reversed: the tourist at home is the travellee and the immigrant is the traveller. Yet the encounter is still characterized by inequality, even more so in Piccolo's subsequent chapter, which describes Mister Piccolo's encounter with a Nigerian prostitute in Rome. Piccolo emphasizes the continuity between inequality at home and abroad, the continuity of responsibility and the role of travel, whether as a tourist or an immigrant, in bringing about these challenging encounters. As we found in Chapter 4, this continuity is usually absent from travel writing, which establishes sharp divisions between home and away, by eliminating the former from the text altogether.

Texts such as Ramazzotti's and Guillebaud's illustrate the complexities of challenging encounters in the context of day-to-day travel, but they remain relatively self-conscious self-representations. Piccolo represents a more self-centred tourist, but perhaps this characterization is more honest. *Allegro occidentale* is unusual in that, unlike most travel books where author, narrator and traveller-protagonist appear to coincide, there is a degree of distance between Francesco Piccolo, the author, and Mister Piccolo, the protagonist, who is presented as more of an alter ego for the author. This is suggested by the blurb on the book jacket: 'Chiamatelo Mister Piccolo. È vostro fratello. Il vostro simile occidentale che va alla scoperta del mondo' (Call him Mister Piccolo. He's your brother. Your fellow Westerner who has set out to discover the world), as well as in the acknowledgements, where 'I', the author, and 'Mister Piccolo' are two separate people (241). It is this distinction between Piccolo and his alter ego protagonist that allows room for a more critical stance. Mister Piccolo is someone who means well, but does not always carry his intentions into practice. Piccolo encourages his readers to identify with the protagonist as fellow tourists, using the first person plural to refer to a collective 'we' and addressing the readers directly as 'you', asking them to imagine themselves in similar situations. Ramazzotti, Guillebaud and other travel writers might not recognize themselves in Piccolo's representation of the Third World package tourist, but the traveller–tourist dichotomy is largely rhetorical. *Allegro occidentale* sheds all pretence at morality or altruism and recognizes the hypocrisy and the malaise of the encounter between the overprivileged tourist and the underprivileged travellee.

✷✷✷

There is an undeniable tension between leisure and poverty, which is all the more manifest in travel encounters between individuals. Since both tourism and the wealth gap are continually expanding, travellers frequently come face-to-face with those whose standard of living is considerably lower than their own, both on their journeys and at home, where they are the travellees and others are the travellers. Whatever the traveller may think about global inequality and its tangled causes and potential solutions, s/he must contend with the individual encountered, within the context of their meeting. Economic inequality places the traveller in a position of unmerited power and hence of responsibility, regardless of how desirable or undesirable that may be.

Travellers may travel to view and to experience, but they cannot expect to remain sealed in a bubble and indeed many deliberately reject such protective environments, as we have seen in Chapter 4. Challenging encounters limit travellers' freedom by forcing choices on them, but this is an inevitable part of the journey. Their simple presence and interaction with travellees entails a degree of responsibility and this is often communicated by the travellee's stare. The encounters in this chapter highlight the limitations of the individual traveller's sense of responsibility. Ramazzotti might not be personally responsible for eradicating Nigerian corruption, but his text briefly explores the idea that perhaps, for a short moment in his journey, he could be responsible for Joseph. The traveller moves quickly on, so the encounter and any sense of responsibility it may evoke are temporary. The travel narrative returns to the episode, however, if not literally then at least textually: the narrative explores the ethical implications of the encounter and renders the traveller responsible before the reader.

Chapter 7
ACCOMPANYING

Fino al momento in cui li ho visti, ora, i miei probabili futuri compagni di viaggio, non sapevo della loro esistenza, nemmeno la presupponevo. […] Essendo domani molto lontano da casa, solo, il mio gruppo si trasformerà immediatamente nella mia improvvisata famiglia, con naturalezza: con loro mangerò, dormirò, camminerò sotto il sole, guarderò il mondo che non ho mai visto. (Piccolo, 14–15)

(Until the moment I saw my probable future travelling companions, until now, I knew nothing of their existence; I did not even suspect it. […] Tomorrow, since I will be very far from home, alone, my group will immediately become my improvised family, naturally: with them I will eat, sleep, walk in the sun and see the world that I have never seen before.)

Sitting in a Malpensa Airport lounge, Francesco Piccolo speculates about the companions who will join him on his package tour, pondering how they will soon be transformed from unknown strangers into intimate acquaintances. Piccolo emphasizes the intensity and intimacy of sharing a journey and its powerful experiences with others, recognizing that such connections form rapidly, but also dissolve equally rapidly at journey's end (15–16). Travel is a temporary and special state, qualities that shape all travel encounters, but perhaps those in this chapter more than others, since the characters who accompany travellers share the intense experiences of the journey.

The typical protagonist of travel writing is a solitary, independent traveller who sets out alone and returns solely in the company of his/her experiences and memories. As David Espey puts it: 'Travel writers tend to face travel as they face writing – alone.'[1] This solitude is usually a deliberate choice, defining a particular shape of journey. Bernard Ollivier, for example, insists on travelling alone since, despite being vulnerable and lonely, he believes his solitude enables encounters (e.g., *Marche I*, 262). As we have seen in previous chapters, the supposedly solitary traveller is rarely completely alone and far from being independent, in fact depends greatly on the advice and hospitality of travellees. Even Ollivier admits that company can have its advantages; isolated by his lack of Chinese, he imagines fictional characters for a novel to accompany him as he walks (e.g., *Marche III*, 208 and 220). Later he accepts human company, pairing up with artist François Dermaut to produce the illustrated *Carnets d'une longue marche*. Tiziano Terzani praises paper companions: the tales of travellers past that provide company and opinion (*Buonanotte*, 359). Nicolas Bouvier meanwhile, crippled by loneliness in Sri Lanka, resorts to insects; as he explains: 'on s'offre les compagnies qu'on peut' (you find whatever company you can) (*Poisson*, 799). Even determinedly independent travellers need some company, but when linguistic and cultural barriers become insurmountable it can seem easier to befriend a dung beetle.

Companions who accompany the traveller for any length of time are usually brought along from home. These are friends, colleagues or partners who participate in the organization and planning of the journey from a start that precedes the beginning of the text. The relationship between traveller and companion may be a long-established friendship, as between Bouvier and childhood friend Thierry Vernet in *L'usage du monde*; or a romantic relationship, as with Corrado Ruggeri and girlfriend Carla in *Farfalle sul Mekong*, or Nicole-Lise Bernheim and her unnamed partner in *Chambres d'ailleurs*. Travellers join forces with other professionals, including other writers, photographers or artists: Jean-Claude Guillebaud collaborates with photographer Raymond Depardon to produce *La colline des anges* and *La porte des larmes*, François Maspero travels with photographer Anaïk Frantz in *Les passagers du Roissy-Express*, Gianni Celati accompanies documentary maker Jean Talon in *Avventure in Africa*, and writers Alberto Moravia and Pier Paolo Pasolini travel together in India, as they recount in their respective narratives *Un'idea dell'India* (1961) and *L'odore dell'India* (1962).[2] Although the actual moment of encounter between traveller and companion usually precedes the journey and is therefore not a travel experience in itself, these characters are travellees and their company is a feature of the journey.

Acquiring travelling companions en route, following unplanned encounters, requires a degree of spontaneity that many itineraries do not permit. As a result fewer companions are picked up on the road, and few for any length of time. Travellers who are always on the move tend to have short-lived encounters, as discussed in Chapter 4, but they are constantly in the company of others, always moving in and out of spaces shared with travellees. Travellees are those who cross travellers' paths, but they are often on their own paths, making every traveller his/her own travellee's travellee. James Clifford reminds us: 'A host of servants, helpers, companions, guides, and bearers have been excluded from the role of proper travelers because of their race and class, and because theirs seemed to be a dependent status in relation to the supposed independence of the individualist, bourgeois voyager.'[3] Mobility is often the norm for those who guide and interpret, and many of the characters encountered in Chapter 3 accompany the travellers, not to mention the riders of rickshaws and drivers of other vehicles. While roles overlap, I focus here on companions who serve only or predominantly that function, rather than those who accompany incidentally to another activity, since these have been covered in previous chapters.

Despite the potential intensity of relationships between travellers and their companions, the latter are often surprisingly absent from travel narratives. Yet their relative presence, or absence, contributes to shaping the concept of travel, both in the sense of demarcating the boundaries of the genre and in defining the identity of travellers as travellers. I begin this chapter by examining the companion's absence, focusing initially on the grammatical visibility and invisibility of companions brought from home and then considering how their absence reflects the limitations of the genre. In Chapter 2, I briefly discussed how tourist characters function in travel writing as opposites against whom traveller characters are constructed and the second section of this chapter examines parallels with the treatment of companion characters. The final section turns to chance companions, those met on the road, whose representation differs from that of companions brought from home, but who also serve to map out the travel in travel writing.

Absent Friends

'That most ambiguous of personal pronouns'

'Les voyageurs se [sont] montrés, dans l'ensemble, assez peu loquaces sur leurs compagnons de voyage' (Travellers have shown themselves, on the whole, to be quite unforthcoming about their travelling companions), remarks Gérard Cogez, citing Claude Lévi-Strauss as an example.[4] Travelling companions, whether brought along from home or met en route, move in and out of visibility in the text, regardless of their presence beside the traveller during the journey. The travelling companion from home is often conspicuously absent, a mere detail among other travel preparations, almost part of the luggage rather than a fully-fledged character. Alisdair Pettinger examines the representation of travelling companions through the use of pronouns, paying particular attention to the first person plural, 'we', which he describes as 'that most ambiguous of personal pronouns', since it is not always clear who 'we' includes.[5] He suggests that the use of 'we' 'would seem to frustrate the conventional ambition of travel writers to represent their own unique experiences (and its corollary: to render generic the experiences of those they meet on the way)'.[6] Pettinger focuses on companions met en route, who share the common spaces of public transport with the traveller. In his examples he shows how fellow passengers are alternately included in 'we', or excluded as 'they'. For Pettinger, 'we' emphasizes shared experience and, to a degree, breaks down the opposition between traveller and travellee.[7] I will consider this kind of interaction in Section 3, but here I wish to examine further uses of 'we' and other pronouns in the treatment of companions who accompany the traveller from the beginning. While, as Pettinger suggests, the move from 'they' to 'we' is one of positive inclusion and recognition for travellees, precisely because it recognizes them as travellers, the use of 'we' for companions brought from home tends, on the contrary, to efface them from the text. 'We' absorbs companions, making them invisible and denying them the separate identity afforded by the third person. In Marco Aime's travel book *Le radici nella sabbia*, for example, his anonymous companions are only ever present as 'we'.[8] He refers to 'nostro gruppetto' (our little group) without identifying any individuals and even dedicates the book to 'tutte le persone che ho incontrato e che mi hanno accompagnato lungo le strade del Sahel' (all the people whom I met and who accompanied me along the roads of the Sahel) without further elaboration (*Radici*, 40 and vii).

Moravia and Pasolini's parallel accounts of their shared journey to India provide contrasting examples in how they treat companions. Moravia makes no mention of Pasolini and Elsa Morante by name, though they are sometimes present as 'we', but he goes further, effacing them altogether by using the impersonal third person 'si'. Pasolini's account of the journey is more personal and makes occasional mention of Moravia. The two styles are illustrated in the following examples, describing the same visit to the funeral pyres of Benares: 'Irresistibile, si insinua nella mente l'idea irriverente che, una volta giunti accanto al rogo, ci si potrà almeno riscaldare al fuoco il corpo intirizzito. Ma una volta arrivati e sbarcati, questo pensiero non pare più tanto irriverente perché si vede che…' (Moravia, *Idea*, 29; Irresistibly, the irreverent idea slips into the mind that, once arrived next to the pyre, one can at least warm one's chilled body by the fire. But once arrived and disembarked, this thought no longer seems so irreverent because one sees that…). 'Siccome l'aria è fredda, Moravia e io ci avviciniamo istintivamente ai roghi, e, avvicinandoci, ci rendiamo presto conto…' (Pasolini, *Odore*, 110; Since the air is cold, Moravia and I draw instinctively closer to the pyres, and, as we approach, we soon realize that…). Moravia's impersonal 'si' speaks to the general rather than the particular, including the reader more than his companions, while Pasolini identifies the individuals present by name and as 'we'. Moravia's style emphasizes the travel experience, but also gives India a timeless quality, as though the same events could be lived again and again by different travellers. Pasolini focuses on specific, subjective details, giving a more personal and individual tone to his text and to the characters and places he describes.

Bernheim's *Chambres d'ailleurs* and Maspero's *Les passagers du Roissy-Express* merit separate attention for their unconventional use of pronouns: Bernheim uses the second person singular to refer to her travelling companion, while Maspero refers to himself and his companion Anaïk Frantz in the third person.

'Pour toi, mon compagnon de route' (*Chambres*, 7; For you, my companion on the road) reads Bernheim's dedication to 'toi', the unnamed partner who accompanies her around Asia. Not only is the book dedicated to him, but throughout he is referred to in the second person, implying that the text also addresses him. The first time Bernheim uses the second person, it presents a certain confusion: 'Je suis à Tokyo, au bout du monde et je suis avec toi' (11; I am in Tokyo, at the end of the world and I'm with you). Here 'toi' could be the reader who does, in a sense, accompany the traveller through the act of reading. This sentence comes at the end of a passage where Bernheim uses the first person plural to talk about the journey in retrospect, so there is less potential for confusion, particularly taking the dedication into account. The text becomes clearer with the next mention of 'toi' a few pages later: 'J'embrasse ton épaule, bonne nuit' (16; I kiss your shoulder, goodnight). The reader thereafter automatically reads 'tu', 'toi' and the second person forms of verbs and pronouns as though they were describing a character, *toi*, not addressing the reader.

Bernheim hints at the intimacy of her relationship with her companion: 'Peu avant l'apparition du soleil, je m'éveille à demi, je m'approche de toi. L'amour sur la plage' (*Chambres*, 26; A little before the sun appears, I half wake up, I draw close to you. Love on the beach). Such details, along with the use of the second person, give the reader the impression of reading a private text, a love letter even, written by Bernheim for *toi*. The final pages of the first edition are also devoted to *toi* and their relationship: the ups and downs of love, hate, desire (253–4). By ending on this note Bernheim emphasizes the importance of her relationship with her companion alongside, or even above, the journey itself. The second edition carries an additional epilogue, reflecting back on the 13 years since the book was first published. The relationship has ended, but she continues to write about *toi* in the second person and addresses her final sentence to him: 'Nous avons fait un beau voyage et je t'en remercie' (258; We had a wonderful journey and I thank you for it).

Bernheim rarely uses the third person for *toi*, and even suggests that *toi* sounds strange as 'lui', when they separate for a while in Nepal: 'Je passe au "Tukche Peak", notre ancien hôtel, vérifier si tu n'es pas rentré. Le patron me dit "non, pas de nouvelles de LUI". Lui, Him, mon Homme, avec H majuscule... je le remercie gravement' (*Chambres*, 173; I pass by 'Tukche Peak', our old hotel, to check whether you have returned yet. The manager says 'no, no news of HIM'. Lui, Him, my Man, with a capital M... I thank him solemnly). This emphasizes the sense of intimacy she creates with the use of 'tu': *toi* as a distanced, separate third person is unnatural; he is the 'you' to whom she addresses herself, part of an exclusive 'we'. However, she does often write about *toi* as though in the third person, describing his actions like those of a character, not a reader: 'Un homme te parle, curieux de rencontrer les inconnus venus de loin' (58; A man speaks to you, curious to meet strangers come from afar). For the reader, this reinforces the sense of *toi* as a character. *Chambres d'ailleurs* combines the intimacy of private correspondence addressed to a lover, with a public, descriptive travel account, in which *toi* is a character. This draws the reader towards the narrator, creating closeness between them, as though speaking over the shoulder of *toi* the companion.

Maspero offers a different solution in *Passagers*: rather than absorbing his companion Anaïk into the first person plural, he instead makes François, his autobiographical protagonist, accompany her in the third person as 'il' and together as 'ils'.[9] While the text of *Passagers* apparently presents Maspero's own account of the journey, he represents his autobiographical protagonist as a character alongside Anaïk, as though seen from a third viewpoint: 'Ils ont fixé pour ce soir un rendez-vous à une amie parisienne. En attendant, Anaïk va continuer seule sa promenade dans les Beaudottes. François la gratifie de consignes de sécurité' (92; Tonight they have arranged a meeting with a Parisian friend. Meanwhile Anaïk continues her walk in the Beaudottes alone. François graces her with security advice).[10] The use of the third person places the two protagonists on an equal footing and gives the text the tone of a novel. Maspero only reverts to the first person singular in the postscript, added in 1993, in which he reflects on the reception of the book, but at this point the change in pronoun serves to clarify the break between the travel text and this additional commentary (331–41). Kathryn Jones suggests that Maspero's use of the third person is a strategy that allows other voices to be heard: 'In contrast to most traditional travel writing which centers on a first-person narrator, the decentered third-person narration of *Les Passagers du Roissy-Express* facilitates the inclusion of these other viewpoints, voices, and intertexts, the most significant of which being the supplementary narration provided by Frantz's photographs.'[11] The use of the third person for François does not prevent Anaïk from disappearing into 'ils' in the same way that travelling companions become invisible in 'we', but her photographs remind us of her constant presence and provide their own parallel account of the journey. As well as granting space and importance to Anaïk's voice, Maspero's choice of style also accommodates the voices of many travellees. In the final pages of the text the narrative deteriorates into a list of scenes, each beginning with the phrase 'On les a vus' (318–26; They were seen; or literally [some] one saw them). This reinforces the impression that the story is told from the viewpoint of a third person: 'on les a vus' is an impersonal construction, but it is also active, with 'on' the subject, the travellee, watching or staring at them ('les'), the objects. In this way Maspero acknowledges the interactivity of the journey – how it is something done to the traveller as much as done by the traveller.

A question of genre

Maspero gives some background to his collaboration with Anaïk, explaining how they met and describing her work as a photographer in detail (16–19). Bernheim, however, gives no context to her relationship with *toi*, and tells us nothing about him, not even his name. Although she is unusual in not naming a companion who is otherwise relatively present in her narrative, she is quite typical in giving him no biography or history. The travelling companion often has no background, no context and even no body, but this absence tells us something about travel writing as a genre. A close examination of Bouvier's treatment of Thierry in *L'usage du monde* will help to elucidate the significance of the absent companion.

Bouvier opens *L'usage du monde* by quoting a letter from Thierry, who had set out ahead of him. The letter describes Thierry's travel experiences in Bosnia: an encounter with a local farmer, the merchandise in the market, listening to gypsies' music, and ends with the exclamation 'L'Orient quoi!' (*Usage*, 79; Is this the Orient or what!). Given its position in the text, but also its content and style, Thierry's letter sets the tone for the book. The rest of the chapter describes the travel project the pair had devised, before moving on to more general reflections on travel and to Bouvier's own situation. The following chapter opens with their meeting in Belgrade, including a brief physical description of Thierry and his current state of mind, his thoughts and doubts about the trip. The description introduces Thierry to the reader and suggests how Bouvier finds his friend after his initial period of travel: 'Le coiffeur de Travnik n'avait pas dû le voir souvent. Avec ses ailerons sur les oreilles et ses petits yeux bleus, il avait l'air d'un jeune requin folâtre et harassé' (*Usage*, 83; The barber in Travnik can't have seen him often. With the tufts over his ears and his little blue eyes he looked like a young shark, lively but exhausted). In the final pages of the text we find another letter from Thierry, now with his fiancée Flo, for whom he had abandoned his journey with Bouvier. This letter, sent from Sri Lanka, provides another list of exotic sights to tempt Bouvier to join them on the island. Thierry therefore frames Bouvier's text with his own texts providing both an initial impetus for Bouvier at the start of his journey and a further call to continue travelling beyond *Usage*. The initial pages emphasize Thierry's presence alongside Bouvier and his collaboration in their common travel plans, suggesting that this companion will be as present in the text as in the journey. Although Thierry and Bouvier rarely part and only go their separate ways towards the very end of the narrative, this presence is not reflected in the written text.[12]

Immediately following Bouvier and Thierry's reunion in Belgrade, they are grammatically united as 'nous'. Symbolically this takes place when Bouvier moves into Thierry's lodgings, which becomes their shared abode. Bouvier describes their neighbours and how they treat the pair: 'Toujours prêts à nous aider, à nous servir d'interprètes, à nous prêter une machine à écrire' (*Usage*, 84; Always ready to help us, to serve as interpreters for us, to lend us a typewriter). Here Bouvier depicts himself and Thierry as one entity, which continues as he describes their routine: 'À cinq heures du matin, le soleil d'août nous trouait les paupières et nous allions nous baigner dans la Save' (88; At 5am the August sun would pierce our eyelids and we would go to bathe in the Sava). For the rest of the text 'je' and 'nous' alternate, with the addition of 'on' for more general comments on travel. What is largely missing is 'il': Thierry.

Thierry is only mentioned by name 72 times in the whole text and even when he is mentioned, he is rarely the focus of attention, which centres instead on his interlocutor, or some cultural aspect that his actions bring to the fore. For example, Bouvier describes Thierry ordering artistic materials to be sent to him in Tabriz, but the passage focuses on the idiosyncrasies of the postmaster, who allows Thierry to see his parcel, but not to take it until the director has returned to give his permission (*Usage*, 212). Later on, when the pair are on the road in Iran, we find: 'En Perse où l'on s'autorise pourtant bien des choses, il est interdit de péter, fût-ce en plein désert. Quand Thierry qui somnole sur le bat-flanc, à demi gâteux de fatigue, enfreint cet usage, la patronne se retourne comme une vipère et le menace de l'index' (289; In Persia, where many things are permitted, it is forbidden to fart, even in the middle of the desert. When Thierry, who is dozing against the partition, half gaga with sleep, infringes this custom, the landlady turns like a viper and points her finger at him threateningly). The paragraph then continues with further description of the landlady. Thierry is quoted in direct speech no more than half a dozen times and only the odd single sentence is given, usually expressing an opinion of a person or situation, as when Bouvier is unexpectedly hugged by an old beggar: 'Thierry riait aux larmes: "Vous auriez dû vous voir, vous aviez l'air de danser le tango"' (191; Thierry laughed till he cried: 'You should have seen yourselves, you looked like you were dancing the tango').

Bouvier is not inclined to outpourings of sentiment about Thierry, though they were very close friends, but when separation becomes an issue he does express his appreciation of their team.[13] When Thierry decides that he will abandon Bouvier earlier than expected to join Flo, Bouvier writes: 'J'étais quand même désemparé: cette équipe était parfaite et j'avais toujours imaginé que nous bouclerions la boucle ensemble' (*Usage*, 208; I was nonetheless distraught: this team was perfect and I had always imagined that we would loop the loop together). After an unsentimental goodbye he adds: 'Je pensais […] à Thierry: le temps d'Asie coule plus large que le nôtre, et cette association parfaite me semblait avoir duré dix ans' (360; I thought […] of Thierry: Asian time flows more fully than our own, and this perfect partnership seemed to have lasted ten years). These comments, along with the various moments along the trip when the two support each other through difficult moments (taking turns to nurse each other through illness, to drive when the other is tired), indicate a solidarity and partnership that is stronger than suggested by Thierry's presence in the text.

Thierry's relative absence from *L'usage du monde* raises the question of why travel writers are so often silent on the subject of their travelling companions. Debbie Lisle discusses the separation of public and private selves, arguing that 'travel writers construct themselves as "public" figures who form impressions about a place by revealing only selected and strategic aspects of their "private" selves'.[14] Since travel writers usually keep details about their private lives out of their texts it is logical that this should extend to the private lives of their travelling companions, especially when those companions are family members, close friends or lovers. When Bouvier joins Thierry and Flo in Sri Lanka, recounted in *Le poisson-scorpion* (1981), he does not write about their reunion, which Olivier Bauer explains thus: 'Trop pudique, trop intime, il n'écrira plus un mot sur son ami' (Too discreet, too private, he will not write another word about his friend).[15] This shyness is symptomatic of the autobiographical nature of travel writing; it suggests wariness about divulging too much of one's own life and the lives of those who are not only characters in texts, but also real people, lest the text disrupt the relationship that exceeds it. Aside from personal motivations, which are external to the text anyway, I would also argue that the treatment of the travelling companion enhances the authenticity and reality effect of the text. The very fact of withholding the relationship from the text implies that there is something significant to withhold, implies the authenticity of the relationship, not only between traveller and companion as characters, but also as real people. The absence of the companion from the text then, ironically, creates the impression for the reader that the companion is important in the real life of the traveller-writer. This might sound contradictory in a case such as Bernheim, who narrates some intimate moments, but she mystifies her relationship with *toi* in other ways: he has no name, no physical appearance, no profession and we never learn anything about the origin, nature or context of their relationship. I should also clarify that the matter of whether traveller and companion are based on real people, or how much character and person correspond, is incidental to this reality effect, which depends not on the reality outside the text, but precisely on the effect created by the text.

The treatment of travelling companions is not simply a matter of autobiographical reticence, however; it is also a question of genre. The relationships between travellers and the companions they bring with them both precede and exceed the text. Unlike many of the other encounters we have considered, they do not belong exclusively to either the journey or the text. Those other travel encounters are not, as a general rule, great love stories; families are neither formed nor broken within the space of travel texts. Lisle argues that the travel writer is silent about his/her private life in order to better maintain a subject position as an autonomous traveller.[16] This identity is central to the travel book: if the travel writer's personal life encroaches too much on the account of the journey, then the text becomes something else: a memoir or autobiography. Lisle herself hints at this interpretation, writing about Paul Theroux: 'The reader gets little information on his life as a teacher, a husband or a father – these are stories for another genre perhaps, but not for the travelogue.'[17] Travel, as it is understood in most travel writing, is a period of limbo, when the traveller is absent from home and all that home entails, including family commitments. The traveller severs those personal links to part and remakes them on his/her return.[18]

The experience of travel described in travel writing differs from tourism in this way. Travel may take tourists away from home and work, but it does not necessarily separate them from family and friends. In fact, holidays are often a time when relationships, such as family ties, are reinforced. This brings us back to Ning Wang's concept of existential authenticity, discussed in Chapter 2. Among tourists, 'interpersonal' existential authenticity tends to occur predominantly within the tourist group (i.e., with the tourist's travelling companions), while travel writing usually represents a time when family ties are temporarily severed. If the traveller is accompanied by a family member or close friend then the relationship is not broken by spatial distance, but rather by its omission from the text. The absence of the travelling companion from the text therefore both emphasizes the authenticity of the relationship and sustains the generic demands of travel writing.

Alter Ego or Mirror?

Although companions are often comparatively absent from travel texts, they are not always completely eclipsed. While their absence might reflect the authenticity of the relationship between traveller-writer and companion, their occasional presence often tells us more about the traveller him/herself. Bauer suggests that Thierry is Bouvier's alter ego: 'Dans le récit que Nicolas Bouvier fait de son voyage, Vernet apparaît très rapidement comme un jumeau psychologique, une sorte d'altérité de l'apprenti écrivain dans les arts et dans le voyage' (In the narrative that Bouvier writes about his journey, Vernet appears very quickly as a psychological twin, a sort of double for the apprentice writer in the arts and in travel).[19] Bauer's analysis certainly reflects what we know about their friendship from other sources, as well as the pair's complementary activities as writer and artist; although he does overemphasize the occasional moments of solidarity in the text, when their experiences or sentiments correspond, such as the powerful and unexpected sense of malaise that they share in Isfahan (*Usage*, 271). There are also moments of discord, for example when Bouvier envies Thierry's letters from Flo (182), or is annoyed that Thierry is able to sleep while he suffers insomnia (295). The abundant use of 'nous' and absorption of Thierry into this common pronoun generally emphasizes their unity. When Thierry is mentioned alone, the focus is usually on his interlocutor or some cultural practice, as I have shown above, rather than his relation to Bouvier.

Travelling companions in other texts do seem to function as alter egos for the travellers, such as Jean Talon in Celati's *Avventure in Africa*. Although Jean and his relationship with Celati are, once more, given no context, *Avventure* does document the documentary maker's actions and reactions throughout their journey, following Jean's unsuccessful efforts to organize his film. In fact, Jean is often the one represented directing the course of events, while Celati tags along, which leads to some tension when Celati feels that Jean is taking command, ironically calling him 'capitano' (captain): 'io non ho obbedito agli ordini del mio capitano' (118; I did not obey my captain's orders). Jean's occupations and preoccupations are noted casually throughout the course of the journey, as though they form part of the travel scenery or the weather. This representation of Jean accords with Charles Klopp's description of the narrative style of *Avventure*: '[Celati] limits himself to describing what he encounters without ascribing a narrative or dramatic structure to it. Instead, Celati, deadpan, simply records what he sees.'[20] While Celati represents himself and Jean bickering mildly and occasionally disagreeing about the style and direction of the journey, there are many common points to both characters. They are both rather bumbling tourists, suffering the same disorientations and irritations, but often at different points in the journey. In this sense Jean acts as a double for Celati: another uncomprehending European lost in the African continent, reinforcing Celati's own self-representation.

The use of 'we' for traveller and companion can render the latter invisible, but it does emphasize complicity and unity between the two. Mentioning the companion separately can create a similar effect, as Guillebaud demonstrates in his representation of Raymond. Like Bouvier and Thierry, Guillebaud and Raymond complement each other in their activities as writer and photographer.[21] Guillebaud highlights their professional differences, focusing on the issues of representation particular to their respective disciplines, for example in the chapter 'L'empire des mots' (The empire of words) (*Porte*, 706–7). However, he also emphasizes their unity, especially in terms of their parallel struggles with representation: 'Quelquefois, une absurde pudeur nous retient. La toile de fond qui défile aux fenêtres du train comme une "transparence" cinématographique est d'une splendeur trop attendue pour que nous osions en parler. Y compris entre nous' (*Colline*, 467; Sometimes, an absurd modesty holds us back. The backdrop that unwinds past the train windows like a cinematographic back projection is of a splendour too long awaited for us to dare speak about it, including between ourselves). Here the writer shows the two travellers responding as one to the same scene. When Guillebaud introduces Raymond into the text on his own, the writer often reinforces his own opinions by showing his companion in agreement: 'Ni Raymond ni moi n'avions imaginé cela' (*Porte*, 714; Neither Raymond nor I had imagined that), 'Ni Raymond ni moi ne songeons à sourire' (732; Neither Raymond nor I would think of smiling). When travelling with the guide Nguyen T. D. (see Chapter 3), Guillebaud shows Raymond also objecting to the choice of itinerary and packing away his camera (*Colline*, 482). Thus the character Raymond strengthens Guillebaud's own position, both through their parallel struggles with representation and by showing them in agreement.

Elsewhere, the figure of the companion serves to define aspects of the traveller's identity by opposition. This is exemplified by Pasolini in his representation of Moravia. The differences between the two writers emerge clearly in the nature of their respective texts: Moravia's *Idea* is a series of well-structured chapters of regular length, discussing various aspects of Indian culture, religion, politics and history in a rather didactic fashion, while Pasolini's *Odore* is a less structured and more spontaneous mixture of impressions and encounters. As we have seen, Pasolini is notably absent from Moravia's account, but Moravia does make the odd appearance in *Odore*, where he cuts a figure that contrasts with Pasolini's autobiographical protagonist. Pasolini draws attention to the differences between their travel texts, telling the reader not to expect detailed information about Indian religion from his own writing, but to read Moravia's articles instead, citing the latter's careful documentation and clear ideas (Pasolini, 32). He also contrasts their ways of travelling: while Moravia takes refuge in the hotel, Pasolini chooses to wander the nocturnal streets: 'a questo punto Moravia decide che è ora di essere stanchi, e, col suo meraviglioso igienismo, prende, e volta deciso verso il Taj Mahal. Ma io no.

Io finché non sono stremato (ineconomico come sono) non disarmo' [Pasolini, 15; at this point Moravia decides that it is time to be tired and, with his marvellous punctiliousness, he takes off and turns decisively towards the Taj Mahal. But I do not. Not until I am exhausted (uneconomical as I am) will I disarm].

Maspero's representation of Anaïk and François also illustrates differences between their styles as travellers. In Aulnay, for example, he refuses an invitation to tea, which Anaïk would have accepted, and later on he is nervous of the men who seem to be following them, while Anaïk is more relaxed: '"Peut-être, dit-elle, qu'ils veulent me demander de faire leur portrait et qu'ils n'osent pas?" Peut-être. François voudrait rejoindre Garonor avant la nuit' (49 and 60; 'Perhaps', she says, 'they want to ask me to take their picture and they don't dare?' Perhaps. François would like to return to Garonor before nightfall). Maspero represents himself as the more nervous traveller, and Anaïk as the one who is more open to encounters, particularly with people from a variety of social backgrounds. Anaïk is the character who facilitates many of the encounters that people Maspero's text, enriching their journey. Jones argues that Maspero's self-portrait is part of his inclusive strategy: 'In line with the author's ethical and humanist agenda, it is significant that he creates for himself the character of François, the prim and anxious traveler.'[22]

On his journey through Thailand and Vietnam Ruggeri is accompanied by his girlfriend Carla, who is introduced on the third page of the text as 'la mia compagna' (11; my partner). From the beginning, Carla's character contrasts with the attitudes and behaviour of Ruggeri's autobiographical protagonist, particularly in terms of gender stereotypes. Like companions in other texts, no context is given for Ruggeri's relationship with Carla; she has no identity other than as his 'compagna'. Ruggeri only gives her physical characteristics to juxtapose them with his own: when the two have massages he reports that their masseuses are amused by his tall, fat, hirsute form in comparison with Carla, who is 'bella, bionda, magra' (15; beautiful, blonde, slim). The contrast in their approaches to travel is established early on, when the couple are faced with the prospect of eating dog meat in a Thai mountain village:

Carla quasi urla. Non riesce a guardarmi mentre mangio le lumache o le rane, figuriamoci se riesce a sopportare l'idea di addentare un pezzo di cane arrostito. Poverina, mi guarda con l'aria smarrita di chi capisce che non c'è soluzione [...]. Io, invece, trovo tutto molto divertente e perfino eccitante. (25)

(Carla almost screams. She can't watch me while I eat snails or frogs, so just imagine how she'd tolerate the idea of biting into a piece of roasted dog. Poor thing, she looks at me with the bewildered air of someone who realizes that there is no way out [...]. I, on the other hand, find everything very entertaining and even exciting).

Carla plays the role of the fearful cautious woman, so that Ruggeri can be the adventurous risk-taking male, as he makes clear when talking to John, one of their guides: '"lei non ha la mia stessa sete d'avventura, non ama mettersi alla prova duramente, preferisce cose più soft"' (88; 'she doesn't have the same thirst for adventure as me, she doesn't like to challenge herself too harshly, she prefers softer things'). Carla comes into her own when she is able to indulge in female stereotypes: '"Shopping!!!" L'urlo del consumismo nell'ultima frontiera del comunismo è la gioia di Carla e la mia disperazione' (217; 'Shopping!!!' The cry of consumerism in the last frontier of communism is Carla's joy and my despair). Once more, the figure of the companion is used as a mirror against which to construct a contrasting traveller identity for the autobiographical protagonist.

As I have discussed in Chapters 1 and 2, travel writers use the figure of the tourist to emphasize their own identity as travellers. Tourists as characters are largely absent from travel books, since travellers usually make a point of avoiding them and the destinations where they congregate. When they do appear, tourists are almost inevitably found committing some travel sin. Such representations allow travel writers to construct a more laudable portrait for their traveller-protagonists, in direct contrast with the tourists. Companions therefore fulfil a similar function when they are treated as opposites that help to define the traveller's own identity. Pasolini, Maspero and Ruggeri all use their companions to assert their own style as travellers. This is particularly clear in Ruggeri, where the distinction he constructs between his protagonist and Carla not only exemplifies stereotypical gender binaries, but also the dichotomy between the traveller and the tourist: the traveller as adventurer, the tourist as consumer. Pasolini and Maspero are both subtler and kinder to their companions; the latter even represents Anaïk as the more daring and himself as the more anxious traveller. As Jones suggests, Maspero's strategy is one of inclusion; he deliberately decentres his protagonist in order to bring forth the voices of other characters.

There is nothing unusual about defining self-identity in opposition to another. It is a common feature of travel writing to compare the writer's home culture with those encountered, defining the one in contrast to the others. Encounter is central to the definition of identity: we have already examined how travel writers react to cultural differences in hospitality, eye contact, racial identities and the use of rickshaws. Yet encounters with travelling companions and tourists are usually encounters with culturally similar others.[23] Like travellers, both tourists and companions travel for leisure and both are therefore used to define the traveller's identity specifically as a traveller, through the play of similarity and difference. This reminds us that travel writing is concerned with the ethics of travel, with evaluating different ways of travelling and exploring answers to the question 'How should one travel?' Pasolini emphasizes spontaneous encounter and sensory perception, Maspero implies the benefits of an openness that he recognizes he may lack, Ruggeri admires masculine adventure. These styles are not outlined in isolation, but in comparison with the styles of other travellers: both their own companions and other tourists.

Chance Companions

It is perhaps no coincidence that Piccolo first meets his companions at an airport terminal, as he describes in the quotation opening this chapter, since transport hubs and means are rich with opportunities for encounter. Pettinger examines the shared spaces of public transport, where travellers are accompanied by and interact with travellees who are also travellers.[24] Long train and bus journeys offer ample time to make acquaintances, though the plane is more controversial as a space of encounter. We have already seen, in Chapter 2, how Paolo Rumiz and Terzani dismiss air travel, but there is no reason intrinsic to the aircraft itself why the plane should not favour sociability, given the forced immobility and close proximity of its passengers. Terzani himself meets a couple of Turkish diplomats on a flight to Turkmenistan (*Buonanotte*, 315). Although travellers share transport with many others, we might ask to what extent they actually accompany each other. Pettinger makes an important distinction between co-presence and interactivity.[25] Although he studies both, I would suggest that for an encounter to happen, mere co-presence is not sufficient. The verb 'to accompany' can imply a degree of passivity, but it also implies a degree of intention. Paolo Proietti suggests that encounter with 'l'Altro' (the Other) is most likely to happen during periods of actual movement, but he complains that these moments are usually omitted from travel texts.[26] I am less convinced that movement is more conducive to encounter than stability; in fact I would suggest that the stability of the traveller within the movement of vehicles or aircraft favours conviviality. Furthermore, interaction between passengers on public transport often occurs when the vehicle is unexpectedly stable: because of delay or breakdown. Pettinger suggests that passengers are drawn together to face shared dangers or resist authority.[27] Sergio Ramazzotti's journey through Africa on public transport provides him with ample opportunity to interact with other passengers and some become significant companions, accompanying him for long stretches of his route. In *Le grand festin de l'Orient*

Olivier Weber is accompanied for most of his journey from Venice to Kabul by Barmak, an Afghan living in France, whom he initially meets on the boat from Italy to Greece. These two texts offer examples of companions met by chance, providing a comparison with the depiction of companions brought from home.

The climactic section of *Vado verso il Capo* covers the most difficult part of Ramazzotti's journey, taking him through Mobutu's Zaire. This is a kind of *via crucis*, where he and his fellow travellers must face pushing a lorry through the thick mud of what they refer to as Mobutu's 'capolavoro' (masterpiece), the Route Nationale 1 (*Vado*, 193–5). Ramazzotti emphasizes the friendship between himself and the other passengers, describing how they adopt him 'come mascotte di bordo: un pazzo o un disperato che, come molti di loro, deve andare con questo trabiccolo […] fino in fondo al paese e oltre, in Zambia' (187; as an on-board mascot: a crazy or desperate man who, like many of them, must travel on this wreck […] to the end of the country and beyond, into Zambia). He is both one of them, sharing their uncomfortable journey, and separate, adopted as their mascot, reflecting his racial and cultural difference. The companionship is sealed when Ramazzotti gives away all the mandarins he has bought and receives back a whole fruit made of donated segments: 'uno dei più bei regali che mi sia capitato di ricevere' (199; one of the most beautiful gifts that I have ever received). Ramazzotti originally planned to cross Africa following the Paris–Le Cap rally route, but using only public transport in contrast to the drivers who travel enclosed in their private vehicles. His solidarity with fellow bus and lorry passengers is a mark of the success of his project. He does maintain a certain distance, in order to sustain a representation of Africa as other and exotic, and to situate himself as witness to the problems he encounters, such as the lamentable state of Zaire. In this role he testifies to his fellow passengers' anger: 'Molte voci imprecano contro il Maresciallo Capitano. "Ladro." "Bastardo." "Guarda in che condizioni…" […]. È la marcia dell'odio' (194; Many voices curse the Captain Marshall. 'Thief.' 'Bastard.' 'Look at the state in which…' […]. It is the march of hatred). The alternation between unity and separation is illustrated in the episode when Ramazzotti and the other passengers push their lorry. At first Ramazzotti describes himself and the passengers separately, in the first person and the third person plural respectively: 'Sessanta mani svegliate dal sonno si appoggiano contro il cassone, si infilano sotto i parafanghi per spingere […]. Appoggio anch'io le mie mani' (193; Sixty hands woken from sleep are placed against the truck and slip under the mudguards to push […]. I also place my hands). He also makes ample use of the impersonal 'si', but on the following page he joins with the passengers grammatically in a collective 'we' effort: 'Spingiamo e spingiamo, spingiamo per un'eternità' (194; We push and we push, we push for an eternity).

Weber describes his first meeting with Barmak on the boat and devotes several pages to the Afghan and his journey, his acrobatics and devotion to the Sufi poet Rumi (*Festin*, 21–5). Weber's travel writing is unusual because of the degree to which he effaces his own presence, opinions and emotions. His travel texts are narrated in the first person and follow his autobiographical protagonist, so his personal point of view colours his narration, but he avoids writing directly about himself and especially his feelings, apart from the odd occasion that arouses a particularly strong sense of fear or wonder, such as when he visits Bamyan, a few years after the destruction of the Buddha statues (359). Weber focuses on the reactions of other characters in place of his own, and although he does not quote Barmak directly, he reports his opinions: in Istanbul, for example, 'Barmak dévore la ville comme un spectateur affamé' (89; Barmak devours the city like a famished spectator), or giving his views on iconoclasm: 'Les mirages, Barmak y songe en chemin car l'iconoclasme d'Orient s'est souvent défié des images trompeuses, des reflets incertains, des miroitements sauvages. L'interdit vient sans doute de là, du moins, Barmak en est certain, de son interprétation' (336; Barmak thinks of the mirages on the road because Eastern iconoclasm has often distrusted deceptive images, vague reflections, wild shimmering. The prohibition derives no doubt from this; at least Barmak is sure of it, in his interpretation). It is not always clear whether Weber is imagining Barmak's feelings, or reporting opinions and sentiments that the Afghan has divulged, as implied in the second quotation. Nonetheless, Weber's account of his journey focuses on the perceptions of his travelling companion rather than his own, decentring his autobiographical protagonist.

These encounters recall those with guides, interpreters and hosts in the sense that they belong to the journey, beginning and ending with the journey, unlike companions brought from home, who have a relationship with the travel writer that precedes and exceeds both journey and text. Weber and Ramazzotti's companions are represented with more context and background, and they are mentioned more frequently and in greater detail. These chance companions are also used as synecdoches to represent the cultures or societies with which they are associated. Furthermore, they allow travel writers to express personal reactions that are not necessarily possible from their own point of view: hence Ramazzotti quotes his companions' criticism of Mobutu and Weber attributes reflections on iconoclasm in Afghanistan to Barmak. In a similar way, in *La porte des larmes*, Guillebaud reports the views of his Ethiopian driver Berhanou and interpreter Amaretch on their own country and Ramazzotti writes about China from the point of view of his interpreter Celia in *La birra di Shaoshan*. Thus the companion allows the writer to depict the journey through the prism of a different perspective. This contrasts with the treatment of companions brought from home, who either share the traveller's perspective or see things from a slightly altered angle, but remain travellers with outside viewpoints. Although companions met en route accompany the traveller and are travellers themselves, they are represented as an integral element of the journey.

While Ramazzotti and Weber's chance companions are used to represent the cultures they travel through, they also provide an opportunity for reflection on what it is to be a traveller. Both texts illustrate the disparity between the status of the European traveller-protagonists and that of their companions. Ramazzotti shares transport with refugees and migrants, constantly reminding us of the traveller's privileged status in terms of his relative wealth and ability to move relatively freely. When Ramazzotti meets Joseph (see Chapter 6) he reflects on the difference between a traveller and a refugee: 'Un viaggiatore ha sempre una casa a cui pensare, e per questo prova la sensazione di trovarsi altrove. Un profugo è un eterno viaggiatore per il quale il concetto di altrove è inesistente' (*Vado*, 129; A traveller always has a home to think about, and for this reason experiences the feeling of being elsewhere. A refugee is an eternal traveller for whom the concept of elsewhere is nonexistent). Ramazzotti's closest companions, François and Kalenga, who accompany him for most of his route through Zaire, perhaps best exemplify such differences. Ramazzotti meets these two trainee policemen on the lorry, on their way home to snatch a few days' respite with their families. At the end of their horrendous journey together the Italian continues on to Cape Town and his plane home, while François and Kalenga, who travel by land because they cannot afford plane tickets, must make the entire journey back the same way to continue their training. At his lowest point in Zaire, when the passengers are pushing the lorry through the mud, Ramazzotti thinks bitterly of the rally: 'Non posso che disprezzare questo stupido e costoso gioco del percorrere le strade dei poveri con i mezzi dei ricchi' (200; I can only despise this stupid and costly game of travelling the roads of the poor with the means of the rich). By taking public transport Ramazzotti shares the means of the poor and undergoes considerable hardship with his fellow travellers, but he always has the means of the rich in his pocket. He occupies an ambivalent position throughout *Vado verso il Capo* between his privileges as a wealthy white European, with a plane ticket home and a commission to write, and his temporary companionship with the African travellers whom he accompanies and whose living conditions he briefly shares.

In Weber's *Le grand festin de l'Orient*, Barmak also suffers the trials of a precarious status: with no visa for Turkey he must sneak across the border from Greece, but is then concerned about how to cross into Iran. Weber manages to convince him that 'un clandestin est sûrement beaucoup moins gênant en dehors qu'en dedans' (181; an illegal immigrant is surely far less troublesome outside than inside), but they must hire the services of a guide to help them out and the crossing takes considerable time and negotiation. Weber is particularly interested in Barmak's feelings about his return to Afghanistan and reflects on his companion's position as an exile: 'Barmak cache une mélancolie, celle de l'exilé, celle du perpétuel voyageur, et cette mélancolie ne peut trouver sa thérapie que dans le cheminement, surtout s'il l'entraîne sur la route de Roumi' (81; Barmak hides a melancholy, that of the exile, that of the perpetual traveller, and the therapy for this melancholy is only found in wandering, especially if it takes him along Rumi's road). As they approach Afghanistan Barmak's reported thoughts turn to his concerns about the state of his country, his worries about what he will find there (e.g., 199 and 289–90). Weber's representation of Barmak also reveals ambivalence: between the romance of the Sufi poet Rumi and the life of the wanderer, the practicalities of visas and crossing borders, and Barmak's concerns and fears about barely post-Taliban Afghanistan.

Lisle argues that travel writers should question their own subject positions, their right to travel and right to represent: 'Travel writers cannot and will not address the ethico-political problems of *encounter* if they are unwilling to question the authority of their own subject positions. Indeed, what *right* do travel writers have to speak for and represent others?'[28] Although Ramazzotti refers to the contribution made by *AutoCapital* to his journey, he does not examine his position as a European in Africa. As we have seen in Chapters 4 and 5, he takes for granted both his right to cross borders and move freely and his right to represent whatever he chooses through photography and writing. Weber goes further, masking the circumstances of his journey. My analysis of his representation of Barmak is based on his presentation of the Afghan in *Le grand festin de l'Orient*, in which he leads the reader to believe that he first encounters Barmak on the boat to Greece. Yet the journey described in *Festin* is in fact the cultural and scientific 'Paris–Kaboul' expedition in which Weber took part, along with forty-odd others, in the summer and autumn of 2003.[29] It is likely that Weber and Barmak had made contact before leaving France, or at least that their encounter was not coincidental. Weber makes no mention of the expedition in *Festin* and his presentation of the journey conceals its true circumstances, hiding the professional motivations and financial backing of the journey from the reader. Weber's autobiographical protagonist in *Festin* appears to wander freely along the Silk Road, as if travelling on a whim. This recalls the way that travellers treat the world as their playground, examined in Chapter 4. Although both Ramazzotti and Weber portray their companions sympathetically and Weber also decentres his own protagonist in order to allow greater space for other characters, they perhaps do not go far enough in questioning their own privileges as travellers, a fact highlighted by the juxtaposition with companions whose own freedom of movement is curtailed.

***

The figure of the travelling companion brings to the fore the question of what constitutes an encounter in travel writing, but also highlights the boundaries of the travel genre. Chance companions, met on the road, represent travel experiences in themselves; they belong to the journey and become synecdoches for the cultures and societies with which they are associated, like guides, interpreters and hosts. The encounter with the individual is once more treated as an opportunity to reflect on a wider social group or cultural entity. Although companions and travellers accompany each other on the same journey, a certain distance is maintained between them, asserting the boundary between same and different, home and away. The companion brought from home, on the other hand, is largely absent from the travel text, despite their presence at the traveller's side during the journey. This figure also helps to define the boundaries of travel: the writer's silence about the relationship implies that it is not a travel experience and therefore does not belong in the travel text. The companion belongs to the home culture and the home life and the encounter does not constitute a travel event. Life may be a journey, but it is not this particular journey that concerns travel writing. Like the much-maligned and shunned tourist, the companion from home serves to hone the representation of the central character's identity as a traveller, through comparison both favourable and unfavourable. To an extent the juxtaposition of leisured traveller-protagonist with travellers whose mobility is not so casual, such as refugees, migrants or exiles, also shapes the boundaries around the travel in travel writing. These associations seem more troubled, suggesting that travel writing has not yet come to terms with the privileged form of mobility that it promotes and its relations to other, less privileged, mobilities.

Chapter 8
CONCLUDING

We began with Sergio Ramazzotti and his collection of beer labels, souvenirs representing his travel encounters. Many of the narratives explored in this study are constructed around a collection of interesting individuals encountered, like a contemporary cabinet of curiosities. At a time when leisured travel has become a mass pursuit and there are few refuges for those who wish to distinguish themselves and return home with a story unique enough to be worth telling, the encounter seems an ideal way of guaranteeing originality. Encounters contradict many of the stereotypes of tourism, which constructs an image of antisocial sheltered travellers, avoiding all contact with the unfamiliar and especially unfamiliar people. Encounters coincide with decelerated methods of travel, both motivating and resulting from the slower journeys that allow more of the time that interaction requires. Encounters are always new; even when the world seems overexplored and homogenized, when places are papered over by their reproducible image, individuals always remain to be discovered. Encounters enable authenticity, through the mediation of travellees who provide information and access, as well as the authenticity of interaction, when genuine relations develop between travellers and travellees. Perhaps the best antidote to the commercialization and mediatization of travel destinations and experiences is spontaneous contact with an individual. Encounter goes to the heart of ethical questions about how one should travel, because how we interact with others is central to ethics and because travel is a highly valued cultural pursuit. Bernard Ollivier's long walk across Asia exemplifies the significance of encounter to contemporary travel. He travels the much-traversed Silk Road, a road overlaid with repetitious journeys and narratives, but by walking he experiences it differently to the tourists who pass him in their jeeps (*Marche I*, 305). At the same time, he acknowledges that the lives and concerns of the people whom he meets ultimately interest him more than the old stones and monuments he passes (*Marche II*, 298). The three volumes of his narrative resound with evocative place names: Istanbul, Teheran, Samarkand, Kashgar, Xi'an, but they are also packed with the less familiar names of the dozens of travellees who populate and shape Ollivier's story.

Ollivier's encounters make his journey and its narrative, but as we have seen throughout this study, they also present him with constant challenges. Travellees offer conflicting versions of the information he needs to navigate the places he visits, he is uncertain whom he can trust and at times his safety is endangered by those he meets. He suffers the discomforts of sharing private spaces, of curious stares, of broken communication. His project, to walk every kilometre of the 12,000-long route he has planned, an assertion of free movement, is threatened by travellees who question his right to that movement either directly or implicitly, intimidating him with their stare. His presence is questioned, as are his motivations, identity and sanity. He uses his camera to reciprocate the generosity he receives, but sometimes his photographs are rejected, while others covet the camera itself. His relative wealth compared to many of those whom he meets presents him with ethical dilemmas and difficult choices. Ollivier is but one example and we have seen many more who undergo similar problems when they encounter travellees, whether intentionally or brought together by a chance crossing of paths. The experiential and narrative value of encounters is undeniable, but the challenges they present are also patent.

One of the principal difficulties of encounter derives from the centrality of the traveller, both during the journey and in the narrative. The term 'independent traveller' is almost an oxymoron: the more independent travellers are of travel agencies and tour operators, the more dependent they are on travellees. Yet travel writers are often reluctant to cede the authority of their traveller-protagonists to travellees. The work of guides and interpreters often goes unacknowledged, the rights of hosts to control travellers is refuted, travellers reject the identities imposed on them by the travellee's stare, while those who challenge travellers are quickly dismissed and companions are rendered invisible. When travellers submit to travellees during their journeys, they often retaliate in their narratives, which undermine travellees and reassert the traveller's authority. Yet some travel writers do acknowledge travellees, recuperating them from the passive implications of that label and asserting their agency: they credit their contributions, recognize their rights to assert authority over the travellers who are their guests and represent those same travellers suffering doubts, questioning themselves and yielding to others.

This study has taken examples from a wide range of travel writing in order to examine the theme of encounters from the different perspectives provided by different texts, but I acknowledge that in so doing I do not provide a thorough analysis of any single text or author. Some of the relative strengths and weaknesses of different texts have emerged in relation to the theme of encounters, though I would not necessarily hold up any single text or author as exemplary. Corrado Ruggeri, for example, cites his guide as an authoritative source, but he also manipulates him in the pursuit of information, while Jean-Claude Guillebaud undermines the authority of several of his guides, asserting his own knowledge, but he is particularly attentive to challenging encounters and moral dilemmas. Olivier Weber masks the financial circumstances of his journey and is silent about language and translation, yet he often effaces himself in order to bring travellees into the foreground of his texts. Ollivier, on the other hand, is far more attentive to language, but sometimes questions the rights of his hosts.

There is a tension in the representation of the travel encounter between the travellee as a means and as an end. Travellees, in their various roles, provide a means to travel experiences, to authenticity and to information. They are a means as synecdoches, made to stand for particular societies, cultures or situations, a tactic exemplified in every chapter: from guides, interpreters, hosts and companions representing their own social groups, political positions or cultural habits, to the stare of the travellee bounced back and reflected onto his/her own culture, to the underclass of beggars and prostitutes symbolizing poverty. Furthermore, travellees are a means to self-representation, a mirror against which the central character is portrayed as traveller, as writer, as European. Yet travellees are not merely a means, just as they are not merely characters in a narrative. When value is bestowed on encounter for the sake of encounter, when a genuine relationship develops between traveller and travellee, when the latter is acknowledged, despite conflict and tension with the former, then travellees become ends in themselves.

The encounters analysed in this study also reflect the limitations of travel and the travel genre. The nature of encounters reinforces the division between home and away that structures travel narratives. This is particularly evident in the lack of reciprocity, discussed in Chapter 4, and the different treatment of companions brought from home and those met on the road, in Chapter 7. The proper subject of travel narratives, it would seem, is everything that is away and not home, and that division is rarely crossed. It is a convention that assumes discontinuity between home and away, that assumes unidirectional movement, of the traveller leaving home to go away and then returning and bringing the narrative home. These assumptions are belied by Stefano Liberti, François Maspero and Francesco Piccolo, who all bring travel home by discussing encounters with immigrants in their home countries, thereby enabling a continuity that much travel writing does not permit. The mobility of travel texts themselves threatens the division; if readerships are no longer reliably monocultural or immobile perhaps they will demand travel books that better reflect their diversity.

This also raises the problem of travel writing as a genre about leisured travel. The tensions between different ways of travelling are evident in the preceding chapters: the paid guide who travels alongside the traveller, the hosts whose mobility is more restricted than the traveller's, the photographees who do not own cameras, the travellees who do not enjoy the same privileges, who travel for different reasons, under different circumstances, with greater restrictions. If travellers usually define themselves in opposition to tourists, it perhaps also reveals a reluctance to scrutinize the others kinds of travellers whose paths they cross. The dichotomy is no longer traveller versus tourist, but traveller versus immigrant, or mobile versus immobile, or tourist versus vagabond, as Zygmunt Bauman puts it.[1]

The temporary nature of travel dictates the temporality of travel encounters, but even brief moments can have sustained significance. The stability of the text provides some compensation for this brevity; it captures the echoes of the moment, testifying to a connection. No matter what technological, social or cultural changes may affect travel in the future, interpersonal encounter will remain a permanent challenge for any kind of traveller. Encounter is not only desirable but also necessary and inevitable. The difficulty of encounters, the discomfort, the power struggles, the conflict, are part of the challenge, part of what makes a journey a story. That story rarely tells the tale that the traveller envisaged from the beginning: s/he may set out with the aim of walking or driving across a continent, but the narrative is comprised of the obstacles that interfere with the achievement of that goal, and those obstacles are largely imposed by travellees. The traveller wrangles with the gatekeeper to gain access to the gate that s/he imagines will open the doors to the country, and this struggle becomes the story narrated in the travel text.

NOTES

Chapter 1: Encountering, Travelling, Writing

1 Sergio Ramazzotti, *La birra di Shaoshan: Viaggio nel paese natale di Mao* (Milan: Feltrinelli, 2002), 59. After an initial long reference, all primary sources will be cited with a short reference in the text. All translations are my own unless otherwise indicated. Celia's real name is Huang Yue, but she uses a Western name when working as an interpreter and insists that Ramazzotti address her thus: *Birra*, 11.
2 Gianni Celati, *Avventure in Africa* (Milan: Feltrinelli, 1998; repr. 2001), 5; and Olivier Weber, *Voyage au pays de toutes les Russies* (Paris: Quai Voltaire, 1992; repr. Payot et Rivages, 2003), 13.
3 Bernard Ollivier, *Longue marche: À pied de la Méditerranée jusqu'en Chine par la Route de la Soie III: Le vent des steppes* (Paris: Phébus, 2003), 333. The other volumes are: *I: Traverser l'Anatolie* (Paris: Phébus, 2000) and *II: Vers Samarcande* (Paris: Phébus, 2001).
4 Pierre Halen remarks that much travel writing is structured in small episodes, often revolving around an individual encountered: 'De deux voyages en terre de génocide: Le Rwanda et la question de l'altérité', in *Récits du dernier siècle des voyages: De Victor Segalen à Nicolas Bouvier*, ed. Olivier Hambursin (Paris: Presses de l'Université Paris-Sorbonne, 2005), 75–90 (88).
5 Nicolas Bouvier, *L'usage du monde* (Geneva: Droz, 1963), reprinted in *Œuvres* (Paris: Gallimard, 2004), 59–388. The quotation is from Bouvier, *Routes et déroutes: Entretiens avec Irène Lichtenstein-Fall* (Geneva: Éditions Métropolis, 1992), reprinted in *Œuvres*, 1249–1388 (1288). On this aspect of Bouvier's writing, see Gérard Cogez, *Les écrivains voyageurs au XXe siècle* (Paris: Seuil, 2004), 203–5; and Olivier Hambursin, 'Sur les traces de Nicolas Bouvier: Portrait et perspectives critiques', in *Récits du dernier siècle*, 223–37 (234–5).
6 François Maspero, *Les passagers du Roissy-Express* (Paris: Seuil, 1990; repr. 2004); and Terzani, *Un indovino mi disse* (Milan: Longanesi, 1995; repr. TEA, 2004).
7 Corrado Ruggeri, *Farfalle sul Mekong: Tra Thailandia e Vietnam* (Milan: Feltrinelli, 1994; repr. 2003); Nicole-Lise Bernheim, *Saisons japonaises* (Paris: Payot et Rivages, 1999; repr. 2002); and Jean-Claude Guillebaud, *La colline des anges: Retour au Vietnam* (Paris: Seuil, 1993), reprinted in *La traversée du monde*, presented by Jean Lacouture (Paris: Arléa, 1998), 419–516.
8 Franco Trequadrini, *Viaggio alienazione ed altro* (Manfredonia: Atlantica, 1980), 19.
9 Hambursin, *Récits du dernier siècle*, 256.
10 Gaia De Pascale, *Scrittori in viaggio: Narratori e poeti italiani del Novecento in giro per il mondo* (Turin: Bollati Boringhieri, 2001), 12–13.
11 Marco Aime, *L'incontro mancato: Turisti, nativi, immagini* (Turin: Bollati Boringhieri, 2005), 47.

12 Mary Louise Pratt, *Imperial Eyes: Travel Writing and Transculturation* (London: Routledge, 1992), 242 and see also 7. Travelee, or the anglicized 'travellee', is an increasingly accepted term in travel writing studies, see, for example: Charles Forsdick, *Travel in Twentieth-Century French and Francophone Cultures: The Persistence of Diversity* (Oxford: Oxford University Press, 2005); and Loredana Polezzi, 'Did Someone Just Travel All Over Me? Travel Writing and the Travelee…', in *Seuils et traverses: Enjeux de l'écriture du voyage: Actes du colloque de Brest (6–8 juillet 2000)*, ed. Jean-Yves Le Disez and Jan Borm, 2 vols (Brest: Université de Bretagne occidentale, 2002), II, 303–12.
13 This is a reference to Polezzi's 'Did Someone Just Travel All Over Me? Travel Writing and the Travelee…'.
14 Nationality, race and/or gender are the focus of many studies of travel and travel writing. Examples include: Olga Augustinos, *French Odysseys: Greece in French Travel Literature from the Renaissance to the Romantic Era* (Baltimore: Johns Hopkins University Press, 1994); Alida D'Aquino Creazzo, *L'io e l'altro: Il viaggio in India da Gozzano a Terzani* (Rome: Avagliano, 2006); Brenda Cooper, *Weary Sons of Conrad: White Fiction against the Grain of Africa's Dark Heart* (New York: Peter Lang, 2002); John Cullen Gruesser, *White on Black: Contemporary Literature about Africa* (Urbana: University of Illinois Press, 1992); Karen R. Lawrence, *Penelope Voyages: Women and Travel in the British Literary Tradition* (Ithaca: Cornell University Press, 1994); Sara Mills, *Discourses of Difference: An Analysis of Women's Travel Writing and Colonialism* (London: Routledge, 1991).
15 Aime, *L'incontro mancato*, 90–2.
16 Ryszard Kapuściński, *The Other*, trans. Antonia Lloyd-Jones (London: Verso, 2008), 31.
17 For more extensive discussions of classification questions, see James M. Buzard, 'What Isn't Travel?' in *Unravelling Civilisation: European Travel and Travel Writing*, ed. Hagen Schulz-Forberg (Brussels: Peter Lang, 2005), 43–61; and Peter Hulme and Tim Youngs, 'Talking about Travel Writing: A Conversation between Peter Hulme and Tim Youngs', *English Association Issues in English* 8 (2007): 1–7.
18 On generic overlapping in general see Glenn Hooper and Tim Youngs, 'Introduction', in *Perspectives on Travel Writing*, ed. Glenn Hooper and Tim Youngs (Aldershot: Ashgate, 2004), 1–11 (2–4). On travel writing and ethnography: Jan Borm, '*In-Betweeners*? On the Travel Book and Ethnographies', *Studies in Travel Writing* 4 (2000): 78–105; Pratt, 'Fieldwork in Common Places', in *Writing Culture: The Poetics and Politics of Ethnography*, ed. James Clifford and George E. Marcus (Berkeley: University of California Press, 1986), 27–50; and Joan Pau Rubiés, 'Travel Writing and Ethnography', in *The Cambridge Companion to Travel Writing*, ed. Peter Hulme and Tim Youngs (Cambridge: Cambridge University Press, 2002), 242–60. On travel writing and journalism: Corinne Fowler, *Chasing Tales: Travel Writing, Journalism and the History of British Ideas About Afghanistan* (Amsterdam: Rodopi, 2007); Catharine Mee, 'Journalism and Travel Writing: From *Grands Reporters* to Global Tourism', *Studies in Travel Writing* 13 (2009): 305–15; and David Spurr, *The Rhetoric of Empire: Colonial Discourse in Journalism, Travel Writing, and Imperial Administration* (London: Duke University Press, 1993). On travel writing and autobiography: Marguerite Helmers and Tilar Mazzeo, eds, *The Traveling and Writing Self* (Newcastle: Cambridge Scholars Publishing, 2007); and Adrien Pasquali, 'Récit de voyage et autobiographie', *Annali d'italianistica* 14 (1996): 71–88. On travel writing and the novel: Percy G. Adams, *Travel Literature and the Evolution of the Novel* (Lexington: University Press of Kentucky, 1983).
19 See, for example: Cogez, *Les écrivains voyageurs*, 11–33; Charles Forsdick, Feroza Basu and Siobhán Shilton, *New Approaches to Twentieth-Century Travel Literature in French: Genre,*

History, Theory (New York: Peter Lang, 2006), 13–57; Odile Gannier, *La littérature de voyage* (Paris: Ellipses, 2001), 5–10 and 91–103; Debbie Lisle, *The Global Politics of Contemporary Travel Writing* (Cambridge: Cambridge University Press, 2006), 27–67; Pasquali, *Le tour des horizons: Critique et récits de voyages* (Paris: Klincksieck, 1994), 91–109; Polezzi, *Translating Travel: Contemporary Italian Travel Writing in English Translation* (Aldershot: Ashgate, 2001), 54–76; and Tzvetan Todorov, 'Le voyage et son récit', in *Les morales de l'histoire* (Paris: Bernard Grasset, 1991), 95–108.

20 Jan Borm, 'Defining Travel: On the Travel Book, Travel Writing and Terminology', in *Perspectives on Travel Writing*, ed. Glenn Hooper and Tim Youngs (Aldershot: Ashgate, 2004), 13–26.

21 Borm, 'Defining Travel', 17.

22 Forsdick also distinguishes between travel literature and travel writing, where the former is the broader category: *Travel in Twentieth-Century French*, xii.

23 Gannier, *La littérature de voyage*, 45–59. See also: Susan Bassnett, 'When is a Translation not a Translation?' in *Constructing Cultures: Essays on Literary Translation*, ed. Susan Bassnett and André Lefevere (Clevedon: Multilingual Matters, 1998), 25–40 (35); Hulme, 'Talking about Travel Writing', 3; and Polezzi, *Translating Travel*, 93–5.

24 On reality effects and fictional devices in travel writing, see Borm, 'Defining Travel', 15–16; and Hulme, 'Patagonian Cases: Travel Writing, Fiction, History', in *Seuils et traverses*, ed. Le Disez and Borm, II, 223–37 (235).

25 See, for example: Stephen Greenblatt, *Marvelous Possessions: The Wonder of the New World* (Oxford: Clarendon Press, 1991), 147; and Pasquali, *Le tour des horizons*, 35–9.

26 For a more detailed discussion see Polezzi, *Translating Travel*, 88–97. Pratt also argues that travel writers construct the 'effect of the real' in deliberate opposition to the glossy representations of a commodified world presented by tourist marketing: *Imperial Eyes*, 221.

27 Paul Lauritzen states the moral case for distinguishing fact and fiction in life writing: 'Arguing with Life Stories: The Case of Rigoberta Menchú', in *The Ethics of Life Writing*, ed. Paul John Eakin (Ithaca: Cornell University Press, 2004), 19–39. Hulme makes a similar argument in relation to travel writing in 'Patagonian Cases', 236–7.

28 Hagen Schulz-Forberg suggests that the 'truth effect' itself is more important than the actual reality of the objects being described: 'European Travel and Travel Writing: Cultural Practice and the Idea of Europe', in *Unravelling Civilisation*, 13–40 (14).

29 Ian Jack insists on this: 'We may have a more sophisticated understanding of that blurred and difficult division between fact and fiction, between what happened and what did not (quite), but we still need to believe that the travel writer, excepting the obviously playful, *did not make it up*.' 'Introduction', in *The Granta Book of Travel* (London: Granta Books, 1991; repr. 1998), vii–xii (xi). Emphasis in the original. Hulme points out that if the writer is proved to have lied, s/he may be discredited: 'Talking about Travel Writing', 3.

30 Bruce Chatwin's *In Patagonia* is a well-known example of a successful travel book that wilfully mixes fact and fiction. See Hulme, 'Patagonian Cases'.

31 Brief biographical notes for each author are also included in the endnotes.

32 The United Nations World Tourism Organisation (UNWTO) ranks tourism as the fourth biggest export category, after fuels, chemicals and food, estimating global international tourist arrivals for 2011 at 983 million and international tourism receipts at 1030 billion US dollars (740 billion euros) in the same year: 'Tourism Highlights: 2012 Edition', online: http://unwto.org/facts/menu.html (accessed 26 May 2013), 2.

33 Erik Cohen, 'Toward a Sociology of International Tourism', *Social Research* 39 (1972): 164–82 (175); and Dean MacCannell, *The Tourist: A New Theory of the Leisure Class* (New York: Schocken Books, 1976; repr. Berkeley: University of California Press, 1999), 171. Jean-Didier Urbain examines this in terms of the conflict between travellers and tourists: *L'idiot du voyage: Histoires de touristes* (Paris: Plon, 1991; repr. Payot et Rivages, 2002), 101 and 276–7. Anthropologist Duccio Canestrini describes unwittingly pioneering tourism through a travel account of his own: *Andare a quel paese: Vademecum del turista responsabile* (Milan: Feltrinelli, 2001; repr. 2003), 57–8.

34 On the influence of travel writing on tourists, see Greg Richards and Julie Wilson, 'Travel Writers and Writers Who Travel: Nomadic Icons for the Backpacker Subculture?' *Journal of Tourism and Cultural Change* 2 (2004): 46–68; John Hutnyk, *The Rumour of Calcutta: Tourism, Charity and the Poverty of Representation* (London: Zed Books, 1996), 81–2; and Urbain, *L'idiot du voyage*, 70 and 156–7.

35 On the development of antitourism in travel literature, see Buzard, *The Beaten Track: European Tourism, Literature, and the Ways to Culture, 1800–1918* (Oxford: Clarendon Press, 1993). See also Urbain's *L'idiot du voyage* and Mee, '"Che brutta invenzione il turismo!" Tourism and Anti-tourism in Current French and Italian Travel Writing', *Comparative Critical Studies* 4 (2007): 269–82.

36 Rachid Amirou points out that the transgressions of antitourism are simply reincorporated into the mainstream: *Imaginaire touristique et sociabilités du voyage* (Paris: Presses Universitaires de France, 1995), 128; and Basu argues that antitourist strategies are conventional in twentieth-century French travel writing, in Forsdick, Basu and Shilton, *New Approaches*, 193. Gianni Celati and Francesco Piccolo are two examples of recent travel writers who distinguish themselves by assuming, rather than denying, their identities as tourists, in *Avventure in Africa* and *Allegro occidentale* (Milan: Feltrinelli, 2003; repr. 2005).

37 See Buzard, *The Beaten Track*; Forsdick, Basu and Shilton, *New Approaches*, 136; Lisle, *The Global Politics*, 77–83; Mee, 'Che brutta invenzione', 273; and Urbain, *L'idiot du voyage*, 67–72.

38 See Patrick Holland and Graham Huggan, *Tourists with Typewriters: Critical Reflections on Contemporary Travel Writing* (Ann Arbor: University of Michigan Press, 1998; repr. 2000), 3.

39 For an overview of interdisciplinary approaches to travel writing, see Mary Baine Campbell, 'Travel Writing and its Theory', in *The Cambridge Companion*, ed. Hulme and Youngs, 261–78; and Youngs, 'Where Are We Going? Cross-Border Approaches to Travel Writing', in *Perspectives on Travel Writing*, ed. Hooper and Youngs, 167–80. Basu provides a precedent with her use of interdisciplinary sources in Forsdick, Basu and Shilton, *New Approaches*, which she justifies on 140 and 147.

40 Buzard's *The Beaten Track* and Urbain's *L'idiot du voyage* provide the most detailed investigations of the subject. Amirou also dismantles the myth of the model traveller: *Imaginaire touristique*, 147–56. Brian Musgrove, among others, points to the inherent snobbism in anti-tourism: 'Travel and Unsettlement: Freud on Vacation', in *Travel Writing and Empire: Postcolonial Theory in Transit*, ed. Steve Clark (London: Zed Books, 1999), 31–44 (33–4).

41 An early classic is Valene L. Smith, ed., *Hosts and Guests: The Anthropology of Tourism*, 2nd edition (Oxford: Blackwell, 1977; repr. Philadelphia: University of Pennsylvania Press, 1989). Others focusing on interpersonal encounter include: Aime, *L'incontro mancato*; Amirou, *Imaginaire touristique*; and Gavin Jack and Alison Phipps, *Tourism and Intercultural Exchange: Why Tourism Matters* (Clevedon: Channel View Publications, 2005).

42 The only Swiss author is Nicolas Bouvier and his writings are often grouped with those of French and other Francophone travel writers.
43 Studies of twentieth-century travel writing in French include: Cogez, *Les écrivains voyageurs*; Forsdick, *Travel in Twentieth-Century French*; Forsdick, Basu and Shilton, *New Approaches*; Gannier, *La littérature de voyage*; Hambursin, ed., *Récits du dernier siècle*; Pasquali, *Le tour des horizons*; Jean-Xavier Ridon, *Le voyage en son miroir: Essai sur quelques tentatives de réinvention du voyage au 20e siècle* (Paris: Éditions Kimé, 2002). On twentieth-century travel writing in Italian: Giorgio Raimondo Cardona, 'I viaggi e le scoperte', in *Letteratura italiana V: Le questioni*, ed. Alberto Asor Rosa (Turin: Einaudi, 1986), 687–716; Luca Clerici, 'La letteratura di viaggio', in *Manuale di letteratura italiana: Storia per generi e problemi*, ed. Franco Brioschi and Costanzo di Girolamo, 4 vols (Turin: Bollati Boringhieri, 1996), III, 590–610; De Pascale, *Scrittori in viaggio*; Monica Farnetti, *Reportages: letteratura di viaggio del Novecento italiano* (Milan: Angelo Guerini, 1994); Elvio Guagnini, *Viaggi d'inchiostro: Note su viaggi e letteratura in Italia* (Pasian di Prato: Campanotto, 2000); Polezzi, *Translating Travel*; Paolo Proietti, *Lontano dalla lingua madre: In viaggio con la narrativa nel secondo Novecento* (Rome: Armando, 2000); Trequadrini, *Viaggio alienazione ed altro*.
44 Michel Le Bris, 'Note de l'éditeur', in *Pour une littérature voyageuse* (Paris: Éditions Complexe, 1992; repr. 1999), 7–15 (13–14); and 'L'étonnant paradoxe de la littérature de voyage', *Livres de France* 208 (1998): 36–8.
45 *Pour une littérature voyageuse*; see also the official website of the festival: http://www.etonnants-voyageurs.com (accessed 18 August 2013).
46 http://www.premioalbatros.org and http://www.festivaletteraturadiviaggio.it (accessed 18 August 2013).
47 'Tourism Highlights: 2012 Edition', 6.
48 On this aspect of travel writing studies in Italian, see Polezzi, *Translating Travel*, 25–34.
49 http://www.crlv.org and http://www.cirvi.it (accessed 18 August 2013).
50 'Effervescence éditoriale' is Pasquali's term to describe the recent abundance of travel literature: *Le tour des horizons*, 1.
51 Italian National Institute of Statistics, 'Viaggi e vacanze in Italia e all'estero', online: http://www.istat.it/it/archivio/81980; and La direction générale de la compétitivité, de l'industrie et des services, 'Chiffres clés du tourisme: Édition 2012', online: http://www.dgcis.redressement-productif.gouv.fr/etudes-et-statistiques/statistiques-tourisme/donnees-cles/chiffres-cles (accessed 18 August 2013). Neither report gives numbers or percentages for how many people went abroad and little detail is given about destinations. The focus of both reports is, unsurprisingly, the economics of tourism in Italy and France.
52 Catherine Bertho-Lavenir provides a long and thorough history of French tourism in *La roue et le stylo: Comment nous sommes devenus touristes* (Paris: Éditions Odile Jacob, 1999).
53 Italian histories of travel and tourism tend to focus on the subject as a broader European phenomenon, or on Italy as host, rather than the specific history of Italians as travellers and tourists. See, for example, Patrizia Battilani, *Vacanze di pochi, vacanze di tutti: L'evoluzione del turismo europeo*, 2nd edition (Bologna: Il Mulino, 2001; repr. 2009).
54 See, for example, Enzo Nocifora, *Itineraria: Dal Grand Tour al turismo postmoderno: Lezioni di sociologia del turismo* (Milan: Le Vespe, 2001).
55 This point is also made by, for example: Forsdick, *Travel in Twentieth-Century French*, vii and xix–xx; Jean-Marc Moura, 'L'exotisme fin-de-(XXe)-siècle', *Revue de littérature comparée* 74 (2000): 533–53 (539); and Proietti, *Lontano dalla lingua madre*, 12–13.
56 Schulz-Forberg, 'European Travel and Travel Writing', 30–33.

57 Syed Manzurul Islam suggests that whether travellers define home and away on regional, national or continental levels depends on where they are travelling to: 'You are a Frenchman/woman when you are in Italy, but you are European while in India', *The Ethics of Travel: From Marco Polo to Kafka* (Manchester: Manchester University Press, 1996), 61–2.

58 Michael Cronin, *Across the Lines: Travel, Language, Translation* (Cork: Cork University Press, 2000). Essay collections and conference proceedings also regularly combine studies of travel writing in a range of different languages.

Chapter 2: Strategy, Authenticity, Ethics

1 Tiziano Terzani (1938–2004) was a correspondent for *Der Spiegel* for 30 years and also wrote for Italian newspapers *La Repubblica* and *Corriere della Sera*. He is particularly known for his profound knowledge of Asia, where he lived and worked, in various countries, for many years. He published a number of books on his travels and experiences as a war correspondent.
2 Tzvetan Todorov, *Nous et les autres: La réflexion française sur la diversité humaine* (Paris: Seuil, 1989), 453.
3 Todorov, *Nous et les autres*, 453.
4 Feroza Basu, in Forsdick, Basu and Shilton, *New Approaches*, 164.
5 There are many examples of this pessimism. Claude Lévi-Strauss's *Tristes tropiques* (Paris: Plon, 1955) has become a staple citation, as has Daniel J. Boorstin's essay 'From Traveler to Tourist: The Lost Art of Travel', in *The Image: A Guide to Pseudo-Events in America* (London: Weidenfeld and Nicolson, 1961), 77–117. Eric J. Leed provides a more recent example in *The Mind of the Traveler: From Gilgamesh to Global Tourism* (New York: Basic Books, 1991), 285–93. Recent Italian examples include Franco Ferrarotti, *Partire, tornare: Viaggiatori e pellegrini alla fine del millennio* (Rome: Donzelli, 1999); and Luigi Monga, 'Travel and Travel Writing: An Historical Overview of Hodoeporics', *Annali d'italianistica* 14 (1996): 6–54 (42–3).
6 Forsdick, *Travel in Twentieth-Century French*.
7 Cogez, *Les écrivains voyageurs*, 20; and Hambursin, ed., *Récits du dernier siècle*, 255–8.
8 Forsdick, *Travel in Twentieth-Century*; and Forsdick, Basu and Shilton, *New Approaches*. Jean-Didier Urbain is particularly resistant to the idea of an end to travel, suggesting that '[la] banalité n'est pas dans le monde. Elle est dans le regard de l'homme' ([the] banal is not in the world. It is in the way we look at it), *Secrets de voyage: Menteurs, imposteurs et autres voyageurs invisibles* (Paris: Payot et Rivages, 1998; repr. 2003), 34. See also Claude Reichler's foreword in Adrien Pasquali, *Le tour des horizons*, xi–xvii (xi–xiii).
9 De Pascale, *Scrittori in viaggio*, 239–40.
10 Cronin, *Across the Lines*, 17.
11 Cronin, *Across the Lines*, 17.
12 Although the human population is not literally infinite, but is currently estimated at 7 billion, this figure is so high that from the perspective of an individual it might as well be infinite. Practicalities, births, deaths and sleep aside, a human life of seventy-five years would allow for less than a third of a second for each encounter if one was to meet the whole of humanity.
13 Gaia De Pascale, *Slow travel: Alla ricerca del lusso di perdere tempo* (Milan: Ponte alle Grazie, 2008).

14 Paolo Rumiz and Francesco Altan, *Tre uomini in bicicletta* (Milan: Feltrinelli, 2002; repr. 2004), 13 and 166; and Rumiz, *È Oriente* (Milan: Feltrinelli, 2003; repr. 2005), 17 and 59. Rumiz (1947–) is a journalist and editor from Trieste, specializing in Italian and European identity and especially the Balkans. He has completed numerous journeys by bicycle and train, narrated in his books and articles.

15 Sergio Ramazzotti, *Vado verso il capo: 13.000 km attraverso l'Africa* (Milan: Feltrinelli, 1996; repr. 2002). Sergio Ramazzotti (1965–) is an Italian reporter and photographer, with a particular interest in Africa. He has also worked in Iraq and Afghanistan.

16 Charles Forsdick, 'A quoi bon marcher: Uses of the Peripatetic in Contemporary Travel Literature in French', *Contemporary French and Francophone Studies* 5 (2001): 47–62; *Travel in Twentieth-Century*, 166–96; 'Projected Journeys: Exploring the Limits of Travel', in *The Art of the Project: Projects and Experiments in Modern French Culture*, ed. Johnnie Gratton and Michael Sheringham (Oxford: Berghahn Books, 2005), 51–65; and Forsdick, Basu and Shilton, *New Approaches*, 159–93.

17 Maspero's and other 'claustrophilic' journeys are also addressed by Urbain in 'Les catanautes des cryptocombes: des iconoclastes de l'Ailleurs', *Nottingham French Studies* 39 (2000): 7–16; and 'Le cogito du voyageur: "Esprit nomade" et "esprit du voyage"', in *Seuils et traverses*, ed. by Le Disez and Borm, II, 21–41.

18 Canestrini, *Andare a quel paese*, 102.

19 Forsdick, Basu and Shilton, *New Approaches*, 187.

20 Jean Chesneaux, *L'art du voyage: Un regard (plutôt...) politique sur l'autre et l'ailleurs* (Paris: Bayard, 1999), 37–8.

21 For a more thorough examination of inauthenticity in tourism see Urbain, *L'idiot du voyage*, 259–70.

22 Buzard, *The Beaten Track*, 6. Wes Williams identifies a 'rhetoric of distinction' already in Montaigne, who 'defines himself as a *real* traveller by searching for authentic otherness': '"Rubbing up against Others": Montaigne on Pilgrimage', in *Voyages and Visions: Towards a Cultural History of Travel*, ed. Jaś Elsner and Joan-Pau Rubiés (London: Reaktion Books, 1999), 101–23 (111–12). Emphasis in the original.

23 Boorstin, 'From Traveler to Tourist'; and MacCannell, *The Tourist*.

24 See, respectively, Erik Cohen, 'A Phenomenology of Tourist Experiences', *Sociology* 13 (1979): 179–201; Donald L. Redfoot, 'Touristic Authenticity, Touristic Angst, and Modern Reality', *Qualitative Sociology* 7 (1984): 291–309; and Jon Abbink, 'Tourism and its Discontents: Suri-Tourist Encounters in Southern Ethiopia', *Social Anthropology* 8 (2000): 1–17 (16).

25 Maxine Feifer, *Going Places: The Ways of the Tourist from Imperial Rome to the Present Day* (London: Macmillan, 1985), 259–68. See also John Urry, *The Tourist Gaze*, 2nd edition (London: Sage, 1990; repr. 2002), 90–92.

26 Subgenres of travel writing address activities associated with recreational tourism, such as mountain climbing, sailing and hiking, but these tend to be more hazardous and involve more physical exertion than the average beach holiday.

27 Basu reports that the self-parody and gimmicky approaches to travel found in anglophone writing are not present in French travel writing: Forsdick, Basu and Shilton, *New Approaches*, 141.

28 Marie-Paule Ha, *Figuring the East: Segalen, Malraux, Duras, and Barthes* (Albany: State University of New York Press, 2000), 110. See also Urbain on this 'vieux mythe de la rencontre et de la pénétration culturelle' (old myth of encounter and cultural penetration): *L'idiot du voyage*, 263–4.

29 Corrado Ruggeri (1957–) is based in Rome where he works as a journalist for *Corriere della Sera*. He has published several travel books and has a particular interest in South-East Asia.
30 MacCannell, *The Tourist*, 3.
31 Bernard Ollivier (1938–), from Normandy, has worked in various professions, including many years as a journalist. In his early sixties he found himself retired and a widower and decided to set out on a 'long walk' of 12,000 kilometres across Asia.
32 See, for example, Gavin Jack and Alison Phipps, *Tourism and Intercultural Exchange*, 6; and Julio Aramberri, 'The Host Should Get Lost: Paradigms in the Tourism Theory', *Annals of Tourism Research* 28 (2001): 738–61 (740).
33 See, for example, Hyounggon Kim and Tazim Jamal, 'Touristic Quest for Existential Authenticity', *Annals of Tourism Research* 34 (2007): 181–201; Nick Kontogeorgopoulos, 'Keeping up with the Joneses: Tourists, Travellers, and the Quest for Cultural Authenticity in Southern Thailand', *Tourist Studies* 3 (2003): 171–203; and Kjell Olsen, 'Authenticity as a Concept in Tourism Research: The Social Organization of the Experience of Authenticity', *Tourist Studies* 2 (2002): 159–82.
34 John Taylor suggests that 'there are at least as many definitions of authenticity as there are those who write about it', in 'Authenticity and Sincerity in Tourism', *Annals of Tourism Research* 28 (2001): 7–26 (8).
35 Ning Wang, 'Rethinking Authenticity in Tourism Experience', *Annals of Tourism Research* 26 (1999): 349–70 (351–6).
36 See also Edward M. Bruner, 'Abraham Lincoln as Authentic Reproduction: A Critique of Postmodernism', *American Anthropologist* 96 (1994): 397–415 (408).
37 MacCannell, *The Tourist*, 92.
38 MacCannell, *The Tourist*, 94.
39 The tourist's desire to access back regions is another use of the common metaphor of penetration evoked by Ha and Urbain above.
40 Cohen also raises the question of whether locals, or 'tourees', use the concept of authenticity and if so, what they consider to be authentic: 'Authenticity and Commoditization in Tourism', *Annals of Tourism Research* 15 (1988): 371–86 (374). Aramberri suggests, rather flippantly, 'As most gatekeepers of authenticity are academics, what they find genuine, engaging, worthwhile, and so on, unsurprisingly coincides with the usually midbrow or mesocratic values that pervade their cultural space': 'The Host Should Get Lost', 740.
41 On the power to authenticate in tourism, see Bruner, 'Abraham Lincoln', 400–401 and 408.
42 Philosophical definitions of authenticity are highly specific and complex, and differ from everyday uses. In philosophy, authenticity is not a quality of objects and it is strictly not synonymous with words such as honesty or sincerity. In the context of tourism, both in terms of the ways tourists and travel writers use the word and in the studies of their beliefs and practices, authenticity has far wider and vaguer applications than in philosophy. In this common, as opposed to philosophical, usage, authentic is more or less synonymous with such terms as genuine, sincere or true. It is the more common use of authenticity that I examine here. For an overview of authenticity in the works of major philosophers, see Jacob Golomb, *In Search of Authenticity: From Kierkegaard to Camus* (London: Routledge, 1995).
43 Philip Pearce and Gianna Moscardo, 'The Concept of Authenticity in Tourist Experiences', *Australian and New Zealand Journal of Sociology* 22 (1986): 121–32. The article receives harsh criticism for its use of Heidegger and Goffman, particularly for reducing philosophical concepts for application to the study of tourism, in Charles

Turner and Phil Manning, 'Placing Authenticity – On Being a Tourist: A Reply to Pearce and Moscardo', *Australian and New Zealand Journal of Sociology* 24 (1988): 136–9.
44 Wang, 'Rethinking Authenticity'.
45 On the search for personal authenticity in travel writing, see Stephen M. Levin, *The Contemporary Anglophone Travel Novel: The Aesthetics of Self-Fashioning in the Era of Globalization* (London: Routledge, 2008).
46 Of course, intrapersonal and interpersonal authenticities are closely connected, both because the former is a necessary basis on which to construct the latter, and because personal authenticity is largely constituted through interpersonal relationships. See, for example, Anthony Giddens, *Modernity and Self-Identity: Self and Society in the Late Modern Age* (Cambridge: Polity Press, 1991), 96–7; and Charles Taylor, *The Ethics of Authenticity* (Cambridge, MA: Harvard University Press, 1991).
47 Wang, 'Rethinking Authenticity', 364–6.
48 As suggested by Pearce and Moscardo, 'The Concept of Authenticity', as well as Olsen, 'Authenticity as a Concept' and Taylor, 'Authenticity and Sincerity'.
49 For the tourists Nick Kontogeorgopoulos interviewed 'spontaneous encounters devoid of commercial transactions between tourist and host embody a fundamental authenticity': 'Keeping up with the Joneses', 183.
50 See especially: Wayne Booth, *The Company We Keep: An Ethics of Fiction* (Berkeley: University of California Press, 1988); and Martha C. Nussbaum, *Love's Knowledge: Essays on Philosophy and Literature* (Oxford: Oxford University Press, 1990). Useful overviews include: Jane Adamson, Richard Freadman and David Parker, eds, *Renegotiating Ethics in Literature, Philosophy, and Theory* (Cambridge: Cambridge University Press, 1998); and Stephen K. George, ed., *Ethics, Literature, and Theory: An Introductory Reader* (Oxford: Rowman and Littlefield, 2005).
51 The few studies of travel literature that do address ethics include Syed Manzurul Islam, *The Ethics of Travel: From Marco Polo to Kafka* (Manchester: Manchester University Press, 1996), 'Travel and Ethics', a special issue of *Journeys* 4 (2003), edited by Corinne Fowler and Ludmilla Kostova; and Charles Forsdick, Corinne Fowler and Ludmilla Kostova, eds., *Travel Writing and Ethics: Theory and Practice* (London: Routledge, 2013).
52 Patrick Holland and Graham Huggan, *Tourists with Typewriters* (Ann Arbor: University of Michigan Press, 1998; repr. 2000); and Debbie Lisle, *The Global Politics of Contemporary Travel Writing* (Cambridge: Cambridge University Press, 2006).
53 On ethics and literary study, see Geoffrey Galt Harpham, 'Ethics', in *Critical Terms for Literary Study*, ed. Frank Lentricchia and Thomas McLaughlin, 2nd edition (Chicago: University of Chicago Press, 1990; repr. 1995), 387–405.
54 Martha C. Nussbaum, *Love's Knowledge: Essays on Philosophy and Literature* (Oxford: Oxford University Press, 1990), 23–9.
55 Nussbaum, *Love's Knowledge*, especially 26–9 and 168–94.
56 Nussbaum, *Love's Knowledge*, 26.
57 Richard Freadman, 'Moral Luck in Paris: *A Moveable Feast* and the Ethics of Autobiography', in *Renegotiating Ethics*, ed. Adamson et al., 134–60 (135); and John Wiltshire, 'The Patient Writes Back: Bioethics and the Illness Narrative', in *Renegotiating Ethics*, ed. Adamson et al., 181–98.
58 See many of the essays in *Ethics, Literature, and Theory*, ed. George, especially Wayne Booth, 'Why Ethical Criticism Can Never Be Simple', 23–35; and Marshall Gregory, 'Ethical Criticism: What It Is and Why It Matters', 37–61. See also Nussbaum, *Love's Knowledge*, 29.

59 See Booth on the connections between reading and conduct, *The Company We Keep*, 277–80.
60 Kwame Anthony Appiah, *Cosmopolitanism: Ethics in a World of Strangers* (London: Norton, 2006).
61 Appiah, *Cosmopolitanism*, xxi, 67, 85, 97.
62 See also Clark, ed. *Travel Writing and Empire*, 1. On the importance of readers in terms of how travel writers construct their narratives to address particular audiences, see, for example, Odile Gannier, *La littérature de voyage* (Paris: Ellipses, 2001), 17–19 and 45–59; and Pasquali, *La tour des horizons*, 47.
63 On the ethics of tourism see, for example, David A. Fennell, *Tourism Ethics* (Clevedon: Channel View Publications, 2006); and Canestrini, *Andare a quel paese*.
64 Duccio Canestrini, *Turistario: Luoghi comuni dei nuovi barbari* (Milan: Baldini e Castoldi, 1993), 48. See also Ian Littlewood, *Sultry Climates: Travel and Sex since the Grand Tour* (London: John Murray, 2001), 183; and Franck Michel, *Désirs d'ailleurs: Essai d'anthropologie des voyages* (Paris: Armand Colin, 2000), 15–16.
65 Zygmunt Bauman, *Globalization: The Human Consequences* (New York: Columbia University Press, 1998), 18.
66 Nussbaum, *Love's Knowledge*, 47–8. See also Gregory, 'Ethical Criticism', 57.
67 Nussbaum, 'The Literary Imagination in Public Life', in *Renegotiating Ethics*, ed. Adamson et al., 222–46 (234).
68 Nussbaum, *Love's Knowledge*, 69.
69 Nussbaum, *Love's Knowledge*, 36–44 and 66–75.
70 Nussbaum, 'The Literary Imagination', 242.
71 Nussbaum, *Love's Knowledge*, 40–3 and 75–82. See also Simon Haines, 'Deepening the Self: The Language of Ethics and the Language of Literature', in *Renegotiating Ethics*, ed. Adamson et al., 21–38.
72 Nussbaum, *Love's Knowledge*, 43–4.
73 Holland and Huggan, *Tourists with Typewriters*, viii, see also xiii. Lisle also complains that travel writers often fail to take account of their influence, *The Global Politics*, 261.
74 Holland and Huggan, *Tourists with Typewriters*, xiii.

Chapter 3: Guiding

1 Nicolas Bouvier, *Journal d'Aran et d'autres lieux* (Paris: Payot, 1990), reprinted in *Œuvres*, 945–1037 (1035–6).
2 Nicolas Bouvier (1929–98) was a writer, photographer and iconographer from Geneva. In his early twenties he undertook a journey from Europe to Japan, which formed the basis for his most notable and celebrated book, *L'usage du monde* (1963). He wrote several other travel narratives, as well as poetry and essays.
3 Adrien Pasquali, *Le tour des horizons*, 52. See also several of the essays in *Pour une littérature voyageuse* (Paris: Éditions Complexe, 1992; repr. 1999), e.g., 19, 85–6 and 120.
4 It seems that it was ever thus: Stephen Greenblatt describes how Columbus's expectations shaped his experience of the New World: *Marvelous Possessions*, 86–91. On the importance of books to travel and particularly how reading influences experience see: Edward Said, *Orientalism* (London: Routledge and Kegan Paul, 1978; repr. Penguin, 1995), 94 and 177; Pasquali, *Le tour des horizons*, 51–9 and 85, and Christine Montalbetti, *Le voyage, le monde et la bibliothèque* (Paris: Presses Universitaires de France, 1997).

5 James Buzard, *The Beaten Track*, 65–79 and Michael Cronin, *Across the Lines*, 85–6.
6 Gianni Celati (1937–) is an Italian writer, author of novels, story collections, and several translations including, most recently, Joyce's *Ulysses*. He has taught literature at universities in Italy and the US and has published works of literary criticism.
7 Marco Aime reports that it is common for guides in Mali to have read Western ethnographies, but he is concerned that guides then feed tourists what they are expecting to hear: *L'incontro mancato*, 86–9.
8 Heather Henderson, 'The Travel Writer and the Text: "My Giant Goes with me Wherever I Go"', in *Temperamental Journeys: Essays on the Modern Literature of Travel*, ed. by Michael Kowalewski (Athens: University of Georgia Press, 1992), 230–48 (235). Emphasis in the original.
9 Jack and Phipps, *Tourism and Intercultural Exchange*, 124.
10 See Pasquali on this opposition, *Le tour des horizons*, 31–9. Eric Leed provides a useful summary of the role of travel in the development of scientific methods for acquiring knowledge through observation and experience: *The Mind of the Traveler*, 177–215. See also Greenblatt on eye-witnessing and authority in travel narratives going back to Herodotus, *Marvelous Possessions*, 123–8.
11 Jean-Xavier Ridon examines this tension in Victor Segalen's writing on China, *Le voyage en son miroir*, 43–56. See also Henderson, 'The Travel Writer and the Text', 230. Loredana Polezzi argues that travel writers gain authority from both experience and intertextual reference, *Translating Travel*, 93 and 96.
12 Said, *Orientalism*, 94.
13 Jean-Claude Guillebaud (1944–) is a writer, essayist and journalist. He has written for *Le Monde* and *Le Nouvel Observateur* and was president of Reporters sans frontières. He has published a number of travel books and collections of his travel writing. His more recent books address philosophical and religious topics.
14 Sarga Moussa, 'Traduttore, traditore: La figure du drogman dans les récits de voyage en Orient au XIXème siècle', in *Écrire le voyage*, ed. by György Tverdota (Paris: Presses de la Sorbonne Nouvelle, 1994), 101–12 (108–12). Moussa also points out that Chateaubriand privileges written over oral sources.
15 Guillebaud, *La porte des larmes: Retour vers l'Abyssinie* (Paris: Seuil, 1996), reprinted in *La traversée du monde*, 653–763 (e.g., 713); and *Sur la route des croisades* (Paris: Arléa, 1993), reprinted in *La traversée du monde*, 517–652 (e.g., 605–7).
16 Cronin and Charles Forsdick offer different interpretations of the role of the guide as mediator in the search for authenticity. Cronin suggests that interpreters 'confer authenticity and verisimilitude on the [travel writer's] account': *Across the Lines*, 72; while Forsdick, writing about Bouvier's Xi'an text, argues that foregrounding the guide emphasizes the fact that access is mediated and therefore not necessarily authentic: '"(In)connaissance de l'Asie": Barthes and Bouvier, China and Japan', *Modern and Contemporary France* 14 (2006): 63–77 (73–4).
17 Erik Cohen, 'The Tourist Guide: The Origins, Structure and Dynamics of a Role', *Annals of Tourism Research* 12 (1985): 5–29 (11–12).
18 Loredana Polezzi, 'Now You See Them, Now You Don't: The Figure of the Interpreter/Translator in Travel Writing and Migrant Literature' (unpublished article, 18 August 2013), Microsoft Word file. Travel writing testifies to a long tradition of distrust between travellers and their guides and interpreter; see Marie-Christine Gomez-Géraud, 'La figure de l'interprète dans quelques récits de voyage français à la Renaissance', in

Voyager à la Renaissance: Actes du colloque de Tours 1983, ed. by Jean Céard and Jean-Claude Margolin (Paris: Éditions Maisonneuve et Larose, 1987), 319–35.
19 Aime cites examples from Indonesia and Mali: *L'incontro mancato*, 85–6. See also Cohen, 'The Tourist Guide', 15; and Tim Edensor, *Tourists at the Taj: Performance and Meaning at a Symbolic Site* (London: Routledge, 1998), 71. Political authorities are not the only ones who promote consciously constructed narratives; other organizations, such as businesses, tailor their self-presentation for tourists, as Jack and Phipps find in a whisky distillery on Skye: *Tourism and Intercultural Exchange*, 128–35.
20 Tiziano Terzani, *Buonanotte, Signor Lenin* (Milan: Longanesi, 1992; repr. TEA, 2004), 324.
21 Cohen describes how the guides on Thai hill treks are presented as an authentic component of the tour: '"Primitive and Remote": Hill Tribe Trekking in Thailand', *Annals of Tourism Research* 16 (1989): 30–61 (53).
22 Greenblatt uses the term metonymy to describe how travellers represent a whole with perceived fragments: *Marvelous Possessions*, 122. I choose synecdoche because it designates a relation where one thing is a part of the other, while metonym is usually only a relation of association. Guides and interpreters are synecdoches in the sense that they are used to represent groups to which they belong, or at least to which they are perceived to belong. See Corinne Fowler for a critical reading of broader ethnography-inspired uses of synecdoche in travel writing and journalism, *Chasing Tales*, 94–124.
23 James Clifford, *Routes: Travel and Translation in the Late Twentieth Century* (Cambridge, MA: Harvard University Press, 1997), 19. See also Renato Rosaldo on the position of the 'native': *Culture and Truth: The Remaking of Social Analysis* (Boston: Beacon Press, 1989; repr. London: Routledge, 1993), 50–51. Aime also makes the link between anthropological informants and tourist guides: *L'incontro mancato*, 84. 'Informant' is a problematic term; Clifford uses it rarely in *Routes* and applies inverted commas (e.g., 19 and 23). Here he uses 'interlocutor', which has more positive connotations.
24 Valene L. Smith, 'Eskimo Tourism: Micro-Models and Marginal Men', in *Hosts and Guests*, 55–82 (79–81). On 'marginal men', see also Theron Nuñez, 'Touristic Studies in Anthropological Perspective' in *Hosts and Guests*, 265–74 (267–9).
25 Smith, 'Eskimo Tourism', 80.
26 See also Catharine Mee, 'The Myopic Eye: Calvino's Travels in the USA and the USSR', *The Modern Language Review* 100 (2005): 985–99.
27 Cronin addresses this issue in the context of the war in Iraq, in *Translation and Identity* (London: Routledge, 2006), 112–16.
28 François-Olivier Rousseau (1947–) is a French journalist and writer, whose novels have earned him several prestigious awards. He also works as a screenwriter. He has lived in the Isle of Mann and Morocco.
29 François-Olivier Rousseau, *Le plaisir de la déception* (Paris: Stock, 2003), 135.
30 Kontogeorgopoulos, 'Keeping up with the Joneses', 187. The term 'adventurers' refers to one of the groups of tourists in Kontogeorgopoulos' study.
31 Peter Hansen, 'Partners: Guides and Sherpas in the Alps and Himalayas, 1850s–1950s', in *Voyages and Visions*.
32 Once more, the economics of the relationship between interpreter and traveller seem to be a long-standing problem, as suggested by Gomez-Géraud in 'La figure de l'interprète', 330, though Renaissance travellers feared greed and trickery rather than the commoditization of relationships.
33 Francesco Piccolo (1964–) is an Italian writer and screenwriter, based in Rome. He has published novels and collections of short stories.

34 Bernard Ollivier, *Carnets d'une longue marche: Nouveau voyage d'Istanbul à Xi'an* (Paris: Phébus, 2005), 86.
35 So-Min Cheong and Marc Miller, 'Power and Tourism: A Foucauldian Observation', *Annals of Tourism Research* 27 (2000): 371–90.
36 On the role of guides in controlling (and sometimes protecting) tourists, see also Edensor, *Tourists at the Taj*, 107–12; Jack and Phipps, *Tourism and Intercultural Exchange*, 131–3; and Kjell Olsen, 'Authenticity as a Concept, 176.
37 Moussa describes how travellers in the nineteenth century put themselves entirely in the hands of their guides, 'Traduttore, traditore', 107. The same is often the case today.
38 Nicole-Lise Bernheim, *Couleur cannelle* (Paris: Arléa, 2002), 17 and 21–2. Bernheim (1942–2003) was a writer and journalist, notably for *Le Monde* and *L'Express*. She also worked as a producer for French radio and director for television. She published three travel books.
39 Olivier Weber, *Le grand festin de l'Orient* (Paris: Robert Laffont, 2004), 182–227. Weber (1958–) is French writer, novelist and reporter, particularly known for his work as a war correspondent. He has won a number of prestigious prizes for his journalism. He is a specialist on Afghanistan and has published several travel books, as well as biographies of Lucien Bodard and Ella Maillart.
40 Cronin draws attention to conflict over control between interpreters and their employers, in *Translation and Identity*, 101. Cohen also examines the issue of relative authority between tourists and their guides in 'The Tourist Guide', 23. See also Rosaldo on ethnographers' relations with their 'informants', *Culture and Truth*, 173–5.
41 Michel Déon, *Pages grecques* (Paris: Gallimard, 1993), 259. Déon (1919–) is a member of the Académie française. He is the author of an extensive œuvre and has received several prestigious awards for his novels. He has spent long periods living in Greece and Ireland.
42 Similarly, Aime describes the impact of his own writing on a guide in Mali, who received visits from Italian tourists as a result and wrote to Aime to thank him for the publicity, *L'incontro mancato*, 142–3.
43 Jean-Claude Guillebaud, *Un voyage vers l'Asie* (Paris: Seuil, 1979), reprinted in *La traversée du monde*, 95–208 (169).
44 Olivier Weber, *Chasseurs de dragons: Voyage en opiomie* (Paris: Arléa, 1996; repr. Payot et Rivages, 2000), 30–1 and 156–60.
45 Cronin examines this lacuna in travel writing: *Across the Lines*, 41–2 and 51. Polezzi also criticizes the lack of attention to issues of language and translation in travel literature and the lack of space given to translators and interpreters: 'Now You See Them'. On the invisibility of the translator see Lawrence Venuti, *The Translator's Invisibility: A History of Translation* (London: Routledge, 1995).
46 Italics in the original.
47 Moussa suggests that the invisibility of the translator is part of the travel writer's strategy to legitimate him/herself as mediator: 'Traduttore, traditore', 111.
48 Cronin, *Across the Lines*, 40. Cronin analyses different translation strategies used in travel writing in 'Travelling Minorities: Language, Translation and the Global', in *Seuils et traverses*, I, 249–60.
49 Montalbetti examines the use of such borrowed terms at length, and suggests they confer authenticity on the account: *Le voyage*, 162–71; as does Odile Gannier, *La littérature de voyage*, 85. Giorgio Raimondo Cardona argues that they have a displacing effect ('spaesamento'), 'I viaggi e le scoperte', 703.

50 See also Cronin on the ambiguous translation of direct and indirect speech: *Across the Lines*, 41–3.
51 On foreign language terms as souvenirs, see also Montalbetti, *Le voyage*, 170–71.
52 See also Cronin, *Across the Lines*, 41–2.
53 Bassnett, 'When is a Translation, 36.
54 Bassnett, 'When is a Translation', 35. See also Polezzi, *Translating Travel*, 86.
55 Fabrizia Ramondino, *Polisario: Un'astronave dimenticata nel deserto* (Rome: Gamberetti, 1997). Ramondino (1936–2008) was an Italian writer, author of a number of novels, as well as essays on social and political themes and books on her native Naples.
56 Kapuściński, *The Other*, 13–14.
57 The 'crisis of representation' began in cultural anthropology in North America in the 1980s. For a discussion of its nature and impact see Michael G. Flaherty et al., 'Review Symposium: Crisis in Representation', in *Journal of Contemporary Ethnography* 31 (2002): 478–516.
58 James Clifford, 'Introduction: Partial Truths', in *Writing Culture*, 1–26 (17). Clifford also analyses the strategies of various ethnographies in 'On Ethnographic Authority', in *The Predicament of Culture: Twentieth-Century Ethnography, Literature, and Art* (Cambridge, MA: Harvard University Press, 1988), 21–54.
59 Jack and Phipps, *Tourism and Intercultural Exchange*, 42. Attempting to overcome some of these problems, Jack and Phipps develop a style of writing with a heavy emphasis on personal anecdote and subjective impressions. At times this makes their anthropological text closely resemble travel writing.
60 Hansen mentions the autobiographies of alpine guides and their desire to express their opinions of their employers: 'Partners', 219–20.
61 Other guides or interpreters may have been given pseudonyms, but this is not always clear.
62 Sergio Ramazzotti, *Afrozapping: Breve guida all'Africa per uomini bianchi* (Milan: Feltrinelli, 2006), 72–5.
63 Johannes Fabian analyses the use of the first, second and third person in ethnography in *Time and the Other: How Anthropology Makes its Object* (New York: Columbia University Press, 1983; repr. 2002), 83–6. See also Polezzi, *Translating Travel*, 92–3.
64 See Marie-Paule Ha on different reader positions in relation to both literature and its study, *Figuring the East*, 10–17.
65 James Clifford, 'On Ethnographic Allegory', in *Writing Culture*, 98–121 (116–19).
66 Loredana Polezzi, 'Non solo colonie: "Africa" in the Work of Contemporary Italian Women Writers', in *Borderlines: Migrazioni e identità nel Novecento*, ed. Jennifer Burns and Loredana Polezzi (Isernia: Cosmo Iannone, 2003), 309–21 (320).
67 The same applies to ethnography, see Clifford: 'Indigenous control over knowledge gained in the field can be considerable, and even determining': 'On Ethnographic Authority', 45.
68 Pratt, *Imperial Eyes*, 135–6.
69 Fowler, *Chasing Tales*, 128–9. See also Clifford: 'One may also read against the grain of the text's dominant voice, seeking out other half-hidden authorities, reinterpreting the descriptions, texts, and quotations gathered together by the writer': 'On Ethnographic Authority', 53.
70 Fowler, *Chasing Tales*, 134.
71 Adapted from *The Chambers Dictionary* (Edinburgh: Chambers, 1993; repr. 1998), 1764.

Chapter 4: Hosting

1 On the history of commercial hospitality see, for example, John K. Walton, 'The Hospitality Trades: A Social History', in *In Search of Hospitality: Theoretical Perspectives and Debates*, ed. Conrad Lashley and Alison Morrison (Oxford: Butterworth-Heinemann, 2000), 56–76. On hospitality and duty, see also Heidrun Friese, 'The Limits of Hospitality', *Paragraph* 32 (2009): 51–68.
2 Friese, 'The Limits of Hospitality', 51.
3 Émile Benveniste, 'L'hospitalité', in *Le vocabulaire des institutions indo-européennes I: Économie, parenté, société* (Paris: Éditions de Minuit, 1969), 87–101 (88).
4 Benveniste, 'L'hospitalité', 94.
5 Jacques Derrida, *De l'hospitalité: Anne Dufourmantelle invite Jacques Derrida à répondre* (Paris: Calmann-Lévy, 1997), 25–7.
6 Jennie Germann Molz and Sarah Gibson provide a summary of the use and criticism of discourses of hospitality in tourism and migration: 'Introduction: Mobilizing and Mooring Hospitality', in *Mobilizing Hospitality: The Ethics of Social Relations in a Mobile World*, ed. Jennie Germann Molz and Sarah Gibson (Aldershot: Ashgate, 2007), 1–25 (6–10).
7 See Julio Aramberri, 'The Host Should Get Lost'; Germann Molz and Gibson, eds, *Mobilizing Hospitality*; and Mireille Rosello *Postcolonial Hospitality: The Immigrant as Guest* (Stanford: Stanford University Press, 2001).
8 The metaphor is widely used; see, for example, Rachid Amirou, *Imaginaire touristique*, 130 and 175; Erik Cohen, 'Toward a Sociology', 171; and Claudio Minca, 'Percorsi dell'autentico', in *Spazi effimeri: Geografia e turismo tra moderno e postmoderno* (Padova: CEDAM, 1996), 103–38 (120).
9 Boorstin, 'From Traveler to Tourist', 99–109; and MacCannell, *The Tourist*, 91–107.
10 Erving Goffman, 'Regions and Region Behavior', in *The Presentation of Self in Everyday Life* (New York: Anchor Books, 1959; repr. London: Penguin, 1990), 109–40 (124–5).
11 See, for example, Leed, who connects the 'objective' viewpoint with the exclusion of travellers from interiors: *The Mind of the Traveler*, 66.
12 Elizabeth Telfer, 'The Philosophy of Hospitableness', in *In Search of Hospitality*, ed. Lashley and Morrison, 38–55.
13 Nicole-Lise Bernheim, *Chambres d'ailleurs* (Paris: Arléa, 1986; repr. Payot et Rivages, 1999).
14 For analysis of hospitality in the 'commercial home', see: Paul Lynch, Maria Laura Di Domenico and Majella Sweeney, 'Resident Hosts and Mobile Strangers: Temporary Exchanges within the Topography of the Commercial Home', in *Mobilizing Hospitality*, ed. Germann Molz and Gibson, 121–43.
15 Boorstin, 'From Traveler to Tourist', 85. He takes the word back to its original root *tripalium*, a torture instrument. Others highlighting the etymology of the term include Leed, *The Mind of the Traveler*, 5–6; Franco Ferrarotti, *Partire, tornare*, 31; and Luigi Monga, 'Travel and Travel Writing', 11–12.
16 Rosello highlights the problems when people with different ideas about hospitality are brought together by tourism, *Postcolonial Hospitality*, 69–70.
17 Charles Forsdick analyses the body in travel writing featuring walking journeys, in *Travel in Twentieth-Century French*, 179–80. On the body in tourism, see Adrian Franklin and Mike Crang, 'The Trouble with Tourism and Travel Theory?' *Tourist Studies* 1 (2001): 5–22 (12–14); and John Urry, *The Tourist Gaze*, 152–6.

18 Conrad Lashley, 'Towards a Theoretical Understanding', in *In Search of Hospitality*, ed. Lashley and Morrison, 1–17 (12). See also Telfer: 'There can be a certain intensity about private entertaining which stems from this intimacy and heightens the experience. But [...] we do not always want this. For a relaxing evening which makes no demands, commercial hospitality, if it is hospitable in its own way, comes into its own', 'The Philosophy of Hospitableness', 51.
19 Lashley, 'Towards a Theoretical Understanding', 13–14.
20 Tom Selwyn, 'An Anthropology of Hospitality', in *In Search of Hospitality*, ed. Lashley and Morrison, 18–37 (27).
21 Benveniste, 'L'hospitalité'.
22 Selwyn, 'An Anthropology of Hospitality', 20.
23 Leed, *The Mind of the Traveler*, 97.
24 Rosello, *Postcolonial Hospitality*, 171.
25 See also Rosello on the risks of hospitality for both host and guest, *Postcolonial Hospitality*, 11–14 and 172–5.
26 Jane Darke and Craig Gurney, 'Putting Up? Gender, Hospitality and Performance', in *In Search of Hospitality*, ed. Lashley and Morrison, 77–99 (96).
27 Alain Borer, 'L'ère de Colomb et l'ère d'Armstrong', in *Pour une littérature voyageuse*, 17–40 (28).
28 Michel Le Bris, 'Fragments du royaume', in *Pour une littérature voyageuse*, 119–40 (126).
29 Michel Chaillou, 'La mer, la route, la poussière', in *Pour une littérature voyageuse*, 57–81 (81).
30 UN General Assembly, Resolution 217 A (III), 'Universal Declaration of Human Rights', 10 December 1948. Online: http://www.un.org/en/documents/udhr/ (accessed 18 August 2013). My emphasis.
31 Bauman, *Globalization*, 2.
32 Bauman, *Globalization*, 92–3. Emphasis in the original.
33 Germann Molz and Gibson, 'Introduction', 9.
34 Shannon Sullivan, *Revealing Whiteness: The Unconscious Habits of Racial Privilege* (Bloomington: Indiana University Press, 2006), 10.
35 Sullivan, *Revealing Whiteness*, 163.
36 Fatou Diome, *Le ventre de l'Atlantique* (Paris: Anne Carrière, 2003), 288.
37 Stefano Liberti, *A Sud di Lampedusa: Cinque anni di viaggi sulle rotte dei migranti* (Rome: Minimum fax, 2008). Liberti (1974–) is an Italian journalist with a particular interest in immigration and neocolonialism.
38 Sullivan, *Revealing Whiteness*, 164.
39 Writing about the context of immigration, Rosello also comments on the overlapping of state and private hospitality: *Postcolonial Hospitality*, 6–7 and 10–11.
40 See also Patrick Holland and Graham Huggan on the need to adjust views of travel writing as a celebration of freedom: *Tourists with Typewriters*, 4.
41 Rosello argues that a balance is not only desirable, but also necessary: *Postcolonial Hospitality*, 167–8.
42 Michel, *Désirs d'ailleurs*, 202–3.
43 I will return to Ollivier's use of the camera in Chapter 5.
44 Lynch, Di Domenico and Sweeney, 'Resident Hosts and Mobile Strangers', 129.
45 I will return to these issues in Chapter 7.
46 Rosello, *Postcolonial Hospitality*, 81.
47 Aime, *L'incontro mancato*, 40.

48 Aime, *L'incontro mancato*, 48. Others are also critical of the tight time limits imposed on encounters in tourism and encourage longer contact. When promoting slow travel Duccio Canestrini mentions the benefits to encounter: *Andare a quel paese*, 100–3. Daniel Elouard is particularly critical of brief encounters, questioning the value of such 'moments forts' (powerful moments) and complaining that without cultural depth, travel 'glisse à la surface des êtres et des choses' (slips on the surface of beings and things): 'Culture en poche', in *Tourismes, touristes, sociétés*, ed. Franck Michel (Paris: L'Harmattan, 1998), 19–24 (21).

49 Bernheim is conscious of this and she is sensitive to the Imai's feelings about her representing them: *Saisons*, e.g., 37, 105–6, 230–31.

50 Bouvier is perhaps more realistic about the fate of travel encounters: 'La dialectique de la vie nomade est faite de deux temps: s'attacher et s'arracher. [...] On se dit, si cette amitié doit durer, elle durera Inch'Allah. Dans la plupart des cas, elle ne dure pas' (*Routes*, 1290–91; The dialectic of the nomadic life is made of two phases: connecting and separating. [...] You say to yourself, if this friendship is to last, it will last Insha'Allah. In most cases, it doesn't last).

51 Cronin, *Across the Lines*, 19. Cronin stresses that vertical travel is temporary, as opposed to residence, in order to maintain the distinction between dwelling and travelling.

52 Amirou states that 'Les sociabilités touristiques ne sont pas seulement une copie conforme du lien social existant dans la société. Le tourisme offre un lieu où les rapports à soi et aux autres subissent une forme de redéfinition' (*Imaginaire touristique*, 53; The social habits of tourists are not simply copied from the social connections that exist in society. Tourism offers a space where relations to oneself and others undergo a kind of redefinition). Cronin also points out that travellers often have greater social mobility, in the sense of having access to different racial groups or classes: *Across the Lines*, 21.

53 Malcolm Crick, 'The Anthropologist as Tourist: An Identity in Question', in *International Tourism: Identity and Change*, ed. Marie-Françoise Lanfant, John B. Allcock and Edward M. Bruner (London: Sage Publications, 1995), 205–23 (216).

Chapter 5: Staring

1 Italo Calvino, *Collezione di sabbia* (Milan: Mondadori, 1994), 168.
2 Judith Adler, 'Origins of Sightseeing', *Annals of Tourism Research* 16 (1989): 7–29.
3 This is not only true for tourists but is a general feature of Western culture, as notably analysed by Michel Foucault. For critical analysis of reliance on the visual in anthropology and journalism (two disciplines closely related to travel writing) see, respectively: Johannes Fabian, *Time and the Other*, 105–41, and David Spurr, *The Rhetoric of Empire*, 13–27.
4 Urry, *The Tourist Gaze*.
5 Carol Crawshaw and John Urry, 'Tourism and the Photographic Eye', in *Touring Cultures: Transformations of Travel and Theory*, ed. by Chris Rojek and John Urry (London: Routledge, 1997), 176–95 (179).
6 On the visual in travel writing, see also Gérard Cogez, *Les écrivains voyageurs*, 81–9. Mary Louise Pratt describes one of the key tropes of colonial discourse in travel writing as the 'monarch-of-all-I-survey' scene, where the traveller-explorer describes a 'discovered' landscape from a vantage point, constructing it both aesthetically and in terms of its potential for colonial exploitation. Pratt, *Imperial Eyes*, 201–8.

7 See also Kristi Siegel and Toni B. Wulff on the problematic connection between sight and knowledge: 'Travel as Spectacle: The Illusion of Knowledge and Sight', in *Issues in Travel Writing: Empire, Spectacle, and Displacement*, ed. by Kristi Siegel (New York: Peter Lang, 2002), 109–22.
8 Crawshaw and Urry, 'Tourism and the Photographic Eye', 180; and Susan Sontag, *On Photography* (New York: Picador: Farrar, Straus and Giroux, 1977; repr. 1990), 9.
9 Sontag, *On Photography*, 10.
10 Urry, *The Tourist Gaze*, 128–9.
11 Ludmilla Kostova suggests that there is an overemphasis on the analysis of the traveller's gaze in studies of travel writing: 'Meals in Foreign Parts: Food in Writing by Nineteenth-Century British Travellers to the Balkans', in 'Travel and Ethics', ed. Corinne Fowler and Ludmilla Kostova, special issue, *Journeys* 4 (2003): 21–44 (21). See also Adrian Franklin and Mike Crang on studies of tourism that go beyond the visual: 'The Trouble with Tourism', 12–14; and Gaia De Pascale on slow travel and the senses: *Slow travel*, 76–104.
12 Henri Michaux, *Un barbare en Asie* (Paris: Gallimard, 1967), 121.
13 Cheong and Miller, 'Power and Tourism'.
14 Cheong and Miller, 'Power and Tourism', 383.
15 Maoz, 'The Mutual Gaze', *Annals of Tourism Research* 33 (2006): 221–39.
16 Maoz, 'The Mutual Gaze', 222.
17 Garland-Thomson, *Staring: How We Look* (Oxford: Oxford University Press, 2009), 9.
18 Garland-Thomson, *Staring*, 13–15.
19 Garland-Thomson, *Staring*, 18–19.
20 Garland-Thomson, *Staring*, 19.
21 Garland-Thomson, *Staring*, 40–44.
22 Garland-Thomson, *Staring*, 3–4.
23 David Chaney proposes the 'glance' as an alternative to the gaze: 'The Power of Metaphors in Tourism Theory', in *Tourism: Between Place and Performance*, ed. Simon Coleman and Mike Crang (Oxford: Berghahn Books, 2002), 193–206 (200–204).
24 Christine Jordis, *Bali, Java, en rêvant* (Paris: Éditions du Rocher, 2001; repr. Gallimard, 2005), 99. Jordis (1942–) is a French writer, journalist and editor, specializing in English literature and was for many years director of English fiction at Gallimard.
25 Bernheim is particularly aware of this voyeuristic gaze. Sara Mills suggests that women are more conscious of themselves as the objects of others' gazes: *Discourses of Difference*, 98; and Charles Forsdick identifies this quality in Bernheim: Forsdick, Basu and Shilton, *New Approaches*, 51.
26 For further analysis of white European travellers' encounters and experiences of their identity in the African context (including Celati, Guillebaud and Ramazzotti), see Mee, 'European Travellers in Africa: The Negotiation of Identity', *Forum for Modern Language Studies* 45 (2009): 378–89.
27 Cheong and Miller, 'Power and Tourism', 385.
28 Cheong and Miller, 'Power and Tourism', 385.
29 Gillespie, 'Tourist Photography and the Reverse Gaze', *Ethos* 34 (2006): 343–66.
30 Gillespie, 'Tourist Photography', 360.
31 Alexandre Kauffmann (1975–) is a freelance reporter from France, specializing in travel and tourism and is the author of a collection of short stories and a novel.
32 Alexandre Kauffmann, *Travellers* (Paris: Éditions des Équateurs, 2004), 64.
33 *Gaijin* and *farang* are both terms used for foreigners, especially Westerners. *Farendj* is, as Guillebaud explains: 'utilisé dans toute la Corne de l'Afrique pour désigner le Blanc.

On ignore souvent qu'il signifie textuellement le "Franc". Il fut en effet introduit au Moyen Orient et dans la Corne à l'époque des croisades' (*Porte*, 664; used throughout the Horn of Africa to designate white people. It is often forgotten that it literally means 'Franc'. It was actually introduced to the Middle East and the Horn at the time of the Crusades).

34 Marc Boulet (1959–) is a freelance journalist and writer. He studied languages and has written extensively on China. He is particularly known for his *Dans la peau de…* books about his undercover experiences in various places and social milieu.
35 Marc Boulet, *Dans la peau d'un intouchable* (Paris: Seuil, 1994). For an analysis of Boulet's transvestic travel, see Feroza Basu in Forsdick, Basu and Shilton, eds, *New Approaches*, 154–8.
36 Garland-Thomson, *Staring*, 185.
37 Sontag, *On Photography*, 14.
38 Aime, *L'incontro mancato*, 95.
39 Michel, *Désirs d'ailleurs*, 109.
40 Michel, *Désirs d'ailleurs*, 112.
41 See also Edward M. Bruner, 'The Ethnographer/Tourist in Indonesia', in *International Tourism*, ed. Lanfant, Allcock and Bruner, 224–41 (234–6).
42 François Maspero (1932–) is a writer, translator and editor. He founded left-wing press Editions Maspero, publishing works on the Third World and neocolonialism in the 1960s and 1970s. He is the author of several novels and travel books, most notably *Les Passagers du Roissy-Express*.
43 Aime, *L'incontro mancato*, 97.
44 Canestrini, *Andare a quel paese*, 109–10.
45 See, for example, Nick Kontogeorgopoulos, 'Keeping up with the Joneses', 179–80.
46 See, for example, Luigi Monga, 'Travel and Travel Writing', 42; and Jean-Didier Urbain, 'Sémiotiques comparées du touriste et du voyageur', *Semiotica* 58 (1986): 269–86 (278).
47 Images may be publically available elsewhere, but the point here is that they are not always presented with the text.
48 Sontag, *On Photography*, 28. See also Roland Barthes, *La chambre claire: Note sur la photographie* (Paris: Cahiers du cinéma, Gallimard, 1980), 60.
49 See Abbink, 'Tourism and its Discontents'; Bouvier, *Routes*, 1311; Erik Cohen, Yeshayahu Nir and Uri Almagor, 'Stranger-Local Interaction in Photography', *Annals of Tourism Research* 19 (1992): 213–33; Marie-Odile Geraud, 'L'image de soi au miroir de l'autre: Une ethnographie des pratiques touristiques dans un village Hmong de Guyane Française', in *Le tourisme local: Une culture de l'exotisme*, ed. Rachid Amirou and Philippe Bachimon (Paris: L'Harmattan, 2000), 93–120; Gillespie, 'Tourist Photography'; and Valene Smith, 'Eskimo Tourism', 63–4.
50 Cohen, Nir and Almagor highlight 'the importance of social interaction between photographer and photographee prior to the taking of the picture, even if such interaction may not bear directly on the very act of photography'. 'Stranger-Local Interaction', 222.
51 Nicolas Bouvier, *Chronique japonaise* (Paris: Payot, 1989), reprinted in *Œuvres*, 495 669 (585).
52 Bouvier also describes photography as a 'sésame très intéressant' (*Routes*, 1311–12; very useful 'open sesame').
53 Edensor, *Tourists at the Taj*, 137.
54 Canestrini provides another parody in *Andare a quel paese*, 110.
55 Cohen, Nir and Almagor mention that Polaroid photography was popular among some photographees as it enabled an immediate exchange: 'Stranger-Local Interaction', 221.

56 Ridon, *Le voyage en son miroir*, 90.
57 See Chapter 4; and Mireille Rosello, *Postcolonial Hospitality*, 81.
58 W. J. T. Mitchell, 'The Photographic Essay: Four Case Studies', in *Picture Theory* (Chicago: University of Chicago Press, 1994), 281–322 (289–92).
59 Kathryn Jones, 'Voices of the *Banlieues*: Constructions of Dialogue in François Maspero's *Les Passagers du Roissy-Express*', *Contemporary French and Francophone Studies* 8 (2004): 127–34 (128–9).
60 Aime, *L'incontro mancato*, 95.
61 Bouvier mentions that establishing contact with the photographee is necessary to the success of the photograph: *Routes*, 1309.
62 In Japan Bouvier finds himself being photographed often by his own photographees and attributes the relaxed attitude of the Japanese to photography to the common ownership of cameras: *Routes*, 1311.

Chapter 6: Challenging

1 Muriel Cerf, *L'antivoyage* (Paris: Mercure de France, 1974; repr. Éditions J'ai lu, 1995). Cerf (1950–2012) was a French novelist who published thirty-odd books. *L'antivoyage*, her first book, was published when she was 24, to critical acclaim.
2 Patrick Holland and Graham Huggan highlight the masking of finances by travel writers and the privilege that wealth grants them: *Tourists with Typewriters*, e.g., 31 and 133.
3 Aime, *Incontro mancato*, 37–8. Franck Michel highlights the elitism of tourism and points out that it also circulates images of Western wealth and leisure to those without such privileges: *Désirs d'ailleurs*, 26–7.
4 For Aime this disparity puts into question the very possibility of an encounter based on an ethical relationship: *L'incontro mancato*, 37.
5 Canestrini, *Turistario*, 48.
6 Rob Gallagher, *The Rickshaws of Bangladesh* (Dhaka: University Press Limited, 1992), 25–8.
7 Gallagher, *Rickshaws*, 43–52.
8 Gallagher, *Rickshaws*, 37.
9 Such vehicles are principally used in Asia, but some are also found in parts of Latin America and Africa: Gallagher, *Rickshaws*, 55.
10 Tony Wheeler and Richard I'Anson, *Chasing Rickshaws* (Hawthorn, Victoria: Lonely Planet Publications, 1998). Although a number of different terms exist for this group of vehicles, which are variously translated into French and Italian, I will use the generic term rickshaw for the sake of simplicity.
11 Wheeler and I'Anson, *Chasing Rickshaws*, 185.
12 The vast majority of rickshaw riders are male, though Wheeler and I'Anson do mention a few cases of female riders: 7; as does Gallagher: *Rickshaws*, 60–1.
13 Gallagher, *Rickshaws*, 26.
14 Gallagher, *Rickshaws*, 39, quoting Unnayan in association with T. H. Thomas, *Rickshaws in Calcutta* (Calcutta: Unnayan, February 1981), 46.
15 See, for example, Holland and Huggan's analysis of Peter Mayle's *A Year in Provence*, in *Tourists with Typewriters*, 40–2.
16 There are exceptions, of course. Terzani, who lived in different parts of Asia for much of his adult life, expresses no moral hand-wringing when he employs a rickshaw in Hanoi: *Indovino*, 319.

17 Pier Paolo Pasolini, *L'odore dell'India* (Milan: Longanesi, 1962; repr. Parma: Ugo Guanda, 2003), 45. Pasolini (1922–75) was a film director, poet and writer and a major intellectual and cultural figure in Italy. He often caused controversy with his radical views on politics and society.
18 Littlewood, *Sultry Climates*, 93.
19 Franck Michel, *Voyage au bout du sexe: Trafics et tourismes sexuels en Asie et ailleurs* (Quebec: Les Presses de l'Université Laval, 2006). On the ethics of sex tourism, see Canestrini, *Andare a quel paese*, 111–12; and David Fennell, *Tourism Ethics*, 288–94.
20 Littlewood, *Sultry Climates*, 4.
21 Nicolas Bouvier, *Le poisson-scorpion* (Vevey: Bertil Galland, 1981), reprinted in *Œuvres*, 721–811 (781–2).
22 Holland and Huggan, *Tourists with Typewriters*, 31–6.
23 Michel, *Voyage au bout du sexe*.
24 Hutnyk, *The Rumour of Calcutta*, vii.
25 Canestrini, *Turistario*, 48–9.
26 Hutnyk describes travellers in Calcutta debating how to respond to beggars: *The Rumour of Calcutta*, 67–9.
27 See Nussbaum, *Love's Knowledge*; and Chapter 2 above.
28 See also Hutnyk: 'It is often those in the most need who are least able to utilize the established avenues, forms and protocols of tourist begging': *The Rumour of Calcutta*, 69.

Chapter 7: Accompanying

1 David Espey, 'The Wilds of New Jersey: John McPhee as Travel Writer', in *Temperamental Journeys*, ed. Kowalewski, 164–75 (167).
2 Alberto Moravia, *Un'idea dell'India* (Milan: Bompiani, 1961; repr. 2001). Moravia (1907–1990) was a major Italian novelist. His most famous works include *Gli indifferenti* (1929) and *Il conformista* (1947). He was known for his stark style and engagement with moral and political themes.
3 Clifford, *Routes*, 33.
4 Cogez, *Les écrivains voyageurs*, 152. Adrien Pasquali also names Chateaubriand, Maxime du Camp and Nerval as examples of writers who efface their travelling companions, though he does not go into detail on the subject: *Le tour des horizons*, 104.
5 Alisdair Pettinger, '"Trains and Boats and Planes": Some Reflections on Travel Writing and Public Transport', in *Seuils et traverses*, ed. Le Disez and Borm, II, 107–15 (110).
6 Pettinger, 'Trains and Boats and Planes', 108.
7 Pettinger, 'Trains and Boats and Planes', 115.
8 Marco Aime, *Le radici nella sabbia: Viaggio in Mali e Burkina Faso* (Turin: EDT, 1999).
9 In order to distinguish between travelling companions as characters in the written text and as authors of photographs or drawings, I use their first names, as used in the text, in the first instance and surnames in the latter. Here I refer to Anaïk, the character in *Passagers*, as opposed to Frantz, the author of the photographs discussed in Chapter 5. I apply the same rule to Raymond/Depardon in Guillebaud, Jean/Talon in Celati and Thierry/Vernet in Bouvier. Pasolini only refers to Moravia by his surname, so I do the same.
10 Mireille Rosello discusses the ambiguity of viewpoint caused by the unclear division between Maspero and Frantz's voices: *Postcolonial Hospitality*, 72.

11 Jones, 'Voices of the *Banlieues*', 128–9. See also Jones, '*Le voyageur étonné*: François Maspero's Alternative Itineraries', *Studies in Travel Writing* 13 (2009): 335–44.
12 Vernet is, of course, very present through his own contribution to the travel narrative: his drawings, which are printed alongside the text.
13 On Bouvier's friendship with Vernet, see also his comments in *Routes*, 1303.
14 Lisle, *The Global Politics*, 90.
15 Bauer, 'Le compagnon', in *Autour de Nicolas Bouvier: Résonances*, ed. Christiane Albert, Nadine Laporte and Jean-Yves Pouilloux (Carouge-Genève: Éditions Zoé, 2002), 148–56 (155).
16 Lisle, *The Global Politics*, 90–95. Cogez suggests that travel writers efface their companions to better emphasize their own solitary confrontation with the world: *Les écrivains voyageurs*, 152.
17 Lisle, *The Global Politics*, 91.
18 Eric Leed discusses this understanding of travel at length in *The Mind of the Traveler*.
19 Bauer, 'Le compagnon', 149.
20 Charles Klopp, 'Buster Keaton Goes to Africa: Gianni Celati's *Avventure in Africa*', in *ItaliAfrica: Bridging Continents and Cultures*, ed. Matteo Sante (New York: Forum Italicum, 2001), 337–47 (339).
21 On Guillebaud and Depardon's collaboration, see Danièle Méaux, 'Récit de voyage et photographie: Le dialogue du texte et des images', in *Miroirs de textes: Récits de voyage et intertextualité*, ed. Sophie Linon-Chipon, Véronique Magri-Mourgues and Sarga Moussa (Nice: Publications de la Faculté des Lettres, Arts et Sciences Humaines de Nice, 1998), 169–83.
22 Jones, 'Voices of the *Banlieues*', 128. On the contrast between the characters of François and Anaïk, see also Jones, '*Le voyageur étonné*'; and Rosello, *Postcolonial Hospitality*, 68–77.
23 Culturally similar often simply means other Westerners with the means to travel, though it is not incidental to the traveller–tourist dichotomy that the two often belong to different social classes.
24 Pettinger, 'Trains and Boats and Planes'.
25 Pettinger, 'Trains and Boats and Planes', 109.
26 Proietti, *Lontano dalla lingua madre*, 18.
27 Pettinger, 'Trains and Boats and Planes', 111 and 113.
28 Lisle, *The Global Politics*, 270. Emphasis in the original.
29 See Olivier Weber and Samuel Douette, eds, *Routes de la soie: La mémoire retrouvée de l'Afghanistan* (Paris: Mille et une nuits, 2004); and Samuel Douette, ed., *Paris–Kaboul: Expédition scientifique et culturelle sur les routes de la soie* (Paris: Hoëbeke, 2004), which contains a text written by Barmak Akram himself, 116–23. Although no mention of Paris–Kaboul is made in *Festin*, the latter is advertised in both of the other texts on the expedition.

Chapter 8: Concluding

1 Bauman, *Globalization*, 77–102.

BIBLIOGRAPHY

Primary Texts

Aime, Marco. *Le radici nella sabbia: Viaggio in Mali e Burkina Faso*. Turin: EDT, 1999.
Bernheim, Nicole-Lise. *Chambres d'ailleurs*. Paris: Arléa, 1986; repr. Payot et Rivages, 1999.
_____. *Saisons japonaises*. Paris: Payot et Rivages, 1999; repr. 2002.
_____. *Couleur cannelle*. Paris: Arléa, 2002.
Boulet, Marc. *Dans la peau d'un intouchable*. Paris: Seuil, 1994.
Bouvier, Nicolas. *L'usage du monde*. Geneva: Droz, 1963. Reprinted in *Œuvres*. Paris: Gallimard, 2004, 59–388.
_____. *Le poisson-scorpion*. Vevey: Bertil Galland, 1981. Reprinted in *Œuvres*. Paris: Gallimard, 2004, 721–811.
_____. *Chronique japonaise*. Paris: Payot, 1989. Reprinted in *Œuvres*. Paris: Gallimard, 2004, 495–669.
_____. *Journal d'Aran et d'autres lieux*. Paris: Payot, 1990. Reprinted in *Œuvres*. Paris: Gallimard, 2004, 945–1037.
_____. *Routes et déroutes: Entretiens avec Irène Lichtenstein-Fall*. Geneva: Éditions Métropolis, 1992. Reprinted in *Œuvres*. Paris: Gallimard, 2004, 1249–1388.
Celati, Gianni. *Avventure in Africa*. Milan: Feltrinelli, 1998; repr. 2001.
Cerf, Muriel. *L'antivoyage*. Paris: Mercure de France, 1974; repr. Éditions J'ai lu, 1995.
Déon, Michel. *Pages grecques*. Paris: Gallimard, 1993.
Guillebaud, Jean-Claude. *Un voyage vers l'Asie*. Paris: Seuil, 1979. Reprinted in *La traversée du monde*, presented by Jean Lacouture, 95–208. Paris: Arléa, 1998.
_____. *La colline des anges: Retour au Vietnam*. Paris: Seuil, 1993. Reprinted in *La traversée du monde*, presented by Jean Lacouture, 419–516. Paris: Arléa, 1998.
_____. *Sur la route des croisades*. Paris: Arléa, 1993. Reprinted in *La traversée du monde*, presented by Jean Lacouture, 517–652. Paris: Arléa, 1998.
_____. *La porte des larmes: Retour vers l'Abyssinie*. Paris: Seuil, 1996. Reprinted in *La traversée du monde*, presented by Jean Lacouture, 653–763. Paris: Arléa, 1998.
Jordis, Christine. *Bali, Java, en rêvant*. Paris: Éditions du Rocher, 2001; repr. Gallimard, 2005.
Kauffmann, Alexandre. *Travellers*. Paris: Éditions des Équateurs, 2004.
Liberti, Stefano. *A Sud di Lampedusa: Cinque anni di viaggi sulle rotte dei migranti*. Rome: Minimum fax, 2008.
Maspero, François. *Les passagers du Roissy-Express*. Paris: Seuil, 1990; repr. 2004.
Moravia, Alberto. *Un'idea dell'India*. Milan: Bompiani, 1961; repr. 2001.
Ollivier, Bernard. *Longue marche: À pied de la Méditerranée jusqu'en Chine par la Route de la Soie I: Traverser l'Anatolie*. Paris: Phébus, 2000.

_____. *Longue marche: À pied de la Méditerranée jusqu'en Chine par la Route de la Soie II: Vers Samarcande*. Paris: Phébus, 2001.
_____. *Longue marche: À pied de la Méditerranée jusqu'en Chine par la Route de la Soie III: Le vent des steppes*. Paris: Phébus, 2003.
_____. *Carnets d'une longue marche: Nouveau voyage d'Istanbul à Xi'an*. Paris: Phébus, 2005.
Pasolini, Pier Paolo. *L'odore dell'India*. Milan: Longanesi, 1962; repr. Parma: Ugo Guanda, 2003.
Piccolo, Francesco. *Allegro occidentale*. Milan: Feltrinelli, 2003; repr. 2005.
Ramazzotti, Sergio. *Vado verso il capo: 13.000 km attraverso l'Africa*. Milan: Feltrinelli, 1996; repr. 2002.
_____. *La birra di Shaoshan: Viaggio nel paese natale di Mao*. Milan: Feltrinelli, 2002.
_____. *Afrozapping: Breve guida all'Africa per uomini bianchi*. Milan: Feltrinelli, 2006.
Ramondino, Fabrizia. *Polisario: Un'astronave dimenticata nel deserto*. Rome: Gamberetti, 1997.
Rousseau, François-Olivier. *Le plaisir de la déception*. Paris: Stock, 2003.
Ruggeri, Corrado. *Farfalle sul Mekong: Tra Thailandia e Vietnam*. Milan: Feltrinelli, 1994; repr. 2003.
Rumiz, Paolo and Francesco Altan. *Tre uomini in bicicletta*. Milan: Feltrinelli, 2002; repr. 2004.
Rumiz, Paolo. *È Oriente*. Milan: Feltrinelli, 2003; repr. 2005.
Terzani, Tiziano. *Buonanotte, Signor Lenin*. Milan: Longanesi, 1992; repr. TEA, 2004.
_____. *Un indovino mi disse*. Milan: Longanesi, 1995; repr. TEA, 2004.
Weber, Olivier. *Voyage au pays de toutes les Russies*. Paris: Quai Voltaire, 1992; repr. Payot et Rivages, 2003.
_____. *Chasseurs de dragons: Voyage en opiomie*. Paris: Arléa, 1996; repr. Payot et Rivages, 2000.
_____. *Le grand festin de l'Orient*. Paris: Robert Laffont, 2004.

Secondary Texts

Abbink, Jon. 'Tourism and its Discontents: Suri-Tourist Encounters in Southern Ethiopia'. *Social Anthropology* 8 (2000): 1–17.
Adams, Percy G. *Travel Literature and the Evolution of the Novel*. Lexington: University Press of Kentucky, 1983.
Adamson, Jane, Richard Freadman and David Parker, eds. *Renegotiating Ethics in Literature, Philosophy, and Theory*. Cambridge: Cambridge University Press, 1998.
Adler, Judith. 'Origins of Sightseeing'. *Annals of Tourism Research* 16 (1989): 7–29.
Aime, Marco. *L'incontro mancato: Turisti, nativi, immagini*. Turin: Bollati Boringhieri, 2005.
Amirou, Rachid. *Imaginaire touristique et sociabilités du voyage*. Paris: Presses Universitaires de France, 1995.
Appiah, Kwame Anthony. *Cosmopolitanism: Ethics in a World of Strangers*. London: Norton, 2006.
Aramberri, Julio. 'The Host Should Get Lost: Paradigms in the Tourism Theory'. *Annals of Tourism Research* 28 (2001): 738–61.
Augustinos, Olga. *French Odysseys: Greece in French Travel Literature from the Renaissance to the Romantic Era*. Baltimore: Johns Hopkins University Press, 1994.
Baine Campbell, Mary. 'Travel Writing and its Theory'. In *The Cambridge Companion to Travel Writing*, ed. Peter Hulme and Tim Youngs, 261–78. Cambridge: Cambridge University Press, 2002.
Barthes, Roland. *La chambre claire: Note sur la photographie*. Paris: Cahiers du cinéma, Gallimard, 1980.
Bassnett, Susan. 'When is a Translation Not a Translation?' In *Constructing Cultures: Essays on Literary Translation*, ed. Susan Bassnett and André Lefevere, 25–40. Clevedon: Multilingual Matters, 1998.

Battilani, Patrizia. *Vacanze di pochi, vacanze di tutti: L'evoluzione del turismo europeo*, 2nd edition. Bologna: Il Mulino, 2001; repr. 2009.
Bauer, Olivier. 'Le compagnon'. In *Autour de Nicolas Bouvier: Résonances*, ed. Christiane Albert, Nadine Laporte and Jean-Yves Pouilloux, 148–56. Carouge-Genève: Éditions Zoé, 2002.
Bauman, Zygmunt. *Globalization: The Human Consequences*. New York: Columbia University Press, 1998.
Benveniste, Émile. 'L'hospitalité'. In *Le vocabulaire des institutions indo-européennes I: Économie, parenté, société*, 87–101. Paris: Éditions de Minuit, 1969.
Bertho-Lavenir, Catherine. *La roue et le stylo: Comment nous sommes devenus touristes*. Paris: Éditions Odile Jacob, 1999.
Boorstin, Daniel J. 'From Traveler to Tourist: The Lost Art of Travel'. In *The Image: A Guide to Pseudo-Events in America*, 77–117. London: Weidenfeld and Nicolson, 1961.
Booth, Wayne C. *The Company We Keep: An Ethics of Fiction*. Berkeley: University of California Press, 1988.
———. 'Why Ethical Criticism Can Never Be Simple'. In *Ethics, Literature, and Theory: An Introductory Reader*, ed. Stephen K. George, 23–35. Oxford: Rowman and Littlefield, 2005.
Borer, Alain. 'L'ère de Colomb et l'ère d'Armstrong'. In *Pour une littérature voyageuse*, 17–40. Paris: Éditions Complexe, 1992; repr. 1999.
Borer, Alain, Nicolas Bouvier, Michel Chaillou et al. *Pour une littérature voyageuse*. Paris: Éditions Complexe, 1992; repr. 1999.
Borm, Jan. 'In-Betweeners? On the Travel Book and Ethnographies'. *Studies in Travel Writing* 4 (2000): 78–105.
———. 'Defining Travel: On the Travel Book, Travel Writing and Terminology'. In *Perspectives on Travel Writing*, ed. Glenn Hooper and Tim Youngs, 13–26. Aldershot: Ashgate, 2004.
Bruner, Edward M. 'Abraham Lincoln as Authentic Reproduction: A Critique of Postmodernism'. *American Anthropologist* 96 (1994): 397–415.
———. 'The Ethnographer/Tourist in Indonesia'. In *International Tourism: Identity and Change*, ed. Marie-Françoise Lanfant, John B. Allcock and Edward M. Bruner, 224–41. London: Sage Publications, 1995.
Buzard, James M. *The Beaten Track: European Tourism, Literature, and the Ways to Culture, 1800–1918*. Oxford: Clarendon Press, 1993.
———. 'What Isn't Travel?' In *Unravelling Civilisation: European Travel and Travel Writing*, ed. Hagen Schulz-Forberg, 43–61. Brussels: Peter Lang, 2005.
Calvino, Italo. *Collezione di sabbia*. Milan: Mondadori, 1994.
Canestrini, Duccio. *Turistario: Luoghi comuni dei nuovi barbari*. Milan: Baldini e Castoldi, 1993.
———. *Andare a quel paese: Vademecum del turista responsabile*. Milan: Feltrinelli, 2001; repr. 2003.
Cardona, Giorgio Raimondo. 'I viaggi e le scoperte'. In *Letteratura italiana V: Le questioni*, ed. Alberto Asor Rosa, 687–716. Turin: Einaudi, 1986.
Chaillou, Michel. 'La mer, la route, la poussière'. In *Pour une littérature voyageuse*, 57–81. Paris: Éditions Complexe, 1992; repr. 1999.
Chaney, David. 'The Power of Metaphors in Tourism Theory'. In *Tourism: Between Place and Performance*, ed. Simon Coleman and Mike Crang, 193–206. Oxford: Berghahn Books, 2002.
Cheong, So-Min and Marc L. Miller. 'Power and Tourism: A Foucauldian Observation'. *Annals of Tourism Research* 27 (2000): 371–90.
Chesneaux, Jean. *L'art du voyage: Un regard (plutôt...) politique sur l'autre et l'ailleurs*. Paris: Bayard, 1999.

Clark, Steve, ed. *Travel Writing and Empire: Postcolonial Theory in Transit*. London: Zed Books, 1999.
Clerici, Luca. 'La letteratura di viaggio'. In *Manuale di letteratura italiana: Storia per generi e problemi*, ed. Franco Brioschi and Costanzo di Girolamo, 4 vols, III, 590–610. Turin: Bollati Boringhieri, 1996.
Clifford, James. 'Introduction: Partial Truths'. In *Writing Culture: The Poetics and Politics of Ethnography*, ed. James Clifford and George E. Marcus, 1–26. Berkeley: University of California Press, 1986.
_____. 'On Ethnographic Allegory'. In *Writing Culture: The Poetics and Politics of Ethnography*, ed. James Clifford and George E. Marcus, 98–121. Berkeley: University of California Press, 1986.
_____. 'On Ethnographic Authority'. In *The Predicament of Culture: Twentieth-Century Ethnography, Literature, and Art*, 21–54. Cambridge, MA: Harvard University Press, 1988.
_____. *Routes: Travel and Translation in the Late Twentieth Century*. Cambridge, MA: Harvard University Press, 1997.
Clifford, James and George E. Marcus, eds. *Writing Culture: The Poetics and Politics of Ethnography*. Berkeley: University of California Press, 1986.
Cogez, Gérard. *Les écrivains voyageurs au XXe siècle*. Paris: Seuil, 2004.
Cohen, Erik. 'Toward a Sociology of International Tourism'. *Social Research* 39 (1972): 164–82.
_____. 'A Phenomenology of Tourist Experiences'. *Sociology* 13 (1979): 179–201.
_____. 'The Tourist Guide: The Origins, Structure and Dynamics of a Role'. *Annals of Tourism Research* 12 (1985): 5–29.
_____. 'Authenticity and Commoditization in Tourism'. *Annals of Tourism Research* 15 (1988): 371–86.
_____. '"Primitive and Remote": Hill Tribe Trekking in Thailand'. *Annals of Tourism Research* 16 (1989): 30–61.
Cohen, Erik, Yeshayahu Nir and Uri Almagor, 'Stranger-Local Interaction in Photography'. *Annals of Tourism Research* 19 (1992): 213–33.
Cooper, Brenda. *Weary Sons of Conrad: White Fiction against the Grain of Africa's Dark Heart*. New York: Peter Lang, 2002.
Crawshaw, Carol and John Urry. 'Tourism and the Photographic Eye'. In *Touring Cultures: Transformations of Travel and Theory*, ed. Chris Rojek and John Urry, 176–95. London: Routledge, 1997.
Crick, Malcolm. 'The Anthropologist as Tourist: An Identity in Question'. In *International Tourism: Identity and Change*, ed. Marie-Françoise Lanfant, John B. Allcock and Edward M. Bruner, 205–23. London: Sage Publications, 1995.
Cronin, Michael. *Across the Lines: Travel, Language, Translation*. Cork: Cork University Press, 2000.
_____. 'Travelling Minorities: Language, Translation and the Global'. In *Seuils et traverses: Enjeux de l'écriture du voyage: Actes du colloque de Brest (6–8 juillet 2000)*, ed. Jean-Yves Le Disez and Jan Borm, 2 vols, I, 249–60. Brest: Université de Bretagne occidentale, 2002.
_____. *Translation and Identity*. London: Routledge, 2006.
D'Aquino Creazzo, Alida. *L'io e l'altro: Il viaggio in India da Gozzano a Terzani*. Rome: Avagliano, 2006.
Darke, Jane and Craig Gurney. 'Putting Up? Gender, Hospitality and Performance'. In *In Search of Hospitality: Theoretical Perspectives and Debates*, ed. Conrad Lashley and Alison Morrison, 77–99. Oxford: Butterworth-Heinemann, 2000.
De Pascale, Gaia. *Scrittori in viaggio: Narratori e poeti italiani del Novecento in giro per il mondo*. Turin: Bollati Boringhieri, 2001.

_____. *Slow travel: Alla ricerca del lusso di perdere tempo*. Milan: Ponte alle Grazie, 2008.
Derrida, Jacques. *De l'hospitalité: Anne Dufourmantelle invite Jacques Derrida à répondre*. Paris: Calmann-Lévy, 1997.
Diome, Fatou. *Le ventre de l'Atlantique*. Paris: Anne Carrière, 2003.
Douette, Samuel, ed. *Paris-Kaboul: Expédition scientifique et culturelle sur les routes de la soie*. Paris: Hoëbeke, 2004.
Edensor, Tim. *Tourists at the Taj: Performance and Meaning at a Symbolic Site*. London: Routledge, 1998.
Elouard, Daniel. 'Culture en poche'. In *Tourismes, touristes, sociétés*, ed. Franck Michel, 19–24. Paris: L'Harmattan, 1998.
Espey, David. 'The Wilds of New Jersey: John McPhee as Travel Writer'. In *Temperamental Journeys: Essays on the Modern Literature of Travel*, ed. Michael Kowalewski, 164–75. Athens: University of Georgia Press, 1992.
Fabian, Johannes. *Time and the Other: How Anthropology Makes its Object*. New York: Columbia University Press, 1983; repr. 2002.
Farnetti, Monica. *Reportages: Letteratura di viaggio del Novecento italiano*. Milan: Angelo Guerini, 1994.
Feifer, Maxine. *Going Places: The Ways of the Tourist from Imperial Rome to the Present Day*. London: Macmillan, 1985.
Fennell, David A. *Tourism Ethics*. Clevedon: Channel View Publications, 2006.
Ferrarotti, Franco. *Partire, tornare: Viaggiatori e pellegrini alla fine del millennio*. Rome: Donzelli, 1999.
Flaherty, Michael G., Norman K. Denzin, Peter K. Manning and David A. Snow. 'Review Symposium: Crisis in Representation'. *Journal of Contemporary Ethnography* 31 (2002): 478–516.
Forsdick, Charles. '*A quoi bon marcher*: Uses of the Peripatetic in Contemporary Travel Literature in French'. *Contemporary French and Francophone Studies* 5 (2001): 47–62.
_____. 'Projected Journeys: Exploring the Limits of Travel'. In *The Art of the Project: Projects and Experiments in Modern French Culture*, ed. Johnnie Gratton and Michael Sheringham, 51–65. Oxford: Berghahn Books, 2005.
_____. *Travel in Twentieth-Century French and Francophone Cultures: The Persistence of Diversity*. Oxford: Oxford University Press, 2005.
_____. '"(In)connaissance de l'Asie": Barthes and Bouvier, China and Japan'. *Modern and Contemporary France* 14 (2006): 63–77.
Forsdick, Charles, Feroza Basu and Siobhán Shilton. *New Approaches to Twentieth-Century Travel Literature in French: Genre, History, Theory*. New York: Peter Lang, 2006.
Fowler, Corinne. *Chasing Tales: Travel Writing, Journalism and the History of British Ideas about Afghanistan*. Amsterdam: Rodopi, 2007.
Fowler, Corinne and Ludmilla Kostova, eds. 'Travel and Ethics'. Special issue, *Journeys: The International Journal of Travel and Travel Writing* 4 (2003).
Franklin, Adrian and Mike Crang. 'The Trouble with Tourism and Travel Theory?' *Tourist Studies* 1 (2001): 5–22.
Freadman, Richard. 'Moral Luck in Paris: *A Moveable Feast* and the Ethics of Autobiography'. In *Renegotiating Ethics in Literature, Philosophy, and Theory*, ed. Jane Adamson, Richard Freadman and David Parker, 134–60. Cambridge: Cambridge University Press, 1998.
Friese, Heidrun. 'The Limits of Hospitality'. *Paragraph* 32 (2009): 51–68.
Gallagher, Rob. *The Rickshaws of Bangladesh*. Dhaka: University Press Limited, 1992.
Galt Harpham, Geoffrey. 'Ethics'. In *Critical Terms for Literary Study*, ed. Frank Lentricchia and Thomas McLaughlin, 2nd edition, 387–405. Chicago: University of Chicago Press, 1990; repr. 1995.

Gannier, Odile. *La littérature de voyage*. Paris: Ellipses, 2001.
Garland-Thomson, Rosemarie. *Staring: How We Look*. Oxford: Oxford University Press, 2009.
George, Stephen K., ed. *Ethics, Literature, and Theory: An Introductory Reader*. Oxford: Rowman and Littlefield, 2005.
Geraud, Marie-Odile. 'L'image de soi au miroir de l'autre: Une ethnographie des pratiques touristiques dans un village Hmong de Guyane Française'. In *Le tourisme local: Une culture de l'exotisme*, ed. Rachid Amirou and Philippe Bachimon, 93–120. Paris: L'Harmattan, 2000.
Germann Molz, Jennie and Sarah Gibson, eds. *Mobilizing Hospitality: The Ethics of Social Relations in a Mobile World*. Aldershot: Ashgate, 2007.
———. 'Introduction: Mobilizing and Mooring Hospitality'. In *Mobilizing Hospitality: The Ethics of Social Relations in a Mobile World*, ed. Jennie Germann Molz and Sarah Gibson, 1–25. Aldershot: Ashgate, 2007.
Giddens, Anthony. *Modernity and Self-Identity: Self and Society in the Late Modern Age*. Cambridge: Polity Press, 1991.
Gillespie, Alex. 'Tourist Photography and the Reverse Gaze'. *Ethos* 34 (2006): 343–66.
Goffman, Erving. 'Regions and Region Behavior'. In *The Presentation of Self in Everyday Life*, 109–40. New York: Anchor Books, 1959; repr. London: Penguin, 1990.
Golomb, Jacob. *In Search of Authenticity: From Kierkegaard to Camus*. London: Routledge, 1995.
Gomez-Géraud, Marie-Christine. 'La figure de l'interprète dans quelques récits de voyage français à la Renaissance'. In *Voyager à la Renaissance: Actes du colloque de Tours 1983*, ed. Jean Céard and Jean-Claude Margolin, 319–35. Paris: Éditions Maisonneuve et Larose, 1987.
Greenblatt, Stephen. *Marvelous Possessions: The Wonder of the New World*. Oxford: Clarendon Press, 1991.
Gregory, Marshall. 'Ethical Criticism: What It Is and Why It Matters'. In *Ethics, Literature, and Theory: An Introductory Reader*, ed. Stephen K. George, 37–61. Oxford: Rowman and Littlefield, 2005.
Gruesser, John Cullen. *White on Black: Contemporary Literature about Africa*. Urbana: University of Illinois Press, 1992.
Guagnini, Elvio. *Viaggi d'inchiostro: Note su viaggi e letteratura in Italia*. Pasian di Prato: Campanotto, 2000.
Ha, Marie-Paule. *Figuring the East: Segalen, Malraux, Duras, and Barthes*. Albany: State University of New York Press, 2000.
Haines, Simon. 'Deepening the Self: The Language of Ethics and the Language of Literature'. In *Renegotiating Ethics in Literature, Philosophy, and Theory*, ed. Jane Adamson, Richard Freadman and David Parker, 21–38. Cambridge: Cambridge University Press, 1998.
Halen, Pierre. 'De deux voyages en terre de génocide: Le Rwanda et la question de l'altérité'. In *Récits du dernier siècle des voyages: De Victor Segalen à Nicolas Bouvier*, ed. Olivier Hamburgin, 75–90. Paris: Presses de l'Université Paris-Sorbonne, 2005.
Hamburgin, Olivier, ed. *Récits du dernier siècle des voyages: De Victor Segalen à Nicolas Bouvier*. Paris: Presses de l'Université Paris-Sorbonne, 2005.
———. 'Sur les traces de Nicolas Bouvier: Portrait et perspectives critiques'. In *Récits du dernier siècle des voyages: De Victor Segalen à Nicolas Bouvier*, ed. Olivier Hamburgin, 223–37. Paris: Presses de l'Université Paris-Sorbonne, 2005.
Hansen, Peter H. 'Partners: Guides and Sherpas in the Alps and Himalayas, 1850s–1950s'. In *Voyages and Visions: Towards a Cultural History of Travel*, ed. Jaś Elsner and Joan-Pau Rubiés, 210–31. London: Reaktion Books, 1999.
Helmers, Marguerite and Tilar Mazzeo, eds. *The Traveling and Writing Self*. Newcastle: Cambridge Scholars Publishing, 2007.

Henderson, Heather. 'The Travel Writer and the Text: "My Giant Goes with me Wherever I Go"'. In *Temperamental Journeys: Essays on the Modern Literature of Travel*, ed. Michael Kowalewski, 230–48. Athens: University of Georgia Press, 1992.

Holland, Patrick and Graham Huggan. *Tourists with Typewriters: Critical Reflections on Contemporary Travel Writing*. Ann Arbor: University of Michigan Press, 1998; repr. 2000.

Hooper, Glenn and Tim Youngs, eds. *Perspectives on Travel Writing*. Aldershot: Ashgate, 2004.

———. 'Introduction'. In *Perspectives on Travel Writing*, ed. Glenn Hooper and Tim Youngs, 1–11. Aldershot: Ashgate, 2004.

Hulme, Peter. 'Patagonian Cases: Travel Writing, Fiction, History'. In *Seuils et traverses: Enjeux de l'écriture du voyage: Actes du colloque de Brest (6–8 juillet 2000)*, ed. Jean-Yves Le Disez and Jan Borm, 2 vols, II, 223–37. Brest: Université de Bretagne occidentale, 2002.

Hulme, Peter and Tim Youngs, eds. *The Cambridge Companion to Travel Writing*. Cambridge: Cambridge University Press, 2002.

———. 'Talking about Travel Writing: A Conversation between Peter Hulme and Tim Youngs'. *English Association Issues in English* 8 (2007).

Hutnyk, John. *The Rumour of Calcutta: Tourism, Charity and the Poverty of Representation*. London: Zed Books, 1996.

Islam, Syed Manzurul. *The Ethics of Travel: From Marco Polo to Kafka*. Manchester: Manchester University Press, 1996.

Jack, Gavin and Alison Phipps. *Tourism and Intercultural Exchange: Why Tourism Matters*. Clevedon: Channel View Publications, 2005.

Jack, Ian. 'Introduction'. In *The Granta Book of Travel*, vii–xii. London: Granta Books, 1991; repr. 1998.

Jones, Kathryn. 'Voices of the *Banlieues*: Constructions of Dialogue in François Maspero's *Les Passagers du Roissy-Express*'. *Contemporary French and Francophone Studies* 8 (2004): 127–34.

———. '*Le voyageur étonné*: François Maspero's Alternative Itineraries'. *Studies in Travel Writing* 13 (2009): 335–44.

Kapuściński, Ryszard. *The Other*, trans. Antonia Lloyd-Jones. London: Verso, 2008.

Kim, Hyounggon and Tazim Jamal. 'Touristic Quest for Existential Authenticity'. *Annals of Tourism Research* 34 (2007): 181–201.

Klopp, Charles. 'Buster Keaton Goes to Africa: Gianni Celati's *Avventure in Africa*'. In *ItaliAfrica: Bridging Continents and Cultures*, ed. Matteo Sante, 337–47. New York: Forum Italicum, 2001.

Kontogeorgopoulos, Nick. 'Keeping up with the Joneses: Tourists, Travellers, and the Quest for Cultural Authenticity in Southern Thailand'. *Tourist Studies* 3 (2003): 171–203.

Kostova, Ludmilla. 'Meals in Foreign Parts: Food in Writing by Nineteenth-Century British Travellers to the Balkans'. In 'Travel and Ethics', ed. Corinne Fowler and Ludmilla Kostova. Special issue, *Journeys: The International Journal of Travel and Travel Writing* 4 (2003): 21–44.

Kowalewski, Michael, ed. *Temperamental Journeys: Essays on the Modern Literature of Travel*. Athens: University of Georgia Press, 1992.

'L'étonnant paradoxe de la littérature de voyage'. *Livres de France* 208 (1998): 36–8.

Lashley, Conrad. 'Towards a Theoretical Understanding'. In *In Search of Hospitality: Theoretical Perspectives and Debates*, ed. Conrad Lashley and Alison Morrison, 1–17. Oxford: Butterworth-Heinemann, 2000.

Lashley, Conrad and Alison Morrison, eds. *In Search of Hospitality: Theoretical Perspectives and Debates*. Oxford: Butterworth-Heinemann, 2000.

Lauritzen, Paul. 'Arguing with Life Stories: The Case of Rigoberta Menchú'. In *The Ethics of Life Writing*, ed. Paul John Eakin, 19–39. Ithaca: Cornell University Press, 2004.

Lawrence, Karen R. *Penelope Voyages: Women and Travel in the British Literary Tradition*. Ithaca: Cornell University Press, 1994.
Le Bris, Michel. 'Note de l'Éditeur'. In *Pour une littérature voyageuse*, 7–15. Paris: Éditions Complexe, 1992; repr. 1999.
———. 'Fragments du royaume'. In *Pour une littérature voyageuse*, 119–40. Paris: Éditions Complexe, 1992; repr. 1999.
Le Disez, Jean-Yves and Jan Borm, eds. *Seuils et traverses: Enjeux de l'écriture du voyage: Actes du colloque de Brest (6–8 juillet 2000)*, 2 vols. Brest: Université de Bretagne occidentale, 2002.
Leed, Eric J. *The Mind of the Traveler: From Gilgamesh to Global Tourism*. New York: Basic Books, 1991.
Levin, Stephen M. *The Contemporary Anglophone Travel Novel: The Aesthetics of Self-Fashioning in the Era of Globalization*. London: Routledge, 2008.
Lévi-Strauss, Claude. *Tristes tropiques*. Paris: Plon, 1955.
Lisle, Debbie. *The Global Politics of Contemporary Travel Writing*. Cambridge: Cambridge University Press, 2006.
Littlewood, Ian. *Sultry Climates: Travel and Sex since the Grand Tour*. London: John Murray, 2001.
Lynch, Paul, Maria Laura Di Domenico and Majella Sweeney. 'Resident Hosts and Mobile Strangers: Temporary Exchanges within the Topography of the Commercial Home'. In *Mobilizing Hospitality: The Ethics of Social Relations in a Mobile World*, ed. Jennie Germann Molz and Sarah Gibson, 121–43. Aldershot: Ashgate, 2007.
MacCannell, Dean. *The Tourist: A New Theory of the Leisure Class*. New York: Schocken Books, 1976; repr. Berkeley: University of California Press, 1999.
Maoz, Darya. 'The Mutual Gaze'. *Annals of Tourism Research* 33 (2006): 221–39.
Méaux, Danièle. 'Récit de voyage et photographie: Le dialogue du texte et des images'. In *Miroirs de textes: Récits de voyage et intertextualité*, ed. Sophie Linon-Chipon, Véronique Magri-Mourgues and Sarga Moussa, 169–83. Nice: Publications de la Faculté des Lettres, Arts et Sciences Humaines de Nice, 1998.
Mee, Catharine. 'The Myopic Eye: Calvino's Travels in the USA and the USSR'. *The Modern Language Review* 100 (2005): 985–99.
———. '"Che brutta invenzione il turismo!" Tourism and Anti-tourism in Current French and Italian Travel Writing'. *Comparative Critical Studies* 4 (2007): 269–82.
———. 'European Travellers in Africa: The Negotiation of Identity'. *Forum for Modern Language Studies* 45 (2009): 378–89.
———. 'Journalism and Travel Writing: From *Grands Reporters* to Global Tourism'. *Studies in Travel Writing* 13 (2009): 305–15.
Michaux, Henri. *Un barbare en Asie*. Paris: Gallimard, 1967.
Michel, Franck. *Désirs d'ailleurs: Essai d'anthropologie des voyages*. Paris: Armand Colin, 2000.
———. *Voyage au bout du sexe: Trafics et tourismes sexuels en Asie et ailleurs*. Quebec: Les Presses de l'Université Laval, 2006.
Mills, Sara. *Discourses of Difference: An Analysis of Women's Travel Writing and Colonialism*. London: Routledge, 1991.
Minca, Claudio. 'Percorsi dell'autentico'. In *Spazi effimeri: Geografia e turismo tra moderno e postmoderno*, 103–38. Padova: CEDAM, 1996.
Mitchell, W. J. T. 'The Photographic Essay: Four Case Studies'. In *Picture Theory*, 281–322. Chicago: University of Chicago Press, 1994.
Monga, Luigi. 'Travel and Travel Writing: An Historical Overview of Hodoeporics'. *Annali d'italianistica* 14 (1996): 6–54.

Montalbetti, Christine. *Le voyage, le monde et la bibliothèque*. Paris: Presses Universitaires de France, 1997.
Moura, Jean-Marc. 'L'exotisme fin-de-(XXe)-siècle'. *Revue de littérature comparée* 74 (2000): 533–53.
Moussa, Sarga. 'Traduttore, traditore: La figure du drogman dans les récits de voyage en Orient au XIXème siècle'. In *Écrire le voyage*, ed. György Tverdota, 101–12. Paris: Presses de la Sorbonne Nouvelle, 1994.
Musgrove, Brian. 'Travel and Unsettlement: Freud on Vacation'. In *Travel Writing and Empire: Postcolonial Theory in Transit*, ed. Steve Clark, 31–44. London: Zed Books, 1999.
Nocifora, Enzo. *Itineraria: Dal Grand Tour al turismo postmoderno: Lezioni di sociologia del turismo*. Milan: Le Vespe, 2001.
Nuñez, Theron. 'Touristic Studies in Anthropological Perspective'. In *Hosts and Guests: The Anthropology of Tourism*, ed. Valene L. Smith, 2nd edition, 265–74. Oxford: Blackwell, 1977; repr. Philadelphia: University of Pennsylvania Press, 1989.
Nussbaum, Martha C. *Love's Knowledge: Essays on Philosophy and Literature*. Oxford: Oxford University Press, 1990.
———. 'The Literary Imagination in Public Life'. In *Renegotiating Ethics in Literature, Philosophy, and Theory*, ed. Jane Adamson, Richard Freadman and David Parker, 222–46. Cambridge: Cambridge University Press, 1998.
Olsen, Kjell. 'Authenticity as a Concept in Tourism Research: The Social Organization of the Experience of Authenticity'. *Tourist Studies* 2 (2002): 159–82.
Pasquali, Adrien. *Le tour des horizons: Critique et récits de voyages*. Paris: Klincksieck, 1994.
———. 'Récit de voyage et autobiographie'. *Annali d'italianistica* 14 (1996): 71–88.
Pearce, Philip L. and Gianna M. Moscardo. 'The Concept of Authenticity in Tourist Experiences'. *Australian and New Zealand Journal of Sociology* 22 (1986): 121–32.
Pettinger, Alasdair. '"Trains and Boats and Planes": Some Reflections on Travel Writing and Public Transport'. In *Seuils et traverses: Enjeux de l'écriture du voyage: Actes du colloque de Brest (6–8 juillet 2000)*, ed. Jean-Yves Le Disez and Jan Borm 2 vols, II, 107–15. Brest: Université de Bretagne occidentale, 2002.
Polezzi, Loredana. *Translating Travel: Contemporary Italian Travel Writing in English Translation*. Aldershot: Ashgate, 2001.
———. 'Did Someone Just Travel All Over Me? Travel Writing and the Travelee…'. In *Seuils et traverses: Enjeux de l'écriture du voyage: Actes du colloque de Brest (6–8 juillet 2000)*, ed. Jean-Yves Le Disez and Jan Borm, 2 vols, II, 303–12. Brest: Université de Bretagne occidentale, 2002.
———. 'Non solo colonie: "Africa" in the Work of Contemporary Italian Women Writers'. In *Borderlines: Migrazioni e identità nel Novecento*, ed. Jennifer Burns and Loredana Polezzi, 309–21. Isernia: Cosmo Iannone, 2003.
———. 'Now You See Them, Now You Don't: The Figure of the Interpreter/Translator in Travel Writing and Migrant Literature'. Unpublished article, 18 August 2013. Microsoft Word file.
Pratt, Mary Louise. 'Fieldwork in Common Places'. In *Writing Culture: The Poetics and Politics of Ethnography*, ed. James Clifford and George E. Marcus, 27–50. Berkeley: University of California Press, 1986.
———. *Imperial Eyes: Travel Writing and Transculturation*. London: Routledge, 1992.
Proietti, Paolo. *Lontano dalla lingua madre: In viaggio con la narrativa nel secondo Novecento*. Rome: Armando, 2000.
Redfoot, Donald L. 'Touristic Authenticity, Touristic Angst, and Modern Reality'. *Qualitative Sociology* 7 (1984): 291–309.

Richards, Greg and Julie Wilson. 'Travel Writers and Writers Who Travel: Nomadic Icons for the Backpacker Subculture?' *Journal of Tourism and Cultural Change* 2 (2004): 46–68.
Ridon, Jean-Xavier. *Le voyage en son miroir: Essai sur quelques tentatives de réinvention du voyage au 20e siècle*. Paris: Éditions Kimé, 2002.
Rosaldo, Renato. *Culture and Truth: The Remaking of Social Analysis*. Boston: Beacon Press, 1989; repr. London: Routledge, 1993.
Rosello, Mireille. *Postcolonial Hospitality: The Immigrant as Guest*. Stanford: Stanford University Press, 2001.
Rubiés, Joan-Pau. 'Travel Writing and Ethnography'. In *The Cambridge Companion to Travel Writing*, ed. Peter Hulme and Tim Youngs, 242–60. Cambridge: Cambridge University Press, 2002.
Said, Edward. *Orientalism*. London: Routledge and Kegan Paul, 1978; repr. Penguin, 1995.
Schulz-Forberg, Hagen. 'European Travel and Travel Writing: Cultural Practice and the Idea of Europe'. In *Unravelling Civilisation: European Travel and Travel Writing*, ed. Hagen Schulz-Forberg, 13–40. Brussels: Peter Lang, 2005.
Selwyn, Tom. 'An Anthropology of Hospitality'. In *In Search of Hospitality: Theoretical Perspectives and Debates*, ed. Conrad Lashley and Alison Morrison, 18–37. Oxford: Butterworth-Heinemann, 2000.
Siegel, Kristi and Toni B. Wulff. 'Travel as Spectacle: The Illusion of Knowledge and Sight'. In *Issues in Travel Writing: Empire, Spectacle, and Displacement*, ed. Kristi Siegel, 109–22. New York: Peter Lang, 2002.
Smith, Valene L., ed. *Hosts and Guests: The Anthropology of Tourism*, 2nd edition. Oxford: Blackwell, 1977; repr. Philadelphia: University of Pennsylvania Press, 1989.
———. 'Eskimo Tourism: Micro-Models and Marginal Men'. In *Hosts and Guests: The Anthropology of Tourism*, ed. Valene L. Smith, 2nd edition, 55–82. Oxford: Blackwell, 1977; repr. Philadelphia: University of Pennsylvania Press, 1989.
Sontag, Susan. *On Photography*. New York: Picador: Farrar, Straus and Giroux, 1977; repr. 1990.
Spurr, David. *The Rhetoric of Empire: Colonial Discourse in Journalism, Travel Writing, and Imperial Administration*. London: Duke University Press, 1993.
Sullivan, Shannon. *Revealing Whiteness: The Unconscious Habits of Racial Privilege*. Bloomington: Indiana University Press, 2006.
Taylor, Charles. *The Ethics of Authenticity*. Cambridge, MA: Harvard University Press, 1991.
Taylor, John P. 'Authenticity and Sincerity in Tourism'. *Annals of Tourism Research* 28 (2001): 7–26.
Telfer, Elizabeth. 'The Philosophy of Hospitableness'. In *In Search of Hospitality: Theoretical Perspectives and Debates*, ed. Conrad Lashley and Alison Morrison, 38–55. Oxford: Butterworth-Heinemann, 2000.
Todorov, Tzvetan. *Nous et les autres: La réflexion française sur la diversité humaine*. Paris: Seuil, 1989.
———. 'Le voyage et son récit'. In *Les morales de l'histoire*, 95–108. Paris: Bernard Grasset, 1991.
Trequadrini, Franco. *Viaggio alienazione ed altro*. Manfredonia: Atlantica, 1980.
Turner, Charles and Phil Manning. 'Placing Authenticity – On Being a Tourist: A Reply to Pearce and Moscardo'. *Australian and New Zealand Journal of Sociology* 24 (1988): 136–9.
Urbain, Jean-Didier. 'Sémiotiques comparées du touriste et du voyageur'. *Semiotica* 58 (1986): 269–86.
———. *L'idiot du voyage: Histoires de touristes*. Paris: Plon, 1991; repr. Payot et Rivages, 2002.
———. *Secrets de voyage: Menteurs, imposteurs et autres voyageurs invisibles*. Paris: Payot et Rivages, 1998; repr. 2003.

_____. 'Les catanautes des cryptocombes: Des iconoclastes de l'Ailleurs'. *Nottingham French Studies* 39 (2000): 7–16.

_____. 'Le cogito du voyageur: "Esprit nomade" et "esprit du voyage"'. In *Seuils et traverses: Enjeux de l'écriture du voyage: Actes du colloque de Brest (6–8 juillet 2000)*, ed. Jean-Yves Le Disez and Jan Borm, 2 vols, II, 21–41. Brest: Université de Bretagne occidentale, 2002.

Urry, John. *The Tourist Gaze*, 2nd edition. London: Sage, 1990; repr. 2002.

Venuti, Lawrence. *The Translator's Invisibility: A History of Translation*. London: Routledge, 1995.

Walton, John K. 'The Hospitality Trades: A Social History'. In *In Search of Hospitality: Theoretical Perspectives and Debates*, ed. Conrad Lashley and Alison Morrison, 56–76. Oxford: Butterworth-Heinemann, 2000.

Wang, Ning. 'Rethinking Authenticity in Tourism Experience'. *Annals of Tourism Research* 26 (1999): 349–70.

Weber, Olivier and Samuel Douette, eds. *Routes de la soie: La mémoire retrouvée de l'Afghanistan*. Paris: Mille et une nuits, 2004.

Wheeler, Tony and Richard I'Anson. *Chasing Rickshaws*. Hawthorn, Victoria: Lonely Planet Publications, 1998.

Williams, Wes. '"Rubbing up against Others": Montaigne on Pilgrimage'. In *Voyages and Visions: Towards a Cultural History of Travel*, ed. Jaś Elsner and Joan-Pau Rubiés, 101–23. London: Reaktion Books, 1999.

Wiltshire, John. 'The Patient Writes Back: Bioethics and the Illness Narrative'. In *Renegotiating Ethics in Literature, Philosophy, and Theory*, ed. Jane Adamson, Richard Freadman and David Parker, 181–98. Cambridge: Cambridge University Press, 1998.

Youngs, Tim. 'Where Are We Going? Cross-Border Approaches to Travel Writing'. In *Perspectives on Travel Writing*, ed. Glenn Hooper and Tim Youngs, 167–80. Aldershot: Ashgate, 2004.

Online

United Nations World Tourism Organization. 'Tourism Highlights: 2012 Edition'. 2012. http://unwto.org/facts/menu.html (accessed 26 May 2013).

Direction générale de la compétitivité, de l'industrie et des services (DGCIS). 'Chiffres clés du tourisme: Édition 2012'. 2012. http://www.dgcis.redressement-productif.gouv.fr/etudes-et-statistiques/statistiques-tourisme/donnees-cles/chiffres-cles (accessed 18 August 2013).

L'istituto nazionale di statistica (Istat). 'Viaggi e vacanze in Italia e all'estero'. www.istat.it (accessed 18 August 2013).

UN General Assembly. Resolution 217 A (III). 'Universal Declaration of Human Rights'. 10 December 1948. http://www.un.org/en/documents/udhr (accessed 18 August 2013).

Étonnants voyageurs. http://www.etonnants-voyageurs.com (accessed 18 August 2013).

L'albatros premio e festival per la letteratura di viaggio. http://www.premioalbatros.org (accessed 18 August 2013).

Festival della letteratura di viaggio. http://www.festivaletteraturadiviaggio.it (accessed 18 August 2013).

Centro interuniversitario di ricerche sul viaggio in Italia (CIRVI). http://www.cirvi.it (accessed 18 August 2013).

Centre de recherche sur la littérature des voyages (CRLV). http://www.crlv.org (accessed 18 August 2013).

INDEX

A Sud di Lampedusa (Liberti) 71
accompanying: absent friends 129–33, 171n4; alter ego or mirror 136–41; chance companions 141–6; contrasting companions 138–40; cultural similarity in 140, 172n23; illustrating disparity 144; perspectives used in 143–4; a question of genre 133–6; synecdoches in 143, 146; types of companions 128–9
Across the Lines (Cronin) 12
Adler, Judith 83
Afrozapping (Ramazzotti) 88–9
agency, attribution of 52–3, 56, 57
Aime, Marco: anonymity of travel companions 130; on anthropological informants vs. guides 162n23; on consciously constructed narratives in guiding 162n19; on disparity and ethics 170n4; on duration of encounters 77, 167n48; guide influenced by writing of 163n42; on guides in Mali 161n7; on photographing travellees 95; on tourism 3, 5–6
air travel 18, 141
Akram, Barmak 142–5
Allegro occidentale (Piccolo) 88, 123–5
Almagor, Uri 169n50, 169n55
Amirou, Rachid 154n36, 154n40, 167n52
antitourism: authenticity as strategy against 21–2; criticism of photography as 95–6, 99; deceleration linked to 21; development of in travel literature 9, 154n35; distancing as strategy against 118; in French travel writing 154n36; as judgement 27; snobbism in 154n40; Terzani exemplifying 17–18
Appiah, Kwame Anthony 28
Aramberri, Julio 158n40
authenticity 21–6; Aramberri on 158n40; authenticating the authenticator 25, 36–8; Cohen on 'tourees' and 158n40; 'The Concept of Authenticity in Tourist Experiences' 158–9n43; in concept of back regions 23–4; in decelerated travel 23; definitions and term usage 23–5, 158n42; of encounters 25–6, 147; existential 24–5, 136; factors interfering with 26; hospitality and 60–62, 66; intrapersonal and interpersonal 25, 159n46, 159n48; Kontogeorgopoulos on 158n49; mediation and 34–8; overview of 11, 14, 18; preventing 39; in representations 57; subjectivity of 25; Taylor on 158n34; Terzani on 18; textual 135; 'The Concept of Authenticity in Tourist Experiences' 158–9n43; of travel texts undermined 51–2; in travel writing 46
authorship and readership 53–7, 67–8, 74
Avventure in Africa (Celati) 2, 137

back regions 13, 22, 24, 39, 61, 158n39
Bassnett, Susan 51
Basu, Feroza 21, 154n39, 157n27
Bauer, Olivier 135, 137
Bauman, Zygmunt 29, 69, 150
beggars 119–25

being away: *see* home
Beneviste, Émile 59–60
Bernheim, Nicole-Lise 163n38;
    experience of with hosts 61, 63;
    financial arrangements of 109;
    guide experience of 45; hospitality
    experience of 62, 73; pronoun usage
    of 131–2, 135–6; reciprocity of
    74–5; relationships and duration of
    encounters 79; representations of
    Imai's family by 79, 167n49; on
    rickshaws 114; *Saisons japonaises* 2,
    78–9, 109; as staree 92, 94; use of local
    words by 50, 92; as vertical traveler 80;
    voyeuristic gazes of 87, 168n25
body and travel 63, 65, 165n17; *see also*
    discomforts of travel
Boorstin, Daniel 22, 61, 62–3, 165n15
Borer, Alain 68
Borm, Jan 7
Boulet, Marc 93–4, 110, 169n34
Bouvier, Nicolas 155n42, 160n2; alter
    ego of 137; attempted brothel
    visit by 116–17; bed and breakfast
    experience of 62; on fate of travel
    encounters 167n50; finances of
    109–10; on group travel 33, 38;
    guide, relationship of 40, 43, 45;
    gypsy, encounter of 66–7, 100;
    photography, experiences of 99–101,
    169n52, 170nn61–2; in *Pour une
    littérature voyageuse* 10; in a question of
    genre 133–5; on reciprocal nature of
    journeys 4; reflecting on fear 71–2;
    as staree 86–7, 90–91; Thierry as
    alter ego of 137
bubble metaphor 61, 165n8
Buzard, James 22, 157n22

Calvino, Italo 83
Canestrini, Duccio 21, 29, 98, 111, 120,
    167n48
Cardona, Giorgio Raimondo 163n49
Carnets d'une longue marche (Ollivier) 78–9,
    102, 128
Celati, Gianni: alter ego of 137;
    biographical notes on 161n6; on
    challenging encounters 111–12;
    financial transactions of 110–11; on
    guides and guidebooks 35; language
    usage of 50–51; on prostitutes 116–
    18; self-identify of tourist assumed
    by 154n36; as staree 87–9
Celia (Ramazzotti's guide) 1–3, 6, 41–2,
    48–50, 52, 54
Centre de recherche sur la littérature des
    voyages (CRLV) 11, 155n49
Centro interuniversitario di ricerche sul
    'Viaggio in Italia' (CIRVI) 11
Cerf, Muriel 107–8, 119, 170n1
Chaillou, Michel 68
challenging encounters: beggars 119–25;
    economic power behind 109–12;
    Guillebaud on 107–8; overview
    of 14, 150; perceptions of wealth
    111; power in 124; prostitutes and
    distancing 115–19; rickshaw riders
    and justification 112–14, 170nn9–
    10, 170n12, 170n16
Chambres d'ailleurs (Bernheim) 62, 131–2
Chaney, David 168n23
chapter overviews 12–15
Cheong, So-Min 44–5, 85, 90
Chesneaux, Jean 21
classifying travel writing 6–7
Clifford, James: on anthropological
    informants 40–41, 162n23; on class
    and travellees 128; on ethnographies
    164n58; on informants as readers
    56, 164n67; on voice 164n69
Cogez, Gérard 19, 172n16
Cohen, Erik 158n40, 162n21, 169n50,
    169n55
colonial nostalgia 69
commercialization 22, 24, 31, 59, 64, 147
commoditization 22, 37, 43–4
'The Concept of Authenticity in Tourist
    Experiences' 158–9n43
concluding 147–50
constructivist approach to authenticity
    24–5, 136
Cosmopolitanism: Ethics in a World of Strangers
    (Appiah) 28
Crawshaw, Carol 83
Cronin, Michael: on fractal geometry 20,
    156n12; on guides 161n16, 163n40;

on horizontal and vertical travel 79–80, 167n51; on social mobility 167n52; on translation strategies 50–51, 163n48; writing style of 12
cultural differences 19, 61, 64, 67, 91, 113

Darke, Jane 67
De Pascale, Gaia 2–3, 20
deceleration of travel 18, 20–21, 23, 72, 87
'Defining Travel' 7
Déon, Michel 46, 55, 163n41
Depardon, Raymond 98–9, 103–4, 138
Dermaut, François 102, 128
Derrida, Jacques 60
Di Domenico, Maria Laura 74
Diome, Fatou 70–71
discomforts of travel 104–5; *see also* body and travel
disguises 93
disparity of personal wealth 29, 69
Duong (Ruggeri's guide) 36–8, 42, 148–9

economic power 109–12, 115, 125–6; *see also* inequality
economics: impacting encounters 29; in relationships 1, 26; of tourism in France and Italy 155n51; of tourism UNWTO on 8, 153n32; of travel impacting relationships 14
Edensor, Tim 101
'effect of the real' 153n26
'effervescence éditoriale' 11, 155n50
Eldem, Edhem 52
Elouard, Daniel 167n48
emigration and emigrants 11, 71, 75–6; *see also* immigration; refugees
emotions 30, 44
encounters: authenticity of 25–6, 147; as backbone of travel narratives 2; characteristics of 81; confrontational 72; deceleration of travel enabling 18, 147; duration of 2, 14, 77–80; economics impacting 29; fractal geometry applied to 20, 156n12; generalization of anthropological 80–81; hosting providing opportunity for 59; intercultural contact in 28; nature of 73–7;

personal attributes as a factor in 5; photography and 94–104; with rickshaw riders 114; staring initiating 94; three-way nature of 55–6; tourist industry preventing 19, 21–2; tourist's lack of interest in 18–19; undermining of 95; usage of term 2–3; *see also specific travellers*
end of travel 18–19, 31
Espey, David 127
Etcharren, Jean-Baptiste 37
ethics 26–31; of agency 57; in challenging encounters 108; contingency in 30; distancing as a comment on 117; genres applicable to 27; implications of in modes of travel 18, 114; overview of 11, 14, 18; responsibilities of writers and readers 57; of travel 141; of travel photography 96, 99; in traveler–travellee relationship 42; *see also* inequality; prostitutes and distancing
ethnographies 53–4, 164n57, 164n58, 164n67
Étonnants voyageurs festival 10

Fabian, Johannes 164n63
fact and fiction 7–8, 153n27, 153n29, 153n30
Farfalle sul Mekong (Ruggeri) 2, 36
fear 110
Feifer, Maxine 22
Festival della letteratura di viaggio 11
financial relationships 29; with guides 43–6, 162n32; between host and guest 62; inauthenticity in 26, 62; traveller–photographee 98
foreigners, terms for 92, 168–9n33
Forsdick, Charles 19–21, 153n22, 161n16
Foucault, Michel 44, 83, 85, 167n3
Fowler, Corinne 56–7
France 11, 19
Frantz, Anaïk 97, 101–3, 132, 139
Freadman, Richard 27
freedom: as a characteristic of travel 68; and hospitality 65–8; limitations on 14; of movement 68–9, 81, 146; questioned by encounters 73; in

traveller–guide relationships 46; *see also* mobility
friendships and time 77–81

Gallagher, Rob 112
Gannier, Odile 7, 163n49
Garland-Thomson, Rosemarie 85–6, 94
gatekeepers 38–43
gazes 83–6, 90; *see also* staring
gender 140, 152n14, 170n12
genres overlapping travel writing 6, 152n18
Gibson, Sarah 165n6
Gillespie, Alex 90–91, 100
Global Politics of Contemporary Travel Writing, The (Lisle) 26
Goffman, Erving 24, 61
Gomez-Géraud, Marie-Christine 162n32
Greenblatt, Stephen 160n4, 162n22
Griaule, Marcel 35
guides: anonymity needed by 54; anthropological informants vs. 162n23; authority over travellers 44–5; distrust between travellers and 39, 161n18; and guidebooks 34–8; manipulation of 42–3; as mediators 24, 41; Ollivier's relationship with 44; as persons 40; pseudonyms used for 164n61; status as 'marginal men' 41; as synecdoches 40–41, 162n21–2; writers' representations of 46
guiding: activities of 33; an authentic encounter 43–7; authorship and readership 53–7; conflict of interests in 39; consciously constructed narratives in 39, 162n19; financial basis of relationship 43–4, 162n32; gatekeepers 38–43; overview of 13, 34; reading influencing experience 35–6, 160n4; representation strategies in translation 50–53; term usage 34; translation and voice 47–50, 54
Guillebaud, Jean-Claude: on beggars 122–3; biographical notes on 161n13; on Calcutta 120; on challenging encounters 107–8, 121–2; collaborations of with Depardon 103; finances of 109–10; guiding tensions illustrated by 36–9, 44–5, 149; linguistic inadequacies of 47; on money's invisible border 111; photography, experiences of 98, 104; on prostitutes 117, 119; on rickshaws 113–14; on synecdoches 40; traveling companion of 43, 138; on Vietnamese 'stringers' 41
Gurney, Craig 67

Ha, Marie-Paule 22, 158n39, 164n64
Halen, Pierre 151n4
Hambursin, Olivier 2, 19
Hansen, Peter 43, 164n60
Henderson, Heather 35
Holland, Patrick 26, 30–31, 166n40, 170n2
home: boundary separating journey from 75, 136, 146, 149, 172n18; continuity between away and 76, 125; defining 156, 156n57; social codes of 63
hosting and hospitality: authenticity in 60–62, 66; back regions in 61; back to the bubble 62–5, 81; in bed and breakfasts 62; benefits of commercial arrangements 64, 166n18; commercialization of 59; cultural differences and 64; etymological roots of 66; etymology of 59–60; examples of hospitality 61; expectations and 67; freedom and 65–8; gaze and 90; hospitality and authenticity 60–62; Japanese 'homestay' schemes 62; motivations in 62; mutual vulnerability in 67; nature of encounters 73–7; overview of 13–14; private arrangements 59, 63–4; reciprocity and obligation in 73, 80; by states 60, 70, 72–3, 165n6, 166n39; texts hosting travelees 76–7; time and friendships 77–81; the uninvited 71; varied ideas about 165n16; the world is my playground 68–73
Huggan, Graham 26, 30–31, 166n40, 170n2
Hulme, Peter 153n29
Hutnyk, John 120

INDEX

Idea (Moravia) 138
identity: assignment of 66; attributes of 5, 152n14; constructed 95; encounters placing stress on 19; interactions of multiple identity 10; racial 88–9; as tourist 154n36
immigration 14, 28, 60, 69, 124, 149; *see also* emigration and emigrants
In Patagonia (Chatwin) 153n30
inequality 29, 69; *see also* economic power; ethics
influence of travel writing on tourists 154n34
intercultural relations 28
interdisciplinary approaches to travel writing 9, 154n39
interpreting: *see* guiding
Islam, Syed Manzurul 156n57
Italian histories of travel and tourism 155n53
Italian National Institute of Statistics 155n51
Italy 10–11

Jack, Gavin 36, 164n59
Jack, Ian 153n29
Jones, Kathryn 103, 132, 139–40
Jordis, Christine 87, 95–6, 101, 113–14, 168n24

Kapuœciñski, Ryszard 53
Kauffmann, Alexandre 91, 117, 168n31
Kerouac, Jack 92
Klopp, Charles 137
knowledge 24–5, 33, 36, 55
Kontogeorgopoulos, Nick 43, 159n49, 162n30
Kostova, Ludmilla 168n11

La birra di Shaoshan: Viaggio nel paese natale di Mao (Ramazzotti) 1, 52
La colline des anges (Guillebaud) 2, 36, 103, 121–2
'La figure de l'interprète' 162n32
La porte des larmes (Guillebaud) 43, 103, 121
L'albatros premio e festival per la letteratura di viaggio 11
language 20–21, 47, 92–3, 164n51, 168–9n33

L'antivoyage (Cerf) 107–8, 170n1
Lashley, Conrad 64
Lauritzen, Paul 153n27
Le balcon de Spetsai (Déon) 55
Le Bris, Michel 10, 68
Le grand festin de l'Orient (Weber) 141–2, 144–5
Le poisson-scorpion (Bouvier) 135
Le radici nella sabbia (Aime) 130
Leed, Eric 66, 161n10
Les passagers du Roissy-Express (Maspero) 2, 76, 102–3, 131–2, 171n10
Liberti, Stefano 71–2, 75–6, 90–91, 149, 166n37
Lisle, Debbie 26, 135–6, 145, 160n73
Littlewood, Ian 115
L'usage du monde (Bouvier) 2, 133–4, 160n2
Lynch, Paul 74

MacCannell, Dean 9, 22–5
Mandelbrot, Benoît 20
Maoz, Darya 85
'marginal men': guides as 41
Maspero, François 131–2, 139, 141, 149, 157n17, 169n42
mediators 24, 25, 38, 163n47
metonymy 162n22
Michaux, Henri 85–6
Michel, Franck 73, 95, 115, 170n3
migrant experiences 75, 146
Miller, Marc 44–5, 85, 90
Mills, Sara 168n25
Mitchell, W. J. T. 103
mobility 69–70, 74, 146; *see also* freedom
modes of travel 18, 21, 141
Moltz, Jennie Germann 165n6
Montalbetti, Christine 163n49
Moravia, Alberto 130, 138–9, 171n2
motivation in voluntary travel 2–3
Moussa, Sarga 38, 45, 161n14, 163n37, 163n47
Musgrove, Brian 154n40

national identity 10
nationality 92, 152n14
Nguyen, T. D. (Guillebaud's guide) 36–7, 39, 44–5, 54, 99, 138
Nir, Yeshayahu 169n50, 169n55
Nussbaum, Martha 27, 29–30, 123

objectivist approach to authenticity 24
Odore (Pasolini) 138
Ollivier, Bernard: as authentic traveller 23; on decelerated travel 21; exemplifying encounters 2, 147–8; on French hospitality 69; as horizontal traveller 80; hospitality experiences of 63–5, 73, 149; influence of writings of 46; knowledge sources used by 25; linguistic inadequacies of 47; movement of restricted 68–9; on photography 96–7, 101–2; on prostitutes 115; reciprocity of 74, 77; relationship of with guide 44; relationships and duration of encounters 78–9; relative wealth of 110, 148; representation of villagers by 67–8; as solitary traveller 127–8; as staree 88, 91; use of reappropriation by 93; vulnerability of 110
'ontological expansiveness' 70
Other, the 2–3, 141; term usage 3–4

Pasolini, Pier Paolo 114, 130–31, 138–9, 141, 171n17
Pasquali, Adrien 155n50
patterns of travel in Western Europe 11–12
penetration metaphor 158n39
Pettinger, Alisdair 129–30, 141
Phipps, Alison 36, 164n59
photography: anthropological studies on 100; bilateral 104; control issues in 96–7; ethics of 96, 99; financial compensation for travelees 98; as interaction 99–104; as intrusion 96–9; opposing aspects of 14; photographic essays 103; refusal to engage in 98–9; sharing photographs 101; textual representation of 99, 103, 169n47; tourists and cameras 83–4, 94–6; *see also* staring; tourists
Piccolo, Francesco 162n33; assuming tourist identity 154n36; on beggars 123–5; on chance companions 127, 141, 149; on commoditization of tourist relations 43–4; financial arrangements of 109; hotel, experience of 60–61; as staree 88, 92
Polezzi, Loredana 39, 161n18, 163n45
Polisario (Ramondino) 52, 164n55
'post-tourists' 22
Pour une littérature voyageuse movement 10
Pratt, Mary Louise 4, 56, 152n12, 167n6
prioritizing encounters 2
Proietti, Paolo 141
pronoun usage 129–33
prostitutes and distancing 115–19; *see also* ethics; sex tourism
'pseudo-events' 61
pseudonyms used for guides 164n61

race 88, 92, 111, 152n14
Ramazzotti, Sergio 157n15; chance companions of 141–2, 144; decelerated travels of 21; encounters of 1–3, 6, 75, 108, 120–21; familial hospitality experiences of 64–5; as horizontal traveler 80; illustrating unity and separation 142; levels of translation and 48–9; methods of recording information 52; movement of restricted 69; photography experiences of 97–100; on prostitutes 115–16; as staree 80, 88; subject position of 145
Ramondino, Fabrizia 52, 61, 63, 74, 164n55
readership and authorship 53–7, 67–8, 74
reality effect 8, 50, 135
reciprocity 57, 73–7, 80, 166n41
refugees 120–21, 144, 146; *see also* emigration and emigrants; immigration
relative wealth 28, 109–11, 144, 148
representation 1–2, 27–8, 53, 57, 67, 145, 164n57
rickshaw riders and justification 112–14, 170nn9–10, 170n12, 170n16
Ridon, Jean-Xavier 103
Rosello, Mireille 67, 76–7, 165n16, 166n41, 171n10
Rousseau, François-Olivier 42, 50–51, 113–16, 162n28

INDEX

Ruggeri, Corrado 158n29; attitude on sex tourism and prostitutes 118–19; on finances in travel 110; food critique by 67; guide of as gatekeeper 39; on inauthenticity 22–3; reciprocity of 74; relationship with Duong (guide) 36–8, 42, 148–9; on rickshaws 113; translation, strategies of 52; travel style of 141; traveling companion of 139–40
Rumiz, Paolo 20–21, 47, 72, 89, 91–2, 157n14

Said, Edward 36
Saisons japonaises (Bernheim) 2, 78–9, 109
Schulz-Forberg, Hagen 12, 153n28
self-development 25, 27
Selwyn, Tom 65–6
sex tourism 115, 117; *see also* prostitutes and distancing
Slow travel (De Pascale) 20; *see also* deceleration of travel
Smith, Valene 41
Sontag, Susan 94–5, 100
souvenirs 1, 50–51, 101
Spiro 46, 55, 77
'staged authenticity' 61
staring 85–6; controlling and directing by 90; the gaze, stare and travel encounter 84–6; glancing 168n23; imposing identity 88–90; interpretation of 90; invisible observers of 91–2; mental perceptions in 85; 'monarch-of-all-I-survey' 167n6; multidirectional power 85; overview of 14; power dynamics in 121; tackling the stare 91; terms for foreigners 92–3, 168–9n33; tourism and photography 83–4; 'tourist gaze' 83; travellees as starers 86–91, 126; travellers as starees 91–4; *see also* gazes; photography
Staring: How We Look (Garland-Thomson) 85
stereotypes 88–9, 140
strategy 18–21
substitution in encounters 1–2

Sullivan, Shannon 70–72
Sultry Climates (Littlewood) 115
Sweeney, Majella 74
synecdoches 40–41, 143, 146, 149, 162nn21–2

Talon, Jean 137
Taylor, John 158n34
Telfer, Elizabeth 62
Terzani, Tiziano 156n1; addressing readers 54–5; on antitourism, end of travel and deceleration 17–18; on beggars 119; bubble metaphor of 61, 165n8; decelerated travel of 20; on encounters 17; guide of marginalized 41; as horizontal traveler 80; on hospitality as control 65–6; on inauthenticity 23, 39; methods of recording information 52; on photography 96; reciprocity of 74; rickshaw use by 170n16; as staree 87; translation strategies of 51–2; travel finances of 110
Theroux, Paul 136
threats to travel 31
time and friendships 77–81
Todorov, Tzvetan 18–19
tourism: Canestrini on 154n33; elitism of 170n3; encounters as contradiction of 147; ethical issues in 29; in France 11, 155n52; inauthenticity and 22–3; MacCannell on motives of 22; ranked by UNWTO 153n32; travel writing and 6–9
tourists: back region access of 13, 22, 24, 39, 61, 158n39; conflict/contrast between travellers and 9, 18–19, 22, 25–6, 140, 154n33; future oriented work of 101; identifying oneself as a 9, 154n36; lack of interest in encounters by 18–19; 'post-tourists' 22; similarity to travellers 22; tourist–host power relations 44–5; 'vagabonds' vs. 69; *see also* photography
Tourists with Typewriters (Holland and Huggan) 26, 31, 166n40
train stations 18

translation: omission of subject in travel writing 47–51, 163n45; Ramazzotti as example of levels of 48–50; representation strategies in 50–53; of travel writing 12, 48; travel writing as series of 57; and voice in guiding 47–50
travel 63, 65, 79–80, 122, 165n17
travel literature 7, 10, 27, 29–30, 38, 153n22
travel writers: constructions of 153n26; devices used by 7, 50, 52, 93, 117, 125, 129–40, 142–3, 163n50; ethical responsibility of 57; as mediators 38; subject positions of 145; *see also specific writers*
travel writing: attribution of agency in 52–3; authenticity in 46, 51–2; autobiographical nature of 135; boundaries in texts 75, 80, 135, 146; cyclical movement of 36; economic outcome of 45–6; ethical dimension of 27; financing of 109; function of 29–30; photographs in 103; representing inner journeys 25; self-legitimazation by 163n47; sources used in 35; studies of 11; subgenres of 157n26; and tourism 6–9; travel literature vs. 7, 153n22; travelees in 28, 148
travellees: appearance of 83; as co-authors 53; powers of 81; role reversal with travellers 124; as synecdoches 40–41, 143, 146, 149, 162nn21–2; tensions of 150; term usage 4–5, 152n12; in travel writing 28, 148; who travel 15
traveller–guide relationships 39–40, 43–7, 57; *see also specific travellers*
travellers: acted upon 4–5, 13, 133; compared to refugees 144; conflict/contrast between tourists and 9, 18–19, 22, 25–6, 140, 154n33; distrust between guides and 39, 161n18 (*see also specific guides and travellers*); 'independent travellers' 148; role reversal with travellees 124; self-identity of French 11; similarity to tourists 22; stressors of 63
Trequadrini, Franco 2
'truth effect' 153n28

Un indovino mi disse (Terzani) 2, 20, 52
Un voyage vers l'Asie (Guillebaud) 109
United Nations' Universal Declaration of Human Rights 69
United Nations World Tourism Organisation (UNWTO) 153n32
Urbain, Jean-Didier 154n33, 157n17, 158n39
Urry, John 83, 85

Vado verso il Capo (Ramazzotti) 21, 72, 99, 108, 120, 142, 144
'vagabonds' 69
Vernet, Thierry 133–5, 137, 172nn12–13
voyage 10–12
Voyage au pays de toutes les Russies (Weber) 2

walking journeys 21; *see also* Ollivier, Bernard
Wang, Ning 24–5
Weber, Oliver 163n39; ambiguity in writings of 52; chance companions of 142–5; guide relationship of 45; language issues ignored in writings of 47–8, 149, 163n45; subject position of 145, 172n29; travel finances of 110
Western culture 83, 167n3
Wiltshire, John 27
Writing Culture (Clifford) 53–4

www.ingramcontent.com/pod-product-compliance
Lightning Source LLC
Chambersburg PA
CBHW021829300426
44114CB00009BA/374